THE UNITED STATES OF ANGER

THE
UNITED STATES
OF ANGER

The People and the American Dream

GAVIN ESLER

MICHAEL JOSEPH
LONDON

MICHAEL JOSEPH LTD
Published by the Penguin Group
Penguin Books Ltd, 27 Wrights Lane, London W8 5TZ, England
Penguin Books USA Inc., 375 Hudson Street, New York, New York 10014, USA
Penguin Books Australia Ltd, Ringwood, Victoria, Australia
Penguin Books Canada Ltd, 10 Alcorn Avenue, Toronto, Ontario, Canada M4V 3B2
Penguin Books (NZ) Ltd, 182–190 Wairau Road, Auckland 10, New Zealand

Penguin Books Ltd, Registered Offices: Harmondsworth, Middlesex, England

First published 1997
10 9 8 7 6 5 4 3 2 1

Copyright © Gavin Esler 1997

A CIP catalogue record for this book is available from the British Library

ISBN 0 7181 4235 7

Set in 12.75/15pt Monotype Walbaum
Typeset by Rowland Phototypesetting Ltd, Bury St Edmunds, Suffolk
Printed in England by Clays Ltd, St Ives plc

The moral right of the author has been asserted

Contents

Acknowledgements

I am deeply indebted to my friend and literary agent Jonathan Lloyd for insisting that I push ahead with this project to record the extraordinary changes in the United States since the end of the cold war. I also owe Jonathan thanks for continually reminding me that as BBC correspondent in Washington I was privileged to travel across the United States with access to those who most reflect these changes – from the White House to the local school house, from members of the Clinton administration to members of street gangs.

I am also thankful for all the assistance, inspiration and encouragement given to me by my friends and colleagues at the BBC. Through working in the United States I have learned that I never secured interviews or access for the BBC. It was always the other way round. The BBC's reputation secures interviews and access for its correspondents and producers. Among those who have been extremely supportive are the staff of the BBC Washington office whose producers, reporters and bureau chief Steve Selman have been continually creative in trying to explain this American continent to our millions of listeners and viewers around the world. Amanda Farnsworth and Beth Miller provided invaluable insights and assistance on the manuscript and with the research. BBC news managers in London, especially Vin Ray and Richard Sambrook, were immediately supportive and enthusiastic. Tony Grant, the editor of that unique programme *From Our Own Correspondent*, and Sian Kevill, encouraged me to create a series of six old-fashioned radio 'talks' entitled *The United States of Anger* which helped sharpen the direction this book eventually took.

At Michael Joseph my editors Luigi Bonomi and Susan Watt suffered my peculiar ways and odd working patterns with exemplary good humour. For their editing and advice I owe a million thanks. My wife, Tricia, as usual, put up with more than anyone should have to bear. She suffered the writing, read the drafts and (even worse) had to endure interminable discussions about the future of the United States with me and our American friends in locations as different as Washington dinner parties and campfires in the Rocky Mountains. To her, my deepest thanks and love.

As I began writing this book my four-year-old daughter asked me if she and her two-year-old brother would be Americans when they grew up, or British. I replied that since she was born in the United States of British parents, technically she could choose to be either American or British when she reached the age of twenty-one.

'But *how* will I choose?' she persisted. I do not know the answer. But I hope this book will help illuminate her choice. If, inevitably, it is an examination of the darker side of American success, it is also an account of the unfulfilled promises of this great continent. It is dedicated to Charlotte and James, my two favourite Americans.

GAVIN ESLER, *Washington DC, March 1997*

PART ONE
AMERICAN DREAMS AND
THE ANXIOUS ECONOMY

'What a century it has been. America became the world's mightiest industrial power, saved the world from tyranny in two world wars and a long cold war, and time and time again reached across the globe to millions who longed for the blessings of liberty. Along the way, Americans produced the great middle class and security in old age; built unrivalled centres of learning and opened public schools to all; split the atom and explored the heavens; invented the computer and the microchip; made a revolution in civil rights for minorities; and extended the circle of citizenship, opportunity and dignity to women. Now, for the third time, a new century is upon us, and another time to choose.'

President Bill Clinton, second Inaugural Address, 20 January 1997

The Rules Have Changed

Sanibel Island, Florida

The middle-aged woman had the kind of New York accent designed to cut through the noise of heavy traffic. She was shrieking at a police officer who stood calmly, staring back at her through black sunglasses. It was early afternoon, the hottest time in the Florida sun, and there was no traffic. Only the woman, shrieking.

'Well, *what* are you *going* to *do* about *it*?' she demanded, stressing alternate words as she shook with rage. The policeman shrugged at this Manhattan meltdown. There was no point getting agitated in the heat. Besides, 'it' was going nowhere. 'It' was an eight-foot-long alligator, basking in the sunshine in a pond on Sanibel Island, a precious little speck of Florida jutting into the Gulf of Mexico.

A flock of a dozen dirty brown pelicans flew languidly towards the sea. The beach on the other side of the dunes was a hundred yards wide and stretched for endless miles. The tide was receding on the powdery sand and groups of wading birds, followed by shell-collecting humans, padded along the shore. The shell-collectors were barefoot, faces hidden under floppy hats, curiously competitive as they searched for rare specimens.

Suddenly, everything went quiet. The New York woman stopped shrieking, the police officer folded his arms and the alligator was motionless as a log. A temporary stand-off. The reptile had chosen to occupy a slimy green pond surrounded by palm trees behind the apartment the woman had rented for a week. The presence of a wild animal had frightened her.

3

She had called the police and wanted it removed. Gone. *Now.*

'Can't you *shoot* it or *something?*' the woman suggested, her voice ripping the air like a saw.

'No, ma'am.'

'Well,' she repeated, jabbing at the police officer with bright red painted nails, 'what *are* you going to *do* about it?'

The policeman sighed as if he would rather deal with an armed bank robber. Outraged taxpayers were definitely the *worst.*

'What I'm gonna do, ma'am,' he said slowly, like Clint Eastwood delivering a punchline, 'is arrest *you* if you harass it.'

The woman blinked in amazement then started to shriek incomprehensibly, calling out to her husband who was circling at a distance, viewing the alligator circumspectly. The beast had sunk a little. Electric blue dragonflies danced in the air where two walnut-sized eyes showed through the green slime. When the woman paused for breath, the policeman explained that the beachfront development in Sanibel was a strip of condominiums along the Ding Darling wildlife refuge. The animals were here first. The original inhabitants of the refuge included alligators, blue herons and ospreys. He pointed to an osprey perched on the roof of a nearby condominium, but the woman was unimpressed.

'So *all* these animals have rights ahead of people?' The cop nodded and quoted various laws in a bored voice.

'The critters were here first, ma'am,' he repeated. No one smiled.

'More than a thousand bucks we paid,' the woman was shrieking again, 'for a week here. Plus the air fare. It's not −' she could not think of the right word at first. 'It's not *fair*. It's not . . . *American.*'

It was coming close to the time when the alligator would *really* scare her, when it began its daily ritual of leaving the pond every evening as the sun sank over the Gulf of Mexico. Locals were so used to the routine that at 4.30 p.m. they would congregate on a wooden bridge over the sand dunes, drink beer and watch it waddle dinosaur-like over the grass, past the swimming-pool, into the sea and off to wherever alligators like to hunt at night. Gator heaven. The woman with the New York accent said she was *trying* to be reasonable. She just could not *believe* that the *government* of the United States had arranged things so that some dumb *brute* took precedence over *people* who had paid *good money* and flown a thousand miles from *Manhattan* to be here, and when she called the *authorities* – here she scowled at the cop – she was *threatened* with *arrest*.

'It's the goddamn spotted owl all over again,' she hissed, referring to the bird whose presence in old growth forests had curtailed logging in the western United States as the government and courts tried to balance environmental interests with those of the lumber companies. The police officer politely suggested that he did not make the laws, but he *would* enforce them. The alligator was not to be molested. If the lady wanted to complain, she could talk to her congressman, or the Interior Department or somebody.

'*Pah*,' she exploded in disgust. 'What good did *government* ever do anybody?' The word 'government' was delivered like a swear-word. The cop shrugged and adjusted his sunglasses. The woman was not finished with him.

'Well, I guess the *rules* have *changed*,' she snapped with withering scorn, stomping off to her apartment with her husband in tow, muttering something about government destroying the country, going to hell in a handbasket. When she had gone from earshot the policeman looked at me.

'Yeah,' he murmured as he walked back to his patrol car. 'I guess the rules *have* changed.'[1]

This book is an account of how the rules of American life have changed profoundly in the 1990s, upsetting the foundations most Americans have taken for granted in the past fifty years. One result is that the US government is now routinely blamed by many of its citizens for every ill which befalls them, from the alligator in the pond of their vacation home to the apparent moral, social and cultural decline they see all around them.

The United States of Anger is an examination of the changes which are sweeping America with a speed that leaves tens of millions of otherwise law-abiding taxpayers disgusted, angry and fearful that the most successful country in the history of the world is on the brink of a cataclysmic failure. Like the woman in Sanibel, many Americans stand in impotent rage that 'the authorities' or 'the government' do not understand or do not care about them, betraying the best traditions of their country. Amid all the successes of what Henry Luce described as the 'American century', many of the country's citizens remain anxious or angry that the lives they lead fall far short of the America of their dreams.

Some of these complaints are uniquely American. Many are not. In our increasingly global culture, what strikes the United States today hits Britain and Europe tomorrow and the rest of the world next week. An examination of American anger at the bewildering changes in their society illuminates the sense of rudderlessness and confusion many Europeans feel about the pace of change on our own continent. In that sense, parts of this book serve as a warning to Britain and Europe as the uneasy trends in American society cross the Atlantic. These trends also reveal the chronic anxieties of a great and dependable ally which may become less dependable in a world in which many of its citizens fear American dominance is being eroded.

At the heart of this unease, there is a profound disconnection between America in the aggregate and America in the anecdotal, between how well the United States appears to be doing as a country and how satisfied many of its citizens are with their lives.

America in the aggregate is booming. The facts and figures about the United States show it as the most successful nation in the world in the 1990s, the statistics of a land overflowing with milk and honey. Newspapers, television reports, government statements and political speeches are full of good news – low unemployment, low inflation, a booming stock market, falling crime figures, the best high-tech health care in the world and the most technologically advanced military-industrial complex in history.

In the twentieth century this America has defeated Nazism, Fascism, Japanese militarism and Communism, exporting democracy around the world. It won the land war in the Gulf in a hundred hours, swatting away the fourth largest army in the world with fewer casualties than an average weekend on the roads. This America has triumphed militarily, politically, economically and culturally in the past fifty years from the beaches of Normandy to the craters of the moon.

American ideas, ideals and products dominate almost everywhere and almost everyone. If you have ever worn blue jeans or listened to rock and roll, flown in an aeroplane, watched a Hollywood movie, made a telephone call by satellite, used Microsoft computer software or eaten a hamburger, then the triumph of the United States has already affected your life.

From Coca-Cola to TV soap operas, Superman comics to Western heroes, Olympic athletes to astronauts and teenagers wearing baseball caps backwards, American culture has so transformed our way of thinking that it has become impossible to separate it from the daily routines of hundreds of millions of people on every continent on earth. In the words of the old British schoolboy book, *1066 and All That*, America has become top nation and history is therefore at an end. So where is the dancing in the streets? The victory parades?

This book is about a simple paradox. America has conquered the world, and yet Americans have found little peace.

Why, in the midst of so much success, are so many ordinary, practical, hard-working Americans anxious about their future, concerned about the fraying of their society, the prospect of social, cultural and military decline? And why are so many patriotic Americans desperately angry with a political system they see in crisis and possibly on the verge of collapse? Why is a country which finds itself at the end of the century without a credible foreign enemy such an obviously troubled superpower? And what are the implications for the rest of the world when this indispensable ally turns inwards to try to fix domestic problems which undercut its success?

In his second Inaugural Address on a freezing January day in 1997, President Clinton stood on the steps of the Capitol and spoke in the uplifting terms customary on such occasions. He listed the triumphs of the American century but nodded towards the unease of many of its people contemplating a difficult future:

America became the world's mightiest industrial power, saved the world from tyranny in two world wars and a long cold war, and time and time again reached across the globe to millions who longed for the blessings of liberty. Along the way, Americans produced the great middle class and security in old age; built unrivalled centres of learning and opened public schools to all; split the atom and explored the heavens; invented the computer and the microchip; made a revolution in civil rights for minorities; and extended the circle of citizenship, opportunity and dignity to women. Now, for the third time, a new century is upon us, and another time to choose.

The choice Mr Clinton posed for the new century, and the new millennium, was stark. 'Will we be one nation, one people, with one common destiny or not? Will we all come together or come apart?'

To foreign ears it may seem extraordinary that, after reciting such a list of triumphs, an American president raised the prospect of his nation coming unglued. But anger, anxiety and apathy are three symptoms of the American disease of disconnection in the dying years of the twentieth century. Though the body looks in rude health, especially to Europeans perplexed by their own problems, the disease is a metastasizing cancer eating away under the skin.

When they think of the future, millions of Americans fear the best days of their country may have passed, that the fabric of daily life is coarsening, racial and class divisions worsening, and that they will not prosper as their parents and grandparents have done. The core of the new anxiety is the recognition – like that of the woman tourist in Florida confronted by the alligator – that 'the rules' which govern what most Americans think is 'normal' have changed irrevocably. Two fundamental American beliefs which helped create the miracle of the American middle class in the past fifty years appear to have collapsed since the end of the cold war. These two beliefs, almost amounting to an American Creed, are that if you work hard you will make it in America, and that each generation will do better than their parents.

But not in the 1990s. At least not for many middle-income Americans. Job insecurity is widespread everywhere in the industrialized world from Munich and Middlesbrough to Miami and Melbourne, as new technologies deliver some of the promise of the information age. Such insecurity is the number one fear of working Americans because technological change has been more rapid in the United States, and because it is more unsettling in a society which does not have the European tradition of welfare state safety nets. To lose a job in Munich or Middlesbrough is bad enough. To lose it in Miami means something worse – losing health care for your entire family and, quite possibly, the threat of losing a middle-class way of life.

In 1996, during the 'good times', the United States reported a record number of bankruptcies, more than a million for the first time in history. Those bankrupted by job loss and health care costs know they could even find themselves homeless. While only a tiny minority of Americans will ever face such a combination of personal calamities, millions more worry about it. Middle-class life has never looked more insecure in a time of unprecedented churning in the workforce, when today's good job may be tomorrow's redundancy.

Moreover, the rich are getting richer while the rest fall behind. This is true of Britain, but it is much more extreme in the United States. One symptom of national disconnection is that more prosperous Americans often cannot understand, or simply deny, the depth of anxiety within the American middle class. Middle-income Americans fear that, for the first time in history, their families may not share a piece of the American pie; that the future of their children may be bleaker than their own. Instead of the economic nirvana of America in the aggregate that they read about every day in their newspapers, in America the anecdotal there is often an impossible squeeze of increased taxes, lower real incomes and harder work, with little chance of sharing in the dream of constantly increasing prosperity.

The British in the 1990s complained of the lack of a 'feel good factor' despite promising economic trends. In the United States this phenomenon is far more brutal. While Britain and other European countries have spent much of this century managing their relative decline from the status of great powers, Americans are only now experiencing the shock of recognition that they, too, may be eclipsed by rising nations in the East. Such unease strikes well beyond the political thinkers in Washington, to ordinary workers who wonder if the national sense of everlasting progress and perfectability captured in the well-worn idea of the 'American Dream' may be fraying beyond recovery.

'Bill Clinton says he has created 11 million new jobs since he became president,' a police officer in Annapolis, Maryland, told me sarcastically in the autumn of 1996, shortly before the presidential election. 'Sure he has. And I have *four* of them.'[2]

The police officer was not joking. He forcefully described the contrasts between America as seen by the politicians and 'experts', and the real America inhabited by ordinary taxpayers like himself. The policeman works six days in a row in uniform and then has three days off. But to reverse what he says is a decline in his family income, he fills each one of those three 'rest' days with part-time jobs as a security guard at a bingo parlour, a yacht harbour and a business complex. Then he goes back to his 'real' job of protecting and serving his community in police uniform, without a break. His wife also works, and they are raising young children, frazzled by the competing demands of earning a living and being with their kids, a tension typical of millions of working Americans in the 1990s, and more extreme here than anywhere else.

Not surprisingly, the police officer and his wife are unimpressed by the wonderful statistics of America in the aggregate, in which the stock market rose by a third in 1995 and a further quarter in 1996.[3] That is a different country. They do not live there. Their home is in America the anecdotal in which two, three or, in this case, five pay cheques are needed to keep alive an American Dream which for their parents' generation, twenty-five years ago, demanded just one wage earner and one good job. Indeed, the long hours of work of Americans in the 1990s suggest the conditions of a century ago, when 1890s trades unions fought against the 'wage slavery' of seventy- and eighty-hour working weeks imposed by their bosses in the big steel factories and on the railroads.

The angriest voices are those who believe American society is in profound decline. Some of these voices are distressingly familiar and uniquely American. They are the preachers and prophets of the religious Right who, almost since the foundation of the United States, have complained that the end is nigh and who, in the 1990s, have declared a cultural and religious war on their fellow Americans. Their legacy has been a decade in which doctors have been murdered for performing legal abortions, abortion clinics bombed and their staff killed because sections of the angriest Americans believe God has told them to kill in the name of being 'pro-life'.

Religious enthusiasms and anxieties have understandably increased on the brink of the new millennium, which some Christian fundamentalists believe will bring about the 'End Time' of tribulations as biblical prophesy is fulfilled by the second coming of Christ. But much more surprising is the extent to which Americans from the Left and Centre as well as those on the Right fear that American society and culture is no longer merely diverse, but divided to the point of Balkanization.

At an apparently trivial level, increased choice on the radio dial means those who like rap, jazz, country and western, metallic rock, classical, new age or oldies, listen to different stations, hear different advertisements and, in some cases, appear to inhabit different Americas. The same is true of television programmes, including — as advertisers notice — a distinct gap between the preferences of blacks and whites, the rich and the middle class.

The criminal and civil trials of O. J. Simpson divided America along racial lines. So does the continuing row over 'affirmative action' policies – what in Britain is called 'positive discrimination' – preferential treatment given to women or minorities to ensure 'balance'. A generation after the disturbances of the civil rights period, black America is far from content with progress towards racial equality and many white Americans are resentful they are being penalized for past injustices. In 1992, three decades after Americans hoped civil rights would lead to domestic tranquillity, Los Angeles became the scene of the most deadly disturbances in an American city this century. Some black commentators called it an 'uprising' rather than a 'riot', and there were gloomy predictions of a bloody racial war, unless relations between Americans of different colours improve. Compounding the sense of disconnection between the races, the board of education in Oakland, California even tried to obtain federal government funding to compensate for what they described as a separate black ghetto language, glorified by the name 'Ebonics'.

Added to the black–white tension, many Americans complain they are being 'swamped' by an unstoppable immigrant tide, legal and illegal, the largest in history, which literally and figuratively is changing the complexion of the great American cities. There is increasing evidence of an anti-immigrant back-lash, especially against those who come from Latin America and who are criticized for not trying to assimilate into mainstream culture.

'The divide of race has been America's constant curse', President Clinton noted in his second Inaugural Speech. 'Prejudice and contempt, cloaked in the pretence of religious or political conviction, are no different. They have nearly destroyed us in the past. They plague us still. They fuel the fanaticism of terror . . . These obsessions cripple those who are hated and those who hate. We cannot – we will not – succumb to the dark impulses that lurk in the far regions of the soul, everywhere.'

Underlying this pattern of social unease and 'dark impulses' is a strong fear of chronic moral decline, from family break-up and the rise in illegitimacy rates in the past generation to the wickedness of some of the most violent criminals, characterized as 'super-predators'. Even as the crime rate stabilized or fell in the mid-1990s, *fear* of crime remains one of America's unconquerable worries. Yet again there was an apparent disconnection between the rosy statistics and what many Americans believed was the reality in their neighbourhood.

According to one of the most detailed surveys of American public opinion, *The State of Disunion*,[4] published in 1996, the majority of Americans admitted they were 'worried' or 'upset' by the condition of their society. Three out of five feared for their families, the ethical condition of society and for the economy. As many as 21 per cent described themselves as 'angry' or 'resentful' about the criminal justice system. Only one in ten thought that the United States was improving while half believed that 'the US is actually in decline'. One in five believed it was a strong decline.

This pessimism has thoroughly infused what Europeans generally assume to be a peculiarly optimistic society. In the 1830s, Alexis de Tocqueville was able to write that 'America is Great because America is Good'. But by the 1990s millions of Americans complained that America was ceasing to be great because Americans were no longer good. The opinion polls showed that in each decade since the 1950s Americans have been less and less trusting of human nature, of each other and of their government.

'Mistrust permeates our society,' is how Senator George Mitchell, one of the shrewdest observers of American public life, puts it, explaining a constant theme in *The United States of Anger*. Senator Mitchell is the former Democratic majority leader in the Senate, and worked as US special envoy on Northern Ireland. He was chosen to play the role of Bob Dole in practice debates with Mr Clinton during the 1996 presidential election campaign. 'The public's trust of *all* institutions, even of friends, neighbours and family, is declining steadily,' he said.[5]

This mistrust is linked to a decline in one of America's most proudly trumpeted core values, self-reliance, or what Theodore

Roosevelt famously called 'rugged individualism'. Many Americans complain of increasing selfishness and self-indulgence, the death of American heroes and the birth of a culture of victims, in which declarations of being a 'victim' are now so commonplace there is almost no group which has not claimed some kind of 'victimhood'.

Anyone who has travelled widely in the United States in the past decade will have heard about this apparent decline in values in conversation with concerned citizens, or will have understood it from the success of bestselling 'moral' books such as Bill Bennett's *The Book of Virtues*. There is one compelling statistical indicator of moral, social and cultural decline: the United States used to boast of being a society under the rule of law; now it is crippled by the rule of lawyers. The number of lawyers in the United States has grown from 250,000 in the 1970s to 800,000 by 1991, with an expectation of exceeding 1 million by the year 2000. This quadrupling in a generation – with, of course, an associated rise in the number of lawsuits on behalf of 'victims' seeking their 'rights' – has nourished a whining culture of self-pity in which the new 'heroes' are those 'victims' who complain most loudly.

This sense that something is seriously wrong at the core of society has even infected the proudest achievement of the American people – American democracy. The system of government is faltering and, to some, seems incapable of reviving itself. 'Sclerotic', 'paralysed', 'gridlocked' are frequently part of the vocabulary of Washington commentators as voter apathy goes hand in hand with anger towards politics and politicians.

President Clinton called his 1996 re-election a 'bridge to the future' and yet a majority of those eligible could not even be bothered to vote. Since Mr Clinton secured less than half of the votes of those who did go to the polls, he has twice been elected to the world's most powerful office with the backing of fewer than one in four of his fellow countrymen. The crisis of American democracy means weak leaders with weak mandates lead weak political parties at a time of great social upheaval, but it extends far further. The federal government, constructed as the servant of the people, is now frequently reviled as an increasingly despotic or greedy master, or alternatively seen as utterly disconnected from the daily lives of most citizens. Government in America has become the alligator in the pond on Sanibel Island. You cannot shoot it, you cannot move it and it appears scary enough that you cannot ignore it.

One result is that fear and hatred of Communism as the greatest threat to the American way of life has given way to fear and hatred of the US federal government itself. Washington has replaced Moscow as the city Americans love to hate. The 'red scare' of anti-Communist witch-hunts of the 1940s and 50s has become the 'fed scare' of anti-government paranoia in the 1990s. The fed scare is most angrily expressed on the far right-wing fringes of anti-government militias and their supporters. But much more significant – though it has received far less attention – is the way in which disgust or anger towards the government has infected the lives of law-abiding average citizens. The angriest Americans turn out to be neither poor nor uneducated nor from racial minorities. They are the white, well-educated middle classes who forcefully argue that government is out of control and that politicians, lobbyists, Washington journalists and government bureaucrats are part of a self-serving, out-of-touch élite.

According to *The State of Disunion* survey, Americans are suspicious of both their local state government and the US federal government in Washington. As many as three out of four (77 per cent) believed that government is usually run by 'a few big interests' looking out for themselves. One in five went so far as to describe the élite of Washington as being 'involved in a conspiracy' against the interests of the American people.

The notion of government as a monstrous conspiracy has become the most dangerous American neurosis of the 1990s. It has seeped into every level of American popular culture, from television shows like the *X Files* which portray top-level government plots against the people of the United States to novels like

David Baldacci's *Absolute Power*, in which a corrupt, drunken, womanizing president encourages the Secret Service to wipe out those who threaten to expose his wickedness.

Listen to America in the 1990s and you hear troubled voices. There is the traditionally deep patriotism which has been associated with this country for two centuries. But you also hear constant attacks on the legitimacy of US government institutions – on the presidency, Congress, the FBI, the CIA, the Bureau of Alcohol, Tobacco and Firearms, the Education Department, the Department of the Interior, the Environmental Protection Agency and, of course, on the tax gatherers of the Internal Revenue Service. Criticizing government is America's best and most noble tradition. But in the angry 1990s some Americans have gone beyond criticism to cynicism, hatred and violence. There have been physical attacks on federal government personnel, bombings of government offices, gunfire and a kamikaze plane crash directed at the White House, a bomb blast at the Atlanta Olympics and in Oklahoma City the most deadly terrorist incident in American history. The titles of a stack of books written about American politics in the 1990s tell part of the story: *Arrogant Capital: Washington, Wall Street and the Frustration of American Politics*; *Dirty Politics*; *The Angry American: How Voter Rage is Changing the Nation*; *Why Americans Hate Politics*; *The Government Racket: Washington Waste from A to Z*.

For a decade unhappy voters have seemed unable to make up their minds what they wanted or who they wanted, churning with anger and irritation as politicians struggled to pander to their latest concerns. Voters opted for George Bush in 1988, turned against him in 1990, threw him out (despite his Gulf War victory) in 1992, while flirting with a third party candidate, Ross Perot, who had never served in any political office.

Then the electorate switched tack and voted overwhelmingly *against* Clinton in 1994, and within a year reacted against Speaker Newt Gingrich's promised Republican revolution by making him as popular as the Ebola virus by the end of 1995. In 1996 Clinton was back in the White House, and Gingrich was back as Speaker. But for the first time in American history the two leaders of the two powerful elected branches of the American government, President Bill Clinton and Speaker Newt Gingrich, simultaneously faced serious ethical questions about their conduct and fitness to hold high public office. It was a symbol of the national mood of pessimism and distaste for political institutions. Mr Clinton and Mr Gingrich were the two flawed men entrusted with leading America towards the new millennium, and yet they had become *causes*, as well as the targets, of the anger they sought to defuse. President Clinton constantly appealed for political reform, though the many scandals which attached to him made him the weakest possible messenger for a campaign to clean up or revitalize Washington.

'And we will reform our politics,' he said at his second Inaugural Address, 'so that in this land the voice of the people will always speak louder than the din of narrow interests, regaining the participation and deserving the trust of all Americans . . . The American people returned to office a president of one party and a Congress of another. Surely they did not do this to advance the politics of petty bickering and extreme partisanship they plainly deplore. No, they call on us instead to repair the breach . . .'

'Repairing the breach', a biblical phrase much used by Mr Clinton, meant healing the disconnection between Americans and their government and between feuding groups of citizens each pursuing their 'rights'. It is the central task of political leadership in the early years of the twenty-first century, otherwise America will not 'come together'. It will surely come apart, riven by racial and ethnic unrest, by competing visions of what it is to be an American, and engulfed in the angry and potentially violent confrontation between the Washington bureaucracy and those who increasingly despise it.

If cynicism, anxiety and anger are so obviously rampant despite the supposedly 'Good Times' of the 1990s, what might happen when the economy of America in the aggregate turns sour? When the irrational exuberance of the stock market ends in an overdue correction? When unemployment or inflation rises? When the massive baby boom generation finally comes to retire and fewer younger working Americans are compelled to support increasing numbers of older Americans? When the cities say they simply cannot absorb any new immigrants?

A central part of the argument which follows is that the end of the cold war not only redrew the boundaries of the Soviet Union and eastern Europe. The end of that fifty-year-long struggle has also had the same effect, in a more subtle way, *within* the United States. The rules of life of America in the 1990s have indeed changed, redrawing the 'boundaries' between regions, classes, racial groups, employers and employees, and, most importantly, between the American people and their capital of Washington.

On a grand scale, the disconnection between the government and the governed neatly parallels the disconnection between the happy statistics about America in the aggregate and the less happy feelings of ordinary Americans across the country. The Washington Beltway is technically Interstate 495, a highway which forms a doughnut-shaped ring around the Washington centre of government. Inside this doughnut live politicians, government workers, economists and journalists, the 'Inside-the-Beltway Tribe' with their own codes, language and social structure. But, as we will hear repeatedly, this Beltway élite is regarded as being as disconnected from the concerns of ordinary citizens as Marie Antoinette was from the problems of the *sans culottes* in pre-revolutionary France.

For example, a month before the November 1996 presidential elections, the *Washington Post* ran a series of articles on the differences between what economists *said* about the American economy and what ordinary people *believed* to be true.[6] The economists could demonstrate that unemployment was at a seven-year low. Inflation was at the lowest level for thirty years. The budget deficit had declined sharply. The economy was creating more jobs than it was losing. But the public saw the alligator in the slime. One in four ordinary people told the survey they believed that unemployment was more like 25 per cent – Great Depression levels. The public thought prices were rising much faster than they really were, that the budget deficit was increasing, not decreasing. And that there were fewer jobs than five years previously.

The evidence of a profound disconnection is clear. Either the public, in this most information-conscious society and on the brink of what President Clinton and others call the information age, is seriously uninformed, misinformed, misled or plain ignorant. Or, alternatively, economic statistics do not measure the lives most Americans believe they live. Or perhaps both.

President Clinton noticed and feared these trends. In informal comments on Air Force One he spoke of the 'tumult and upheaval' of a life in which the rules kept changing. Americans felt 'lost in the fun house. They always feel that living life is like walking across a running river on slippery rocks and you can lose your footing at any time.' He called this disease a nation-wide 'funk'.[7] It was the recognition, at the highest level of government, that behind the peace and prosperity of America's dazzling success there is a truly dangerous disconnection between government and the governed, between the rich and the middle class (not just rich and poor), and between the vast and wonderfully inventive United States and its often arrogant and out-of-touch Washington élite. It is the stunning contrast between the paradise of Sanibel Island and the fear that a rough and threatening beast lurks somewhere in the slime ready to strike.

Finally, there will be those who resent the idea that a foreigner, despite years of living and travelling in the United States, can presume to write about America. In *Democracy in America* Alexis de Tocqueville was much struck by such sensitivities. 'The Americans in their intercourse with strangers,' he wrote, 'appear impatient of the smallest censure and insatiable of praise.'

For those who take offence at my presumption, I apologize. But the old wisdom that war is too important to be left to the generals may be rewritten thanks to America's success. The United States bears the conqueror's burden. It is too important to the rest of the world for its problems to be relevant only to Americans, and the world is too interconnected for America's anxieties to stop at America's shores. Democratic governments everywhere report moods of disillusionment and the questioning of once unchallengeable social structures or national symbols, from the British royal family to the German Deutschmark.

In America the questioning has gone further and faster than anywhere else, undermining the sense of what it is to be an American in a way that many Europeans have failed to recognize. Besides, this is not a mere country. It is a continent and an idea of human progress, bigger, often better, and frequently more colourful and complex than anything foreigners could ever imagine, especially if their knowledge of the United States springs only from Hollywood movies or exported television programmes.

Whatever subject is under discussion there is *more* of it in America: more wealth, more consumption, more freedom, more poverty, more contradictions, more success, more failure, more violence, and, most definitely, more anger and anxiety, but always more, more, more. The ordinary Americans, who make up the bulk of the voices in this book, face this anxious time with their usual practical common sense, good humour and considerable patriotism. But many are pessimistic that the institutions of their government, and those who aspire to political leadership, are irreparably flawed and about as capable of productive change as a wolf is of becoming vegetarian. There are intimations of failure and decline as America shudders with foreboding that the country's best years may no longer lie ahead.

How America solves these problems, or fails to do so, affects Britain and Europe most closely, but also the rest of the world. What goes wrong in America tends to go wrong everywhere. What goes right in America becomes the candle which is lit to prevent the rest of us from cursing the darkness. That is why the journey through a disconnected America begins with a family in rural New Hampshire, anxious that the candle has been blown out.

Freezing the American Dream

'The American economy presents a curious paradox. Employment is high and inflation is low; yet many Americans feel growing economic anxiety.'

Building the Bridge, *Progressive Policy Institute, 1997*[1]

Berlin, New Hampshire

The man walking across the frozen lake is carrying something in his hand, a stick probably. Even at this distance you can see his boots kick up a light dusting of snow on the ice as his dog, a tan-coloured labrador, runs around. It is bitterly cold, at least ten below freezing, with an icy wind from the north like a knife in the ribs. He is bundled up in a goose down parka, so bulky he looks like the Michelin man. Everything is white and frozen, then the man bends down and puts a golf ball on the ice. The stick turns out to be a seven iron and he pitches the ball a hundred yards as the dog runs after it across the ice.

This is New Hampshire where, once every leap year, the fate of American democracy is, by an accident of history, in the hands of the ice golfer and 800,000 other voters in the first in the nation primary election. I am driving on Interstate 93 north to meet a family who say they were once living that cliché, the elusive American Dream, but now the dream is frozen and possibly lost to them and their generation.

The road cuts through the old mill town of Manchester – where mill jobs have mostly gone – along the Merrimack River, past the ice golfer to the White Mountains. The towns thin out and the scenery is spectacular: mixed forests, frozen waterfalls, ski resorts and alpine meadows in valleys they call 'notches'. Locals joke that there are only two seasons: winter and July. This is winter. Snow is forecast and a few flurries begin. The wind-chill is so fierce when I stop to ask for directions that it reminds me of the Jack London story when the Old Timer warns that nobody – *nobody* – goes outside when it is forty below. Except crazy people.

Heavy trucks carrying huge logs roll past, each with number-plates which read 'New Hampshire – Live Free or Die'. Only in America would these be the available choices. Road signs instruct you to brake for moose. 'Hundreds of accidents', they warn, which sounds funny until half a ton of moose emerges from the forest to trot along the roadside and you brake hard because hitting it would be like driving into a brick wall.

By the time the Androscoggin river snakes into view you are in Berlin, a small town of 11,000 people. Bleached smoke from the chimneys of the colossal paper-mills pumps into the sky, then a few houses appear clustered like toys around the mills' feet. Crown Vantage mill is so big that people walking below look like matchstick figures from a Lowry painting.

Berlin's Main Street is one way, running parallel to the river towards a second big mill. The cars are of an older, patriotic America, gas guzzlers, Oldsmobiles and Chevys, pick-up trucks with dogs inside, gun racks for hunting rifles, four-wheel drive Jeeps. Two restaurants face each other competitively, a Country Kitchen which proudly offers its speciality: 'Fried Food'. The alternative is Choo Choo's which boasts meatloaf, mashed potatoes, a vegetable, a small salad and coffee for five dollars.

The owner, a portly sixty-six-year-old with a bald head and a long white chef's apron, is Lionel Caron. Everyone calls him Choo Choo. He is frying eggs and bacon. His daughter is the waitress, and all around the restaurant model aircraft hang from the ceiling. They are made from beer or Coke cans, biplanes, triplanes and sea-planes, expertly built by one of Choo Choo's relatives to earn a little extra cash.

At the counter a handful of locals discuss politics. Betty Jo and James LaRocque are in their late fifties. He is unshaven with a couple of teeth missing and looks cock-eyed through thick glasses with the desperate, kicked-around air of a man who has given up. She has dyed brown hair and a wan smile, and works in a bank. The LaRocques voted for Bill Clinton last time, but not this time. Betty Jo is resentful that she did not find out Clinton was 'in favour of abortion' until after the 1992 election – which is surprising because abortion rights was a major plank of Clinton's campaign.

Betty Jo says, oh, she must have missed it then. She admits she is not well informed, perhaps because politicians disgust her. 'If you want my honest opinion,' she says softly, 'I don't really believe in any of them. I think they're in it for their own benefit. I think I may vote for the one who sounds good.' Her voice trails away. 'And be disappointed later.'

Her husband, James, launches into articulate support of the ultra-right-wing Republican presidential candidate Patrick Buchanan, who claims to be 'a conservative of the heart', though to his critics he is more like a conservative of the lower bowel – visceral, flatulent, grumbling. 'Buchanan,' LaRocque claims, is 'for the working man.'

In fact, Buchanan is a symptom of a very significant return in the 1990s of an old and virulent strain in American history, 1930s' style 'America First' politics. He is a populist exploiting class resentment: anti-foreigner, anti-big government, anti-big business, isolationist and protectionist, a phenomenon which seems to symbolize a return to widening class divisions for the first time since the Second World War. Buchanan's 'America First' rhetoric certainly impressed the diners in Choo Choo's.

'If you're in the poorhouse, you don't help somebody else,' James LaRocque insists, thumping along with Buchanan's nativist beat. I wonder why he thinks America, the richest country in the world, engaging – according to the economists – in a sustained economic recovery, is in the poorhouse. Before I can ask, he continues. 'You help yourself. They can put bridges across

Bosnia, spend money like that ... they should help poor little Berlin, New Hampshire to get back on its feet.'

Buchanan is a hero because the maverick right-winger has done something very un-Republican. In the party of business, Buchanan has attacked the 'Corporate Killers', the big bosses who get fat by firing American workers from what were once assumed to be secure jobs. Men like the Chief Executive of AT&T, Robert Allen, who earns more than $3 million a year and has just fired 40,000 staff. Or Walter Shipley, who piloted the Chemical and Chase Manhattan Bank merger with 12,000 lay-offs. He earns $2.5 million a year. In his presidential campaign speeches Buchanan, like a great tradition of populists, exploits the sense of class division and appeals across party lines to what in the 1990s were called 'angry white men'.

There once was a more familiar name for the same people in industrial America from the 1890s to the 1930s. They used to be called 'working class'. And the Corporate Killers used to be called the 'Robber Barons'. The workers in Choo Choo's speak like echoes of the angry class conflict which, from the Homestead strike of 1892 to the River Rouge Ford plant violence in the 1930s, was once a strong American tradition. The sense of class resentment, if not the violence, appears to be coming back. Every time the corporate bosses kill American jobs, James LaRocque concludes angrily, they make more money because their stock options soar. They earn their millions by destroying working families. 'That's not right,' he shakes his head. 'It's not *right*.'

But it is accurate. By the mid-1990s, according to the Economic Policy Institute, after-tax company profits in America were the highest for a generation, but workers' wages were stagnant or had declined for all except the best paid, for more than twenty years. The average middle-class American, after inflation, was no better paid in 1990 than in 1970, and most lower-class families saw their incomes fall. In the last decades of the twentieth century the United States was witnessing the largest increase in the divide between rich and poor wage earners in any developed nation – an enormous gulf had opened compared to a few years before.

In the 1960s, the typical pay of a chief executive in a big American company was thirty times that of the average worker. By 1990 the ratio had shot up to 135 times. A top company pay survey showed the median salary plus cash bonuses for chief executives was more than $2 million a year. To maximize share options, chief executives were, as everyone in Choo Choo's restaurant knew, slashing jobs.[2]

Bill Clinton used to say that the bosses got the goldmine and the workers got the shaft. But what, the LaRocques wanted to know, is Clinton doing about it? He is with the fat cats down in Washington, they concluded, hand out, asking for campaign contributions. Clinton will never attack the Corporate Killers in favour of the little guy and risk the money for his campaign drying up.

I eat my meatloaf, which was not bad for five bucks, and talk to Choo Choo, who is clearing up. His customers have French-Canadian names – Villeneuve, Vachon, LaRocque – and he bears the wistful air of a provincial French café owner, descended from one Robert Caron who left Normandy 360 years ago for Quebec. In the Roaring Twenties Choo Choo's parents moved down to find work in the New Hampshire paper mills. He was born here in Berlin in 1929 and speaks French as his first language. The paper-mills, he says grimly, once employed 4,400 people. Now it is 1,000 and dropping. Last October another 150 workers were laid off. I respond that economists said unemployment in New Hampshire is low. A Gallic shrug. Economists, like politicians, are disconnected from Choo Choo's America. 'Sure. People move away.'

The politicians don't know or don't care. They read the *Wall Street Journal* which says the stock market is soaring. The Labor Department statistics look good, so the politicians assume everything must be fine. But it is not. The good jobs are going, Choo Choo says, and they are not coming back. The new jobs here are lower paid, lower skilled, part-time and without health care and other benefits, a familiar, depressing litany.

'Give me fifty senators,' Choo Choo demands fiercely, an

articulate example of the new American working-class anger. 'Up here, we'll find 'em jobs. They will have to leave their credit cards, limousines and tuxedos in Washington but they can bring their families. What you earn is what you live on . . . They have no concept of what the value of a dollar is to working people.'

Or a trillion dollars. Underlying the unease of many ordinary American workers is the sense that while they work hard to pay their bills and balance their cheque-books, the US government lives by different rules. Washington consistently spends more than it earns, even in the good times. Choo Choo regards this as a sign of chronic incompetence and moral failure. Ronald Reagan's legacy has been to ensure that no nation in peacetime has ever gone as rapidly as America from being the world's largest creditor to the world's greatest debtor nation – with the possible exception of France in the 1780s, leading up to the French Revolution.[3]

President Reagan would have liked to be remembered as the man who broke the government of the Soviet Union. But his unique position in history is that he destroyed one superpower by virtually bankrupting the other. Historian Garry Wills wrote that 'it is not given to many presidents to spend *two* world empires towards decline'. Reagan's 'supply side economics' meant, according to true believers, that you could cut taxes, increase defence spending and not worry about balancing the budget.

George Bush called it 'Voodoo Economics'. As Wills points out, it was not a coherent economic strategy. Yet as a political plan it was a stroke of genius. For those ideologically committed to dismantling or discrediting the US government, Reaganomics was exactly what was necessary to create such debt that it dried up the resources available. The Reagan Deficit Monster ate Washington. The old critique of Democrats was that they were the party of 'Tax and Spend'. The new Reagan Republican policy was an enormous change of the 'rules' of American political life – 'Spend but do *not* Tax'. The consequences have been profound not merely for the direction of the US government, but also for its reputation for competence.

Reagan rhetoric about 'getting Big Government off your backs' was achieved by trying to render government impotent through lack of money. By the 1990s, that meant taxpayers' money was increasingly committed to programmes the politicians could not, or dared not, change, with serious negative consequences for how Americans have come to regard politics, politicians and the institutions of government. Year after year most of the budget – in 1998 it will be as much as 83 per cent according to White House projections – is already spent, paying the interest on the Reagan debts or funding sacred and uncuttable entitlements like Social Security (state old-age pensions), Medicare (health care for the elderly), or defence. That leaves the politicians a tiny slice – 17 per cent in 1998 – which they can cut if they choose. For good or ill, Reaganomics helped emasculate American political leadership.[4]

Choo Choo Caron folds his arms across his chest and purses his lips angrily at the mere mention of the government in Washington. Like the woman tourist in Florida, and countless other taxpayers throughout this book, for Choo Choo 'government' is almost a swear-word.

He is firmly of the view that politics has become a career, a way of life, for too many people, like welfare at its worst. One estimate says that in the mid-1990s there were 500,000 elected officials in the United States, from local mayors right up to the president. Many of them were, as Choo Choo says, career politicians – what the comedian Will Rogers once called the only 'distinctively native American criminal class'. There were 85,000 different governments from local counties and cities to the federal government in Washington. And there were 19.5 million government workers in a population of 260 million people. In fact, in the 1990s, for the first time in history, the number of Americans working for government was greater than the number in manufacturing industry.

That means the United States has become the most over-governed democracy in the world, at a time when the mountainous federal debt made government often seem impotent. Most days in the 1980s and 90s newspapers and TV news programmes could recount examples of political paralysis in Washington, 'Government Gridlock', the failure of politicians to decide where to cut spending or where to raise taxes. It is hardly surprising citizens concluded that more government was not better government.[5]

By 1993, three-quarters of Americans did *not* trust the federal government to do the right thing when taking decisions. This collapse in trust had happened over one generation: for comparison, in 1958, three-quarters of Americans *did* trust the federal government to do the right thing.[6] Only 5 per cent of Americans admitted to having 'a great deal of confidence' in members of Congress, according to *The State of Disunion* study of 1996. This was down from 42 per cent in 1966.[7] The decline in confidence was an inevitable result of aggressive media scrutiny of scandals after Watergate and the official lies told about the Vietnam war and other matters. But underpinning the collapse in trust is a brutal economic fact. Even if the economy seemed sound, by the 1990s the American government appeared so hamstrung by budget and deficit worries that it had become a pitiful, helpless giant – not a solution, but a problem in itself, a can't-do government in an aggressively and impatiently can-do society.

I finish my coffee and Choo Choo laughs when I step out into the bitter wind. 'Keep cool,' he calls out cheerfully, then returns to cleaning up. My appointment with the American Dream is five miles out of town. I smell it first, wood smoke rising above the snowy fields. The Morin family have built their own log cabin in two acres, surrounded by forests of white birch, oak and pine.[8]

Claude Morin is a thickset man of thirty-two with a walrus moustache and wiry hair like a pot scourer. When he shakes your hand, it stays shook. Your body bounces. His wife, Ann Marie, is an articulate physiotherapist who works in a small local hospital. They have one daughter, Mary, aged three, who peeps out shyly from behind her mother's legs, and a dog, Bayley, who stands accused of gross moral turpitude. Instead of breeding as planned with another thoroughbred spaniel to produce a litter which would make the Morins $250 a head in much needed cash, Bayley has been sleeping around, giving birth to nine mongrel pups. Little Mary shows off the pups anyway.

Claude says he was laid off by the paper-mill last October. He speaks slowly and deliberately, trying to hide his anger. He has spent three months as a house-husband looking after his daughter while his wife is the sole breadwinner, and he knows he is running out of options. He admits with restrained panic that yet another job he applied for told him today that he had not been hired. As a machine operator at the paper-mill he used to work twelve-hour shifts at $13 an hour. Hard work, good money. Now all the jobs are around $7 an hour, even if he could get one. Stacking shelves in a supermarket. Dreary. Dead end. Dismal. He says he might lose the log cabin, and the big man is almost in tears because this really is his American Dream, the home the family built themselves in the forest. The Morins' desperation is part of a pattern which suggests this may become the generation in which − for many average Americans − the venerable cliché of the Dream finally crumbles.

The American Enterprise Institute reported that couples with no children prospered in the past generation because their income rose when women, like Ann Marie Morin, started to work. But, by the mid-1990s, what began as a liberating choice for women to work became a *necessity*. The rules of basic economic life really did change irrevocably when the one-breadwinner family of the 1950s and 60s became transformed into the two-breadwinner families of the 1970s and 80s. By the 1990s, for many families the second breadwinner is now compulsory, and so are extra part-time jobs. Even more unnerving, the AEI study suggested that the more your family looked like the traditional American Dream − mum, dad and the kids − the worse off you became. For all but the top 20 per cent of wage earners, if you dared have more than two children then you were probably not doing as well as a generation ago, even with *both* parents working.[9]

All industrialized countries including, of course, Britain, have experienced a similar dislocation, but it is especially acute in the

United States. At the end of the cold war, at the peak of American military power, there is a sense of decline rather than of triumph. America's decline is 'strong' or 'moderately strong' according to 51 per cent of those surveyed for *The State of Disunion* poll.[10] The rise of the economies of the 'Asian Tigers', and particularly China, has helped the United States' share of world GDP continue to decline since it dominated all world markets at the end of the Second World War. Even if most Americans do not know the economic statistics, they sense trouble ahead for themselves and for the country.

'We were always raised with the ideals that if we wanted something we had to work for it,' Ann Marie says of the basic rules of her life, the social contract which guided generations of Americans to prosperity. 'That was not a problem for us. We want to work . . . We *have* lived the American Dream. We would like to have another child —'

'But not right now,' Claude breaks in. Another child can typically cost $10,000 or more in hospital fees for a normal delivery, plus all the dislocation to the mother's career. Europeans rarely understand this American anxiety.

To lose a job in the United States usually means to lose health insurance, possibly for an entire family. Every industrial society is experiencing 'downsizing' by corporate bosses anxious to boost profits and maximize efficiency. But the United States is the only industrialized country without a health insurance system for all its citizens.

When President Clinton began his abortive effort to introduce comprehensive health care in 1993, an estimated 37 million Americans were without insurance, about 15 per cent of the population. Approximately 72 million had no insurance coverage for frequently expensive prescription drugs. All the good news about low unemployment could not ease the anxiety that losing or changing jobs might mean you were one illness away from bankruptcy. And, up to 1997, if you were unfortunate enough to have what American insurers call a 'pre-existing condition' you were doubly cursed. Even if you could find a new job you might be refused health insurance on the most incredible grounds of all: that you might get sick.[11]

The Morins, fortunately, did not face this anxiety directly. After a while, Claude cheered up. We talked about the economics of the north country — the dead 600-lb moose he found last autumn freshly hit by a truck, and from which he recovered 190 lbs of meat, including sausages and hamburgers. He hunted white tailed deer and pheasant. The freezer was well stocked and he managed to collect free waste wood — three cords, or a small truckload — from local woodyards, enough to heat the house all winter. He offered me water from the tap, cold and fresh from their own artesian well, deep below their property. It was not hard to imagine a similarly intense pride in the first pioneers who shaped the forests of the American frontier. But Claude knew self-reliance was not enough. What made him most angry was the knowledge that his fate was not in his own control.

Like those in Choo Choo's restaurant, Claude turned bitter when he talked of the Corporate Killers and the Washington politicians who were a disconnected élite, as separated from his daily struggles as aliens from another planet. There was some kind of company reorganization, he explained, vaguely referring to the paper-mill's parent company a thousand miles away in Richmond, Virginia. The lay-offs started again.

Downsizing. Whoever it was who fired him, the company still sent him quarterly shareholders' reports showing that the corporation's shares were doing very well on Wall Street, thank you. Claude was baffled and enraged by the morality of a corporate America in which the more jobs the chief executives killed the better they were regarded and the more they were paid. The stock market was booming. The Dow Jones index breached 6,000 for the first time in history in 1996 and roared onwards. Up more than 30 per cent in 1995. Up a further quarter in 1996. Onward and upward, as that great Robber Baron of the 1890s, Andrew Carnegie, used to say. But where was Claude's share of the increasing national prosperity?

We walked outside with the spaniel Bayley barking and running crazily in the snow. With the enthusiasm of a pioneer, Claude explained how he chose the land, cleared the trees, then sank the foundations. They bought logs in a kit but cut every joint themselves, varnished the wood with the help of brothers, sisters, mothers, fathers and cousins. 'I told them I'd get the beer and the food,' he laughed, 'if they helped with the work.'

Then he talked about the pain of selling up and moving away to where the jobs are. The sunbelt, maybe. Texas, the south or south-west, Montana, Wyoming. He did not know where. He and Ann Marie still dared to believe that they might do better than their parents and that three-year-old Mary could do even better still, maybe becoming a doctor – though opinion polls suggest half of all Americans do *not* think the next generation will be better off. In Britain and Europe there are similar worries about the future, but nowhere is there such a sense that the Dream is fading as there is for middle-class Americans. They fear that the sun is setting on a way of life and that able, skilled workers will no longer be able to make it as their parents did.

In October 1996 the *Washington Post* reported that three out of five Americans claimed they did not make enough money to save. One in four had problems with bill collectors.[12] And in 1996 there were a record 1 million bankruptcies. At the height of the supposed boom more citizens were filing for personal bankruptcy than the 900,000 total bankruptcies recorded at the end of the recession in 1992. The prosperity of America in the aggregate was not filtering through to most of its citizens, except those who were already well off.

The Morins and I said farewell. I drove back to my hotel in the darkness hoping they would be lucky. Theirs was the perennial dilemma at the core of American life since the first immigrants left Europe: do you stay among friends and family or do you sacrifice and uproot for the promise that thousands of miles away there really is a better life? The Morins would uproot, I decided, to pursue the Dream. Americans always did.

I reached my hotel optimistic about their spirit, until I switched on the television to catch up with the latest twists in the American presidential election campaign which had rolled into New Hampshire. There had been a lot of talk about 'reviving the American Dream'. It was to become Senator Bob Dole's slogan, though every presidential candidate routinely promised that America's best days were still ahead. Listening to them talk, I was not so sure.

One candidate, TV reporters said, was 'out of touch' because he did not know the price of a dozen eggs or a gallon of milk. Another prospective successor to George Washington and Abraham Lincoln was asked by a reporter – undoubtedly an investigative reporter – what kind of underwear he favoured. A third was giving out a recipe for apple pie. A fourth, Senator Dole, passed around photographs of himself, his wife, his dog called – you could not make this up – Leader. They all had a debate in which they snapped at each other to no real effect. With the snow falling heavily, CBS News concluded it was *Snow White* in New Hampshire and the candidates were all dwarves named Grumpy.

I tried to imagine which one of these performers in the Theatre of the Political Absurd was most likely to get Claude Morin a good job. None of them. Claude would survive, maybe even prosper, but it would have to be by his own efforts.

'I didn't realize,' Senator Dole complained with genuine irritation, 'that jobs and trade and what makes America work would become a big issue in the last few days of this campaign.' Senator Dole came from humble mid-Western stock. But I knew that back in Choo Choo's restaurant they would think that he had spent the past thirty-five years of his life orbiting a distant planet. Maybe he had. For thirty-five years he had been in Congress at the heart of American government, which – the Morins, the LaRocques, Choo Choo Caron and tens of millions of other Americans clearly believed – was equally detached from the cares of this world.

On the local TV news the weatherman said heavy snow was general, blanketing the north country. I looked out of the window wondering whether the tough ice golfer was still at his game on some darkened frozen lake, and whether the Morins were watching the candidates' debate. Probably not. They would be too busy figuring out how to survive in the new America which was decidedly like a much older America. It was suddenly at peace. But not with itself.

America's Fifty Years War

'It is a big idea: a New World Order ... to achieve the universal aspirations of mankind – peace and security, freedom and the rule of law.'

President George Bush, State of the Union speech, January 1991

Floyd County, East Kentucky

It is morning in George Bush's kinder, gentler America. In the Appalachian mountains that run like a spine down the eastern United States, the sun splits the oak leaves and pine branches, warming the mountain hollows. It is 1991, the first spring of what President Bush called the New World Order. From small east Kentucky towns like Beattyville and Barbourville, to big cities like Washington and New York, proud parents, wives and girlfriends are preparing to do what Americans have done for fifty years almost without a break: welcome home local boys who fought in a foreign war. (And some girls, too. The rules really have changed.)

This last war of the Old World Order was against Iraq, and it was fought for the oldest reasons: the security of America, its allies and trading partners depended upon Gulf oil. By invading Kuwait Saddam Hussein had placed a potential choke-hold on the world economy. In early 1991 the United States and its allies released that choke-hold in one of the most decisive military encounters in history.

The day on which victory was declared was unseasonably warm and sunny for February at the White House. Across the street in Lafayette Park anti-war demonstrators continued to pound their drums in protest at the struggle, but no one paid them any attention. Even the German shepherd dogs which patrolled the White House grounds caught the relaxed mood, lolling on the grass by the north-west gate, playing with their black-uniformed Secret Service handlers. There was the promise of magnificent victory parades honouring the Desert Storm heroes. In Beattyville and Barbourville chests were swelling with patriotic pride. In New York there was to be a ticker-tape parade. And in Washington there would be a fly-past of stealth aircraft and an evening of fireworks in the heart of a picture-perfect capital of the Free World. Of the Whole World.

But the war with Iraq marked more than a nasty struggle with a brutish Third World dictator. It did not quite usher in what President George Bush dramatically called the New World Order. But it did bury an old order which had lasted for half a century, with a profound effect on every strand of American life. The old order of the past fifty years created the modern industrial United States. The new order, whatever that might be, does not yet exist. The core of America's anxiety and anger in the 1990s is that Americans live in between, in a new *dis*order.

The old order began when Japan dropped its bombs on Pearl Harbor in December 1941, and did not end until America dropped its cruise missiles on Baghdad in January and February 1991. The end of this old order brought America its first true peace for fifty years. There was no terrifying enemy any more. Yet the Fifty Years War (or near-war) from 1941 to 1991 irrevocably changed the character, economy and sense of purpose of the United States and its citizens. It marked the triumph of democracy as the pre-eminent form of political organization in the world, and the victory of the United States as its pre-eminent salesman.

Above all, the Gulf war was an unequal contest between the future and the past. It was a war between an information-age superpower, using stealth aircraft, computers, unmanned cruise missiles and spy satellites, and an old-fashioned industrial-age military machine relying on big tanks, heavy artillery and almost useless anti-aircraft guns and missiles. The conflict was as one-sided as that between Europeans with rifles and native American Indians with bows and arrows for control of the New World. It was also a symbol of the broader changes sweeping the world as industrial America finally gave way to information-age America. This change is one of most pervasive reasons for the 'funk' noticed by President Clinton.

In the new order, whatever that might prove to be, Americans suddenly have access to hundreds of cable and satellite television channels, radio stations and the Internet. Across the world, even the most mundane jobs involve computers, personal pagers, modems, faxes and mobile telephones for the first time.

These 1990s work tools are so widespread they reach from the most prosperous multinational corporations down to America's least glamorous business, neighbourhood street corner drug dealing. None of us, anywhere, quite understands where these changes are leading, or what is about to change next. The sense of doubt makes all of us anxious.

No American worker wants to go the way of the typewriter or the Iraqi Republican Guard – once all-powerful but suddenly rendered obsolete by computers, stealth aircraft and cruise missiles. We all know there is no going back from these changes. But to understand the real reasons behind America's 'funk', we do have to return to what was considered normal in the Old World Order, the past fifty years of war or near-war which shaped what we assumed were 'the rules' by which we lived in the United States and much of western Europe. And then we have to recognize that many of the stresses of America in the 1990s have strong parallels in the period before the Second World War, most especially the 1890s to the 1930s.

After their defeat in 1945, Japan and Germany were quickly refashioned in America's own image: capitalist powers with democratic constitutions and a free press. It was the start of America's role as the most successful exporter of democracy in the world. Within two years of VJ Day President Truman was forced to switch enemies, trying to contain Communism. He failed in China but succeeded in Greece and Italy. Then, in rapid succession, came the Korean war, the crises over Berlin and Hungary, Cuba and Vietnam, plus all kinds of dirty sideshows in thankless struggles from Nicaragua and Chile to Iran and Ethiopia. To call this period of superpower rivalry the 'cold war' is something of a nonsense. More than 100,000 American military personnel were killed in unglorious conflicts during those fifty years, 58,000 of them in Vietnam. This was a *real* war. Real people died, making real sacrifices. And it was also a *total* war. From the military draft to red scares and McCarthyism, from spy trials to movies like *Dr Strangelove* and bitter rows over the kind of memorial appropriate to the Vietnam conflict, the Fifty Years War affected, or perhaps infected, every aspect of life in the United States.

There was little doubt that the United States was engaged in a life-or-death struggle for control of the planet and beyond. The total war spilled over from proxy struggles in faraway countries to economic rivalry, the space race, athletic contests, cultural competitiveness, even chess matches. Each provided a clue to the relative worth of the two combatants and their political systems.

These fifty years utterly transformed Washington from a sleepy, provincial Southern town into the modern capital of the pre-eminent superpower, the nuclear guarantor of Western freedom. The Capital Beltway was built. So was the Pentagon. So was 'Gucci Gulch' – the lawyer and lobbyist enclave along Washington's K Street. President Eisenhower warned against the permanence of a 'military industrial complex' created to win the superpower struggle, but which would in the end dominate the lives of ordinary Americans. On the face of it, such 'domination' appeared to be benign. As Michael Elliott has shown in his masterly account of what he calls 'the Golden Age' in *The Day Before Yesterday*, America's economy roared to meet the challenges of the cold war struggle. The military draft helped homogenize America. Millions of men who otherwise might not have left their home towns or home states, were posted to Okinawa, Khe Sanh, East Anglia or Naples. Black Americans finally began to serve alongside white Americans in uniform in an integrated military which led the way towards a more integrated society.[1]

Beyond the Beltway, the wartime economy helped create the Interstate system of roads which allowed Americans of modest means to travel their country. And, above all, the economy produced an apparently endless supply of well-paid jobs, even for workers of modest skills. One pay cheque per family – Dad's – built the American Dream. It also built the American middle class. A soldier who had served in Germany or Korea could easily find work as a carpenter or metal worker in a car factory, settle down, buy a home and a car, raise kids and thrive.

In September 1991, the Fifty Years War came to a symbolic end. President Bush finally stood down the American bombers of Strategic Air Command, the nuclear strike force of planes sitting on the tarmac with their engines running ready to pound the USSR into oblivion at a moment's notice.

The 'nuclear clock' of atomic scientists, which for years had instructed us all just how close we were to Armageddon, did the impossible for a timepiece. It ticked backwards. Suddenly the cold war arsenal of nuclear submarines and ICBMs, even the vocabulary of arms control, 'throw-weights' and 'MIRVs', seemed as quaint as the bows and arrows of Agincourt. America and its allies had triumphed. But after years of sacrifice, the end of fifty years of undeclared war would have as profound effects on American society as the struggle itself once had.

For years during the cold war American schoolchildren had been instructed to 'Duck and Cover' – duck down and cover themselves with whatever was at hand to protect from nuclear annihilation. (School desks? Exercise books?) Information films of the period show Jimmy leaping off his bike and crouching with his classmates under desks while a cartoon turtle explains the efficacy of a strong shell against thermonuclear attack. It looks as amusing and as dated as a Charlie Chaplin movie. But for those fifty years *every* American from the Pentagon war room to the local schoolroom was mobilized with considerable unity of purpose in a great struggle which America could not afford to lose. The struggle has gone. So has the unity of national purpose which began to crumble in the divisions over Vietnam and disappeared when what Ronald Reagan saw as the 'evil empire' of Communism finally collapsed.

But there was nothing 'normal' about the period from 1941 to 1991. It was an aberration in American history. The economic growth which touched *all* levels of American society during this period was exceptional, allowing President Kennedy to say that a 'rising tide' will raise 'all boats'. Also exceptional was the idea that the United States had a permanent world role – as guarantor of democracy – and a permanent enemy. From the founding of the Republic the only obvious American 'enemy' was Britain, which mostly acted as a trade rival before becoming the closest possible ally. And the only 'permanent' world role of the United States had been to exploit the great untapped interior of the continent while keeping out of foreign entanglements. America, for most of its history, therefore, was very different from what its citizens who grew up in the past fifty or sixty years have come to take for granted.

From the 1890s, when industrialization gathered pace, to the outbreak of the Second World War, America was, as Michael Elliott demonstrates, riddled with class resentment and division. In 1911 *The Los Angeles Times* printing plant was bombed and twenty-one people were killed. In 1914 company goons and soldiers of the National Guard killed thirteen people (including women and children) at a Colorado mining camp. In 1919 social-ists led a general strike which paralysed Seattle. The Robber Barons – the great corporate interests of the time – built the railroads and steel mills but were even more vilified than today's Corporate Killers.

Ever since the founding of the Republic, Americans have feared class warfare almost as much as racial conflict. Those who drafted the Constitution fretted that too much democracy might subvert the interests of the governing élite. The safety-valve was always the promise that even poor Americans could get ahead and prosper by hard work and thrift. At the turn of the last century there were great gulfs between the wealthiest Americans and the workers they employed. Politicians were regarded with contempt. Journalists raked for muck (and found it). Waves of immigrants threatened to 'swamp' the existing Anglo-Saxon culture with a Babel of foreign tongues. It sounds depressingly familiar. There were other social upheavals including the assassination of President McKinley, culminating in the birth of a progressive movement which led to the reforms of Theodore Roosevelt and Woodrow Wilson. In the period leading up to the Second World War it is fair to describe American society as frequently being swept along by strong currents of isolationism, protectionism and nativism. There was a weak federal government, no obvious foreign enemy, slum-ridden cities replete with racial tensions, endemic poverty and sporadic warfare between criminal gangs. This, also, sounds depressingly familiar. But that America ended with Pearl Harbor. For the next fifty years it was replaced by a different vision of America's world role, a vision quite unusual in the history of the United States.

President John F. Kennedy's Inaugural Address captures exquisitely the tone. On 20 January 1961, on the steps of the Capitol, Kennedy's focus was not on domestic policy, as it would be for Bill Clinton a generation later. Instead, Kennedy followed Roosevelt, Truman and Eisenhower as a leader in time of war, a style adapted and copied by Johnson, Nixon, Ford, Carter, Reagan and Bush.

Addressing himself, significantly, not to 'my fellow Americans', but to 'my fellow citizens of the world', Kennedy announced: 'We shall pay any price, bear any burden, meet any hardship, support any friend, oppose any foe to ensure the success and survival of liberty.'

Americans did *precisely* that. It was the most eloquent statement of American idealism and seriousness of national purpose in the Fifty Years War. But by 1990, with the cold war almost over, the former Kennedy aide, Theodore Sorensen, began adding up the bill:

Through nine administrations and twenty-two Congresses virtually every dimension and deployment of our armed forces, virtually every weapons system developed, diplomatic move taken and foreign dollar expended have been shaped primarily by the need to wage and win the cold war with Communism . . . this nation put up with complaining allies, poured money into ungrateful or undemocratic governments, opened our markets to disagreeable competitors, involved ourselves in other countries' internal matters, and contributed funds to multilateral organizations in which we were consistently outvoted, all in the interests of winning friends against the Soviet empire and keeping others out of the Soviet orbit. Now there is no Soviet empire and no Soviet orbit.[2]

And no sense of triumph either. President Kennedy was speaking at the height of Imperial America, the last, best hope for mankind. Thirty years later Theodore Sorensen was the prophet of Angry America, a grumpy waiter delivering the bill and irritated that the tip is not going to be big enough. By the time Sorensen was writing, America had lost an enemy but failed to find a role. It had constructed a society, from the CIA to the Peace Corps, the military draft to the underlying patriotic values which venerate the American flag, which had made the country more homogeneous and prosperous than ever in history. But the 'peace dividend' that George Bush prophesied at the end of the cold war never arrived. Instead, the United States was hit by the same tectonic shifts which dislocated Europe. The rules changed. Everything changed.

The result of America's victory has been a profound sense of anticlimax as deep as anything which afflicted Britain after the Great War. And yet it was a great victory. Ronald Reagan had demanded 'Mr Gorbachev, tear down that wall', and a few years later you can find bits of the Berlin wall, suitably fossilized in clear hard plastic or on plaques, in the offices of American diplomats, members of Congress and generals in the Pentagon. The Soviet Union had gone. Even the Sandinistas in Nicaragua had fallen. By 1991 it was hardly surprising that George Bush had a personal approval rating of 90 per cent, the highest since opinion polling began. He was confident of re-election and the Democrats could not find even one prominent candidate to run against him. Life was good.

Except that in small-town America, down in Floyd County, east Kentucky, something was wrong. Even in the sunshine, people were not celebrating. The shop fronts on Main Street were bedecked with yellow ribbons and flags. A cascade of red, white and blue signs praised the 'Desert Storm Heroes'. But a few paces further, it was not so colourful. Most of the stores had no decorations, no goods and no customers.

Instead there were boarded-up windows, empty displays, the casualties of a recession which led to old charges being made with new vigour: that America had two presidents, a beguiling George Bush who won the Fifty Years War, and a dismally disconnected president so out of touch with the reality of life for ordinary Americans that when he visited a supermarket he was amazed that prices could be scanned electronically by flashing a light along a bar code. Think about it. George Bush could involve Syria, Saudia Arabia and France in the Gulf war coalition, and persuade Russia and Israel not to make trouble. He could launch an information-age cruise missile strike on Baghdad guided by spy and communications satellites whirling in space. But he did not know that in every supermarket in America bar code scanners could add up the prices at the checkout. If the Gulf war is a symbol of the transition between the industrial age and the information age, then George Bush standing puzzled in the supermarket is the ultimate symbol of the disconnection of the American cold war élite in his promised New World Order. That disconnection was immediately sensed by most Americans. It killed George Bush's presidency.

Like Britain in 1945, America in 1992 would dump the man who led it to victory, making a transition which was inevitable.

The nation moved from the idealism of John F. Kennedy to the grumpiness of Ted Sorensen reckoning up the cost. It dumped the Bush generation of common sacrifice and military service for the Clinton generation which protested against having to serve in Vietnam. It also dumped a habit of mind, by which the worth of America could be measured against the successes or failures of a deadly rival. It dumped arms races and space races, Olympic games rivalry in counting gold medals won against those of the USSR. It replaced the fear of nuclear annihilation with a host of other demons which had always been present but never loomed as large, and which were often strong echoes of America *before* the old order: fear of crime, of gangs, of the government, of economic dislocation, of change, of foreigners, of the future. And, most significantly, America exchanged the paranoia of the red scare fear of Communism with a new paranoia, a fed scare fear of the federal government itself.

In late 1991 the dinner tables of the Washington power élite in Georgetown still buzzed with the usual geopolitical superpower concerns. Should billions of dollars be funnelled into economic aid for the former Communist states? What kind of Soviet Union or Disunion best suited US interests? Might NATO expand? Could Iran and Iraq both be contained? It was as if nothing had changed. But it had in Beattyville and Barbourville and Floyd County, east Kentucky.

The sun has now fully risen over the Appalachian mountain hollows, this glorious spring of 1991. Families begin to stir and make their way towards the Mud Creek health clinic, assembling before 8 a.m. They are raggedy men and women: decent, ordinary, patriotic and, in this case, white Americans who rejoice in the Gulf victory and the prowess of US forces. They fly the stars and stripes from their houses. There is plenty of red, white and blue bunting on the telephone poles around town. But these Kentuckians have climbed from their beds early today not because there is going to be a victory parade, not to celebrate a foreign war, the demise of Communism or the end of fifty years of struggle, but because they are poor and hungry. These spectators on the American Dream are desperate for the free food the clinic can provide. They shuffle away with their hand-outs, ashamed.

In a country in which wealth is often equated with virtue, there is embarrassment in being poor, as if it were a sin. It is now three weeks into the month after the Gulf war victory, March 1991. And at Mud Creek, US federal government assistance – food stamps – have run out. Charity is all that stands between 250 local families and empty bellies for the next ten days. As the doors open, a formidable woman called Eula Hall is helping to distribute food parcels.

She comes from a poor east Kentucky background, and is precisely the kind of person George Bush meant when he talked of 'a thousand points of light' of individual effort, of Americans helping each other to make their country better. The clinic serves an area where half the patients live below the poverty line. Ninety per cent of those here are without any kind of health insurance. The nearest hospital takes only paying or insured patients. And the non-profit hospital is an hour's drive, or $75 cash – in advance, thank you – by the local ambulance company. Yet the plan for the following year, when demand for its services would predictably increase, was for Mud Creek clinic's federal government grant to be cut. The Bush administration, in a familiar budget squeeze, wanted to target money on the inner cities. 'Robbing Peter to pay Paul,' Eula Hall says grimly, knowing she will have to close her doors to new patients.

She lies awake at night tortured by having to decide who should and who should not receive whatever care the clinic can offer. With an estimated three out of five industrial disputes in George Bush's kinder, gentler America involving the issue of who should pay for health care – employers? the government? individuals? or in millions of cases no one at all – from Kentucky to California, from Capitol Hill to the campaign trail, Americans reflected on the paradox of their foreign victories and chronic domestic failures. The 'peace dividend' became an ironic phrase. How come, Eula Hall and millions of other Americans wanted to know, we could win the Gulf war in a hundred hours, yet an estimated one in eight American children went to bed hungry? If the United States could defeat Communism, easily destroy the world's fourth largest army, hit Iraqi SCUD missiles with patriots, why was it not possible for all Americans to be clothed, housed, properly educated, on safe streets in safe cities and in families where children were well treated?

Why was it so difficult for the most successful and richest nation in world history to win the war on drugs, improve education, provide health care, repair the holes in the roads, stitch back the failing fabric of everyday life? Didn't America just beat Communism to prove the American Way was superior?

Lyndon Johnson had declared a war on poverty in the 1960s. (Poverty won.) Ronald Reagan declared war on drugs. (Yes, drugs won.) But by the early 1990s America's successes abroad provoked stinging reassessments of its failures at home. Everywhere the idealism of Kennedy was being replaced by the grumpy settling of accounts of Sorensen as America began the sharpest turn inward since Pearl Harbor.

Outwardly all was joy and celebration. From victory parades in Washington to the ticker-tape reception for General Colin Powell in Manhattan, to the little homecomings in Beattyville and Barbourville, America offered as usual the patriotic welcomes fit for heroes. But they did not return to a home fit for heroes.

By high summer, 4 July 1991, Independence Day – a day on which President Bush wanted Americans to remember again the Gulf war victory – the mood in middle America had changed definitively. I travelled to the small town of Bonaparte, Iowa with the only Democrat to have openly announced he was running for president by that stage, former Massachusetts Senator Paul Tsongas. Tsongas was amiable and intelligent, but he had a serious, professorial air. It meant he looked out of place in the game of soundbites and alarmist issues by which American politics has often become showbusiness for ugly people. So when Tsongas marched in the Bonaparte 4 July parade, few local people had a clue who he was, and even fewer cared. He was the 'stealth' presidential candidate, evading all political radar.

But it soon became obvious that Tsongas had a message which resonated among ordinary people with the perfect pitch of a tuning fork. After the parade, Senator Tsongas stood by a pig barn discussing corn prices with local farmers. Farmers everywhere, and Iowans in particular, have a natural politeness and warmth towards strangers, but nothing quite prepared me for the reception Tsongas received.

The farmers seemed eager to learn what Tsongas, or any Democratic candidate, might do to improve their standard of living. Nobody spoke of George Bush's successful war. Saddam Hussein, like Communism and Hitler, was history. But the anxiety of ordinary Americans was pronounced. They seemed unsure whether that time, 1991, represented the end of Communism and Saddam Hussein, or the beginning of the end for the extraordinary success of their way of life in the United States.

Tsongas gave a short speech, reflecting on America's 215 years of independence that Independence Day. Then he hit the farmers hard in the gut. 'For ten generations,' Tsongas insisted, 'Americans have believed that the next generation will be better off than they are, that children will have a better life than their parents. This is the first generation of Americans for whom that is no longer true.' There was warm applause and cries of approval. Heads nodded. People exchanged glances:

'You said it.'

'That's right.'

Tsongas's main point was that while Communism proved philosophically and literally bankrupt in 1991, American capitalism was not having such a great year either. More applause. More nods and murmurs. He mentioned the Savings and Loan scandal, Wall Street chicanery and the cancerous operations of the Bank of Credit and Commerce International, plus the budget and trade deficits, the seriousness of the recession and the hangover of Reagan's 'Voodoo Economics'. Tsongas's indictment amounted to this: that George Herbert Walker Bush, while engaged on foreign policy objectives and as part of a conspiracy with Ronald Reagan, a well-known old lag, did wilfully and maliciously murder America's irrepressible optimism. At the end of the Fifty Years War, Bush was unwittingly helping to kill the American Dream.

It was a core of discontent and anger at America's neglected domestic problems on which a bold Democratic candidate might build. From the hollows of Kentucky to the plains of Iowa, the great American middle class was waking up to what victory in the Fifty Years War had come to mean, and it was not what George Bush claimed.

'For two centuries,' Mr Bush said, in his 1991 State of the Union address in the middle of the Gulf war to free Kuwait, 'we've done the hard work of freedom ... What is at stake is more than one small country. It is a big idea: a New World Order ... to achieve the universal aspirations of mankind, peace and security, freedom and the rule of law.' In that new world 'brutality will go unrewarded, and aggression will meet collective resistance'. This was John F. Kennedy revisited. But America had moved on.

'If anyone tells you America's best days are behind her, they're looking the wrong way,' President Bush insisted throughout his 1992 campaign, repeating the unquenchable cliché of modern American politics. And yet it proved to be George Bush who was looking the wrong way. As soon as this last president of the Second World War generation could boast that the 'day of the dictator is over', his own day was over and the disconnecting of America set in apace.

Americans in the 1990s were forced to adapt to an inchoate new order which, for the first time in half a century, meant there was no threat of imminent destruction. The glue of a terrifying external enemy had gone. These changes not only allowed the rise of a draft-dodging president in Bill Clinton – something utterly unthinkable during the fifty years of struggle – they also helped create the first Republican-dominated Congress for forty years.

Whatever his flaws, the new aggressive House Speaker, Newt Gingrich, was one of the few thinkers in American public life to have grappled with the profundity of these changes. The end of the fifty years of war or near-war not only changed Russia and eastern Europe, Speaker Gingrich noted, but the shock waves were also felt in mysterious ways all across the world. In the elections of 1993 the Canadian governing party collapsed, from 153 seats to just two in parliament. The Japanese Liberal Democratic Party was shaken out of its forty-year monopoly of power. In Britain the Conservatives managed for a time to cling to office until Labour re-invented itself by throwing overboard its historic commitment to socialism. And in Italy and a united Germany the post-Second World War political structure was utterly transformed.

Most notably in the United States a Texan billionaire, Ross Perot, captured 19 per cent of the vote in the 1992 presidential elections, almost one vote in five. Gingrich compared the political, social, cultural and economic changes of the 1990s to the eclipse of the Middle Ages by the Renaissance. Looking back in history, the Renaissance seems an exciting period of innovation, intellectual ferment and glorious change. But to contemporaries it was a terrifying shattering of the existing, settled order. America in the 1990s appeared on the cusp of precisely this kind of stunning, exciting, frightening change and Americans, reasonably, became fearful of what was to come.

Stealth technology renders old-style defences absolutely useless. The information age sweeps away the industrial age. Bill Gates's Microsoft computer programs are as revolutionary now as Gutenberg's invention of movable type was in creating the literate society that emerged from the Middle Ages. The old order disintegrates, even if the new order has not yet arrived and Americans twist and squirm in the new disorder, where the rules of life continue to change at a bewildering pace. Whatever the statistics of economic prosperity, the neurosis of our times is the fear of being a decent man left standing at the supermarket checkout, bewildered by the bar codes.[3]

Working in the United States of Anxiety

Dayton, Ohio

At first sight, Dayton seems to have died. Heart failure was the cause. Or a neutron bomb. In the sunshine as you approach

over one of the bridges that span the Miami River valley, the city looks pleasant enough. There are flags announcing that the town, founded in 1796, is celebrating its 200th anniversary. It is an average-sized mid-Western city clustered around a few skyscrapers. In the summer humidity, joggers plod along the river walk, T-shirts dark with sweat. A few lazy turtles sit on logs while mallards bicker in the shallows. On the streets, municipal trolleybuses come and go, proudly carrying the symbol of the Miami Valley Regional Transit Authority, the very model of mid-Western efficiency and old-fashioned civic pride. Sort of.

Dayton is a Doughnut City. There must be a better town-planning term for it, but many urban areas in the United States are like ring doughnuts or bagels, cities left without a heart. People who can afford to do so have abandoned the centre to live in a circle of pleasant and prosperous suburbs. The shops have mostly followed their customers, decanted into a loop of suburban malls. What is left in the centre is nothing, or not much. And yet Dayton, and other cities in the industrial mid-West, demonstrate precisely how ordinary Americans have adapted to the collapse of the old order, how it affects their jobs, and how Americans now think about work. The American workforce for the new millennium is turning out to be mobile, adaptable, very hard working, extremely anxious and secretly (or not so secretly) disloyal to its employers.

At one end of Dayton's Main Street, grass grows through the sidewalk until the weeds are almost a foot high. There are boarded-up shops and in the heart of downtown, where Main meets Second, the Rike Kumler Company (whatever that was) boasts it was 'Established 1853'. There is no clue as to when it was disestablished, but it is seriously disestablished now. Gone. A pleading sign says that if you want to rent or buy the space, 'contact Larry Stein Realty, 222 7884'. You do not want to rent or buy the space. Nobody does.

In 1992 the Clinton–Gore campaign battlebus, with its message of 'hope' and 'change' and 'economic growth', rolled through the towns of central Ohio, stopping off in Dayton because Ohio is one of the half-dozen big industrial states which determine the political – as well as economic – destiny of the United States. Dayton is dotted with automobile factories and engineering works, and has been synonymous with mid-Western entrepreneurship ever since Wilbur and Orville Wright ran a bicycle shop here at the end of the nineteenth century. Senator, now Vice-President, Al Gore dropped in on workers being retrained in Sinclair Community College in the centre of the city that summer of 1992, promising that if America threw out George Bush and put a Democrat in the White House the economy would pick up. It did. Though whether Bill Clinton created the prosperity, or merely profited from it politically, depends upon your party allegiance.

By the time the Clinton–Gore campaign rolled through Ohio again in 1996 – this time on a train – Dayton, like America, had certainly changed for the better. Yet Sinclair Community College's president, David Ponitz, argues that the statistics of prosperity are often misleading. Emphasizing, as he put it, that 'America, in the aggregate, is doing rather well', Dr Ponitz admitted that 'America in the anecdotal is not doing so well'. He quoted the statistics about the national economic recovery from the *Wall Street Journal* and Federal Reserve Board officials.

Then he undercut the figures with a string of anecdotes about his anxious neighbours and students, people being 'downsized' or 'outsourced' or any of the other euphemisms we use for being beaten by a rapidly changing economy.

Dr Ponitz mentioned one neighbour, Jeff Woodward, a high-powered businessman who had been 'downsized' in Dayton. When he lost his job Mr Woodward did something remarkable. He decided to keep his home and family in Ohio while commuting to a new job 800 miles away in Florida. The story of this supercommuter seemed to symbolize a national fear of coping with a rapidly changing economy. It had featured in the pages of *The New York Times* as an extreme example of the anxieties of the new order or disorder. I decided I would have to meet the supercommuting Jeff Woodward before I left Ohio.[1]

But I had come to Dayton because President Clinton's advisers had concluded job security was working America's number-one worry, yet in a free market economy the only way government could help was to provide access to training and education, in places like Sinclair Community College. The college is a series of modern concrete buildings connected by well-manicured lawns, trees and shrubs. It was founded by David Sinclair, a Scottish *émigré*, in 1887 as an evening education programme for working people who would be charged modest sums to improve their education. The canny Scottish founder knew that workers would only value that which they paid for. In the rapidly changing American economy of the 1880s a man became 'an investor in his own opportunity', according to the College's official history. A century ago Sinclair and his staff helped ease the way as a generation of Americans moved from working on the land to working in rapidly industrializing American cities like Dayton. Now, in the 1990s, Sinclair Community College was helping make the transition away from the old industrial economy and towards the new information- and computer-based economy of the twenty-first century. In both cases the fears of workers were unchanging – that if they did not retrain, at best they would never improve their standard of living and at worst they would become jobless.

Dr Ponitz, more than six-feet tall with a heavy build and loud voice, fitted squarely into the thrifty, hard-headed, mid-Western tradition of David Sinclair. The good news, he said, was that the area around Dayton contained 25,000 scientists and engineers in well-paid jobs. The bad news was that there were the usual pockets of poverty, plus enormous discontent among unskilled and semiskilled workers who were far from poor but who could not break through into well-paid jobs. These people – the majority of working families and the core of America's middle class – knew they were being left behind and might never catch up.

'You have to know *something* that somebody else doesn't know to get a job and keep a job,' Dr Ponitz explained. Such anxiety allowed Sinclair Community College to prosper. Almost 20,000 people, two-thirds of them women, average age thirty-two, were enrolled in community college classes ranging from robotics and mechanics to basic English. Everybody knew there were plenty of jobs – in much of the mid-West in 1996 unemployment was statistically so low it almost amounted to a labour shortage.

But unlike the boom times in the previous five decades of the old order, in the 1990s the trick was to find a job which paid significantly better than the minimum wage, and which might last longer than two or three years. 'You are in a *funk*,' Dr Ponitz commented, using President Clinton's word to describe the anxiety of working Americans amid so much prosperity, 'if you don't know computers, technology, critical thinking. There are all kinds of jobs in this community that pay $40,000 or $50,000 a year. But you have to have a real skill to get those jobs.'

A 1996 report by the American Enterprise Institute concluded that many Americans were whining inexcusably about working harder for less money in real terms. The selfish baby boom 'Me Generation' had become, in the phrase of conservative writer James Glassman, the even more repellent 'Woe is Me Generation', which complained about everything. But the AEI study also pointed out good reasons to complain.

In 1955, the AEI report says, the average American mum and dad paid about 20 per cent of their family income in taxes. But by 1995 the average Mr and Mrs America saw double that amount, more than 38 per cent of their family income, disappear in taxes. The 1990s complaint, that there was no peace dividend after the cold war, was more than whining. It was perceptive social commentary.[2]

In the 1990s many Americans were looking for a way out of this middle-class income trap. The bottom 60 per cent of workers, including the core of the American middle class, were often working long hours in two or more jobs with little chance of getting ahead. Or they were retraining and working at the same time − putting in so many hours a week that their family life was in chaos. Rush hour at Sinclair College was not in the morning, it was at 5.30 p.m. when those workers in day jobs streamed in for night classes. Juggling two or three jobs per family plus college study at night is, Dr Ponitz says, 'as stressful as you can get. It's very tough'.

I passed the machine shop where, in 1992, Vice-President Al Gore had spoken of the need to make the US workforce competitive through better education. Round the corner a robotics class was beginning. There were six students, all men, ranging in age from early thirties to late fifties. They were studying how robots work on car assembly lines − robots which have made US automobile manufacturers much more competitive by displacing tens of thousands of car workers in Ohio and beyond. The students were making calculations on a computer, pressing buttons and programming the robots to pick up, move, then drop small pieces of metal.

All six of the men, casually dressed in jeans, open-necked shirts and training shoes, were from one of the dozen General Motors automobile plants that ring Dayton. GM was paying for their studies at Sinclair College. All six were skilled electricians, but they readily admitted they knew that to remain in employment they had to keep ahead of their workmates, and ahead of the robots. They had to be skilled enough to do what the machines could not – or at least, not yet.

Gary McCoy, a tall, balding, fresh-faced man, summed up how all of them thought of work in the 1990s: 'I'm making more money [but] I'm working a lot more hours.' Everybody agreed they had to work harder to keep up. And everybody said how proud they were that American automobile manufacturers were – at last – building cars which the American people wanted to buy. But when I asked if that meant they were content living in the paradise of America in the aggregate, as described by Washington economists, their expressions changed.

'Taxes are probably worse,' Carl Webb, the oldest of the group, said. 'You have less to take home.' He estimated – like a walking, talking AEI report – that about 40 per cent of his pay went in one tax or another. Spot on. Then he said, 'Your wife *has* to work to keep going. I think people have to work more just to make ends meet. I think I'm working more hours but I have less in my pocket. It's worse than it used to be.'

The AEI concluded that the typical family of four in 1996 spent more on taxes than on food, clothing and housing combined. The biggest increases since the 1950s had come thanks to contributions for Social Security (pensions for old people), and Medicare (medical treatment for older Americans). Every one of these mature robotics students knew that Americans were ageing as a population. By the time baby boomers like them came to retire it was hard not to believe that Social Security and Medicare would take an even bigger bite out of the remaining workers' pay packets. How could informed citizens not be anxious about the future of a greying America?

Another of the electricians, Terry Chessman, short and dapper with a close-cropped moustache, watched with satisfaction as the computerized grab arm beeped and whirred as it responded exactly as he had programmed it to do.

'I have been working seven days a week now for the last four years,' Terry said in a matter-of-fact way. 'I take a day or two off now and again . . . [but] most days they'll ask us to come in four hours early and work four hours extra — sixteen hours a day.' Terry reckoned that he would usually work sixty-eight hours a week, and that he did so because he needed to make the money while the good times were still around.

Everyone was convinced another economic downturn could not be far away. Electricians and maintenance workers tend to work longer hours than assembly line workers. The six I spoke to were proud to be among the best-paid skilled working men in Dayton.

'I put in sixty hours a week,' Anthony Vance said. 'My wife works forty hours a week. For the younger people it definitely puts a hardship on the house and home.' Gary McCoy, the tall balding man, admitted his family gets upset when he works too hard, though what 'too hard' might be is a matter of opinion. 'Normally I work fifty-four to sixty-eight hours a week, seven days a week, eight hours a day,' he says. 'The money's good. Time away from the family is not.'

None of these men believed in the idea of 'jobs for life' or even in secure employment. They all referred anxiously to the ups and downs of the car industry, the prospect of jobs going overseas, new technology, corporate downsizing and rightsizing, the fancy euphemisms which all mean the same: you get fired.

'I can probably get a new job,' workers would say, 'but how safe is *this* one? And will the next one be any more secure? Will my craft or skill be as needed tomorrow as today, or will it be obsolete?' America is a *carpe diem* economy. It is not only Wall Street traders who want to turn a fast profit and move on. Ordinary workers have recognized they have to seize what they can get today, because tomorrow they might be unemployed and even unemployable. Today's skills are tomorrow's historical curiosity, the typewriter on the scrapheap. That is why so many people are resistant to feeling good about economic good news. Everyone, naturally, asks the same question: 'The statistics look good for *America*. But are they good for *me*?'

On Henry Ford Boulevard on the outskirts of Cleveland, I drove into a massive complex of smokestacks and rail yards known collectively as Brook Park. It rises like an inhuman factory city of Soviet proportions. Dozens of chimneys belch bleached smoke into the air in an area in which, in two desperate weeks in 1980, 4,000 of the 12,000 local car workers were laid off. *Bam!* A third of the workforce gone. Their employers were unable to compete with the Japanese. But by the mid-1990s, the remaining workers of Brook Park were not just competing. They were winning. In a significant change, Japanese engineers toured Ford's 365-acre Cleveland Engine Park to see what *they* might learn from the born-again, highly computerized, extremely efficient, high-quality American industry.

I drove my rented Ford car down Henry Ford Boulevard past the Ford plant and a couple of ugly taverns. Then I came to the union hall of United Auto Workers' Local 1250. There were the usual posters and stickers you find in any trade union office, including a boldly lettered quote from Jack London: 'After God had finished the rattlesnake, the toad and the vampire, he had some awful stuff left with which he made a Scab. A Scab is a two-legged animal with a corkscrew soul, a waterlogged brain, and a combination backbone made of jelly and glue . . . there is nothing lower than a Scab.'

Despite the old-fashioned union rhetoric, the local UAW union president, Nick Parente, could not have been more forward-looking. He is a cheerful, well spoken Italian-American who considered the mid-1990s were the best time for the plant since the lay-offs in 1980.

His biggest worry was that some members were working too hard, grossing $70,000 a year and taking home more than $900 a week. It was hurting their families.

'We work a lot of overtime,' one of the women on the production line, Debby Wowk, admitted with echoes of those in Dayton. 'Nine- or ten-hour days. Some people work twelve hours a day, seven days a week.'

'Thirteen or fourteen hours a day,' another worker, Darrell

Riley chipped in. 'Seven days a week. The money's great but there's not a lot of time for family.'

For employers, boosting overtime obviously avoids the extra training, health and benefit costs of hiring new workers. It also makes it easier to contract in leaner times. The fat years for America in the aggregate are very busy years for skilled working-class America in the anecdotal. Department of Labor statistics showed that by August 1994 the *average* overtime in US manufacturing industry was 4.9 hours a week, the highest since records began in 1956. The result, again with echoes of the 1890s, was that the forty-hour week – for so long a central part of American labour's struggle against 'wage slavery' – is now a historical curiosity for many skilled workers.

Further north through the Car Belt, almost on the Canadian border, you reach the Detroit suburbs of Macomb County, Michigan. Just as in Ohio, there was evidence of ordinary, ambitious people struggling to do better. The first time I met Jerry Dupke he was in a Michigan-sponsored worker training programme. Jerry was forty-two years old, married, with two children aged twelve and five. He had been laid off from the grocery business in October 1995 and decided to retrain as an engineer, hoping for a job in a car factory. A job that might last longer than a few months.

'My kids, I'm really afraid for,' he said. 'At least with my dad's generation they could work thirty, forty years with one company and retire. I was seventeen years with a company called Chatham Supermarkets. When they closed up I've probably had eight jobs in the last ten years. I think it's getting a lot worse.' Jerry admitted he earned *less* in 1996, allowing for inflation, than he did ten years before. Adding up the working hours of the Dupke family makes your head hurt. Jerry's retraining course took thirty-two hours a week. Then, to keep his family housed and fed, Jerry put in another thirty-five hours in what he laughingly called a 'part-time job' at a grocery store.

He had to work all day Saturday and Sunday. Plus his wife worked a forty-hour week in a military factory, with only weekends off. This middle-class American couple put in 107 hours of labour a week. They barely saw each other. Mum and dad were both working to earn what dad alone could have earned a generation before. Jerry felt understandably guilty when he was too tired to read to his kids.[3]

'It's not a real happy home life right now,' he confided with laconic understatement, typical of the dilemma facing millions of American families. Balancing home life and work life did not sound an especially happy task for any of the workers I talked to. And whatever the AEI report might imply with the loftiness of the disconnected Washington élite, Jerry Dupke and the others were *not* whining baby boomers. He is a decent man who was brought up to believe in the social contract of the past fifty years of the old order: if you play by the rules and work hard, all will go well. That rule had applied to his dad. It just did not apply any more.

'I'm working harder than ten years ago and it just don't make any sense,' Jerry said, a common complaint not only among blue-collar workers. The restructuring of AT&T, IBM, countless banks and other white-collar employers has resulted in fear of unemployment, job changes, insecurity or stagnant earnings spreading to the upper-middle class.

At the Macomb County seat in Mount Clemens the local barber Bill Visnaw clips hair in an old-fashioned shop decorated with a red, white and blue rotating pole. As he works behind his barber's chair he says he hears every day from people like Jerry – those who feel their lives are out of control. Like the tourist on Sanibel Island, they see the alligator dozing in the pond but can do nothing about it. The condition of middle-class Americans in the 1990s, Bill decides, is to be frazzled. 'Particularly salaried people. They have to work longer hours, a lot of overtime without extra pay, just so they maintain their job. In many cases it is "voluntary". But they know if they don't [work overtime] they will lose their job.'

Travelling from Dayton to Cleveland to Macomb County through America's industrial heartland, when I talked about jobs, pay and the future I always heard the same vocabulary — 'fear ... frightened ... angry ... anxious ... alarmed'. And, most strikingly, this was not from poor people. These were all people who *had* jobs in a *prosperous* economy. Workers, not welfare recipients. How much worse would it be in the next recession? There was fear and alarm in the least likely places.

Jeanette Pangrazzi is a teacher in Macomb County's McGlinnen Elementary School. When I first met her she was worrying about her looming fiftieth birthday, retirement and the future. But as we talked she revealed a deeper worry, about her husband's job. Jeanette had recently remarried and the couple were planning a first anniversary 'honeymoon' tour of Italy. But the honeymoon was thrown into doubt by a take-over at the accountancy firm where her husband worked. The result was that Jeanette's husband decided it would be unwise to go on holiday after the take-over because he would be expected to demonstrate loyalty to his new bosses. Jeanette went on her honeymoon trip without him, like all prudent American workers living defensively, battening down in choppy seas.

From the car workers in Ohio to the school teacher and self-employed barber in Michigan, working in the United States of Anxiety meant that nobody expected to stay for forty years, or even ten years, with the same employer any more. The unwritten social contract between Americans and their employers of the past fifty years had broken irretrievably. No one expected to receive an award for loyal service. And no one believed the big corporations had any sense of loyalty to their workforce. There was, workers repeatedly suggested, pride in doing a good job, but no loyalty in return.

Every American worker could recite the bovine corporate credos pinned like religious observances on management notice-boards: 'People are our most important resource'. And everyone knew it was untrue. The most important resource of corporate America was not people. It was money. 'When I was a young boy,' Senator George Mitchell, the former majority leader, said of the rules of employment in the old order, 'men were expected to work their lifetime for a single employer, and people were expected to live their lives in the same community, even in the same home. The mobility of American life has increased dramatically. Even though the economy is very good, people are still fearful.'

Ask Claude Morin in New Hampshire as he studies the stock reports on the company which fired him, and plans where to move next. Or the car workers who know they could be out of a job tomorrow, even though they are making huge amounts of money making bestselling cars today. Or Jeanette Pangrazzi who took her honeymoon trip without her new husband. Or – if you can catch him between Florida and Ohio – ask Dr Ponitz's neighbour, Jeff Woodward.

The Woodwards live in a pleasant suburb, in one of the most sought after sections of the doughnut of prosperity around Dayton. An expensive Volvo station-wagon and an Isuzu Trooper sit outside their comfortable, large family home. Inside, a peculiar ritual is taking place. Jeff is getting ready to leave for work. Not in Dayton. Not in the State of Ohio. Not even in that huge region known as the mid-West. It is Monday night and he is packing a garment bag, because every Tuesday Jeff leaves at 5.30 a.m., drives to the airport and commutes to work 800 miles away in Gainesville, Florida.

This might be a glimpse of the future in the increasingly mobile American workforce of the new millennium. Jeff and his wife Cinda are both in their mid-forties, well educated, high achievers. They are at the top end of the middle class in America, the people who economists say have done so well. The top fifth. And both are scared.

For thirty-five years Jeff's father worked for the big Dayton employer National Cash Register. NCR's eventual 'rationalization' helped take the heart out of Dayton city centre. But Jeff's father's story is familiar to anyone in the post-Second World War generation. You fought against Hitler or the Japanese. You came out of the military in 1945 or '46, joined a big corporation.

You did your job. They looked after you. Gave you health benefits. A pension plan. Everybody got rich and happy. This cartoonish social contract was more or less the story of the old order from the 1940s to the 1990s for tens of millions of Americans – a chicken in every pot, a car in every driveway, a secure job in every home. 'The thought was that you would work hard and be promoted,' Jeff says of the old order and his hopes when he started a career after university. 'Upward mobility. Security.'

Jeff took an MBA then joined National Cash Register just like dad. He eventually moved on to become chief financial officer of an electronic information company in Dayton, a whiz-kid in a whiz market with whiz products. He made so much money the Woodwards could afford a big house in the suburbs, the fancy cars and even a small private plane. Then a take-over killed Jeff's unspoken belief that in America you could defy gravity and go onward and upward forever. The new parent corporation decided it could get along without Jeff and most of the other senior people in his company. All but three or four of the top thirty-five managers were 'let go', 'downsized', 'rightsized' or 'dislocated'. Jeff says he was 'phased out'. The result was the same: he had to find a new job.

Jeff found one as chief financial officer of Gold Standard Multimedia Inc. in Gainesville, Florida, a medical information service. But seeing many of his friends face this same dilemma, Jeff concluded that high-paying corporate jobs had become about as long-lasting as disposable tissues. He could not face the idea of uprooting his family. His wife Cinda was a teacher with her own career. Their teenage children, Paul and Leslie, were still at school. Jeff decided he could not drag them away from their home in Dayton to a new job which might 'phase him out' again as soon as the economy sneezed. And so Jeff Woodward has become a symbol of working in the United States of Anxiety, an American supercommuter who flies down to Florida every Tuesday and back late every Thursday night. Mondays and Fridays he works by fax, modem or telephone from home in Ohio.

'Of course it's difficult,' Jeff admits. 'It was not a decision taken lightly.'

'It was a very difficult decision,' Cinda agrees. 'Teenagers should have both parents around. That's a time when they need a lot of attention . . . we were coming from a generation in which people were in a job for twenty-five years. That changed five years ago.'

Six years ago, 1991, was the year George Bush defeated Saddam Hussein and declared the promise of the New World Order and the peace dividend. The changes which began with the progressive collapse of fifty years of rules and beliefs have been especially daunting, Cinda says, for the baby boom generation to which she and Jeff belong and who came of age in the 1960s. Cinda says they were 'the ones who had the hopes they could charge into life and change everything'. Instead, life has charged into them. And changed them.

After ten months of interregional commuting Jeff says he is used to it. They have moved to a smaller house, though it is big and comfortable by most people's standards. And Jeff betrays no bitterness about being 'phased out'. But when I asked him about the relationship between big corporations and their workers, he turned as fiery as Claude Morin in New Hampshire or Jerry Dupke in Michigan. 'The degree of loyalty that once was there will not be again,' he insisted. His friends 'are very, very aware that their obligation to the corporation and the corporation's obligation to them ends with the paycheck'. That means, he accepts ruefully, that each month at work is like the first month − or possibly the last month − in a job.[4]

But unemployment is low, I persisted. Inflation is low. 'Americans are *not* unemployed,' Jeff nods. He reads the news about America in the aggregate every day in the *Wall Street Journal*. 'But they *are* anxious. Anxiousness does not show up on unemployment charts and personal income charts.'

And the future? Jeff sighs. He can foresee only one result − a decline for most Americans and the decline of the United States. He calls it a 'slide down' from that 'vast middle class which has made America so strong'. A 'slide down' sounds exactly what Senator Paul Tsongas most feared – the end of the American Dream of constant optimism that the next generation will be better off, a continuing reduction in the US share of world GDP and a slow erosion of the superiority of the superpower.

Before I left Dayton I wanted to check in with the *Daily News* to see if this anxiety, fear and anger was typical of their sense of the mood in Ohio. Local newspapers in America are usually plugged in to their communities, and that is especially true in Dayton. The *Daily News* is in the centre of the doughnut, on Ludlow Street, in an old-fashioned Victorian building remodelled to become the computerized newsroom of the 1990s. Max Jennings, the editor, taught journalism at the University of Arizona and had strong views about 'public journalism'. This is an attempt by journalists to connect more strongly with their readers by using, for example, panels of local people to discuss their hopes and fears or to talk about controversial issues. The *Daily News* had created such panels and conducted what was almost a rolling social survey of reader opinion.

Americans, Max Jennings said, had far deeper problems than what was reflected in much of the national media coverage of politics, economics and society in the 1990s. 'There's a lot of fear out there. I think they are very much worried about the future.' It used to be, Max said, that you could 'work your way up as a part-time worker' into a full-time job, then from the full-time job into management. Now corporations saw part-time workers as a permanent way to undercut full-time employees. The social contract that had held in Dayton and everywhere else in industrial America for fifty years exploded in the 1990s. The workers of Dayton, Max concluded, are absolutely convinced 'that the rules are changing. They are not loyal to the company and the company is not loyal to them. They think the rules of the American workplace have changed. And I think it's creating a great deal of angst.'

Many workers could not or would not turn to trades unions for help. They felt alone, even though tens of millions of other

Americans had the same problems and felt the same way. The political system was being blamed because politicians could not solve this or any of the other enormous problems caused by the changing of the 'rules'. Middle-income Americans were caught in a trap: they were working hard to make money for their families. But that meant putting in such long hours at work, family life suffered anyway.

These dilemmas, of course, are not uniquely American. Many British and European families, blue collar and white collar, have bounced through the changes in the workplace in the past two recessions and will recognize immediately the stresses on family life. But the United States and its disappointments are different. It is not merely that those who fall in America fall further and faster and have little in the way of a welfare safety net to catch them. It is also that Americans have, in the expanding economy since the Second World War, come to *expect* better. The Founding Fathers created a society in which it was possible to believe in the perfectability of human experience and the *entitlement* to happiness, rather than, as the Declaration of Independence asserts, the *right* to pursue it. The gap between expectations that in America every man can be a king, and the grimmer reality of everyday life, makes the inevitable disappointments more difficult to bear.

On my way out of Dayton I stood again at the riverbank watching the sweating joggers and the turtles on the log in the river. The sun was still strong and the city, from this angle, looked rather grand. The morning paper had spoken about a further drop in unemployment. There was speculation that interest rates might have to rise a little, but the great beast of inflation seemed asleep. America in the aggregate was a paradise. It must be nice to live there. But like Jerry and Jeff and Max and Jeanette, Choo Choo Caron and the Morins, people live in America the anecdotal, working hard because they suspect that around the next corner, or the one after that, something awful will happen. The alligator will bite.

Of course the United States is prospering. But America is also the sum of the anecdotes of its people. Loyalty, as great an American virtue as hard work, has evaporated from the workplace. Anxiety has taken its place. The morality of the big corporations now is not much different from that of the railroad and steel barons of the nineteenth century, maximizing profits in a free-wheeling economy. That is justifiable. But treating workers as a disposable commodity is not. After fifty years of an economy distorted by cold war struggles, it is not simply that the rules of the old order have changed. It is even worse. No one knows what the rules *are* any more. Our moral compass is spinning in confusion. America has failed to build the Great Society President Johnson hoped for in the 1960s. Instead it has created the Angry Society of wild conspiracies and ugly hatreds.

PART TWO
THE ANGRY SOCIETY

'The challenge of our past remains the challenge of our future: will we be one nation, one people, with one common destiny, or not? Will we all come together, or come apart? The divide of race has been America's constant curse. Each new wave of immigrants gives new targets to old prejudices. Prejudice and contempt, cloaked in the pretense of religious or political conviction, are no different. They have nearly destroyed us in the past. They plague us still. They fuel the fanaticism of terror . . . These obsessions cripple both those who are hated and, of course, those who hate.'

President Bill Clinton, second Inaugural Address, 20 January 1997

'It doesn't matter to them [members of Congress] that the semi-auto ban gives jack-booted government thugs more power to take away our constitutional rights, break in our doors, seize our guns, destroy our property and even injure or kill us.'

Wayne LaPierre, executive vice-president of the National Rifle Association in a letter to his members dated May 1995

The Death of the American Hero and the Rise of the Culture of Victims

Kitty Hawk, North Carolina

Twisting across the Great Dismal Swamp in North Carolina the road eventually reaches the Currituck Sound. You feel relief in the sea breeze. It is heavy with salt but anything is better than the dead, humid air that in summer-time hangs over the swampland like a curse. Driving along the spine of the Outer Banks, on your left behind the sand dunes you can smell the freshness of the Atlantic. The endless beaches that greeted the first Europeans in the New World begin around Cape Cod and end up dribbling into the soupy water off Florida. Here in the middle, the giant sandbanks and low scrub are connected by a series of bridges and defend the rest of the United States from bad weather in the Atlantic. At the elbow of the Outer Banks, Cape Hatteras attracts so many shipwrecks that quaint lighthouses string the coast like glittering beads on a necklace of rock and sand, while road signs remind you this is the principal evacuation highway to escape hurricanes.

Little towns of wooden holiday homes appear with folksy names like Duck, Sanderling and Kill Devil Hills. Along the strip of Anywhere, USA, tourist hotels, fast-food joints and gas stations, there are drive-through liquor stores, known as 'Bru Thrus', where you can have your beer loaded without the unspeakable inconvenience of getting out of your car. And then there is a strange piece of sand staked out grandly as a National Memorial.

69

Here at Kitty Hawk in 1903 the American century began with a very American story. To the amusement of locals, Wilbur and Orville Wright moved down from Dayton, Ohio to test their heavier-than-air machine on the blustery Carolina coast. The Wright brothers were confident, despite all previous evidence, that they would make it fly. In 1899 Wilbur wrote from his Dayton bicycle shop to the Smithsonian Institution in Washington for information about the new 'science' – actually not much more than dreams and hocus-pocus – of aeronautics.

Just four years later on 17 December 1903, with the promise of a soft crash landing on sand, Orville took the flyer aloft for twelve seconds, covering a distance of 120 feet at a walking pace. 'They have done it,' a witness said. 'Damned if they ain't flew.' Damned if they ain't.

No nation has ever marketed its heroes so assiduously. Like most British boys, I grew up on Hawkeye, Superman, Batman, Rawhide, the Wright Brothers, John Glenn, John Wayne, Clint Eastwood and Neil Armstrong. They were all so magnificent I doubt if I could have separated the real from the fictional, and I still marvel at the way Americans live up to their myths, combining – like Wilbur and Orville – imagination, talent and persistence in the face of conventional wisdom which argues only a nut would try to fly.

All along this coast are testaments to heroism and ruthlessness, from the north in Massachusetts where the Pilgrim Fathers landed, to Jamestown in Virginia where in 1607 the first settlers saw their numbers cut by disease and starvation from 105 to just thirty-two in one winter, yet they struggled on. Or further south at Cape Canaveral where the space programme, a mere sixty years after the Wright brothers, ensured, as President Kennedy demanded, that the first (and only) footprints on the moon would be American.

Driving to Kitty Hawk, thinking about American heroes, I catch a preacher on the car radio, a crackly AM station. He is ranting about the decline of American virtue. He clearly thinks that the rules of American life have changed for the worse and he is getting excited about a display of pornographic art which he calls '*un*-American'. Does any other country use its name this way, as a compliment or, negatively, as the worst criticism? In Tokyo are inefficient workers regarded as 'un-Japanese'? Do the Parisians criticize unromantic souls as 'un-French'?

The radio preacher is moving rapidly to attack a profound moral decline in American life, quoting Alexis de Tocqueville's observation that 'America is Great because America is Good'. American greatness is under threat because American goodness is being undermined, and the preacher cites the usual suspects – pornography, crime, illegitimacy, Hollywood. But he adds a few others: a decline in self-reliance, a rise in vexatious lawsuits, a lack of personal responsibility, loss of the sense of community.

If he is correct, then the rules in America really have changed. American society has entered an angry and destructive phase. There is no scientific proof, but in conversations with Americans politically from the Left, Right and Centre, of different races and social backgrounds, from California to New England and the mid-West, I have heard similar complaints. Americans' image of themselves as can-do, hardy, 'rugged individualists' is disintegrating. There are no more American heroes. Everyone has feet of clay. The sense of 'community', of civil society, the pleasant small-town America idealized by Norman Rockwell paintings and Thornton Wilder's *Our Town*, is under siege. Heroes like the Wright brothers have been replaced by a new national anthem of whining. Individualism has become egocentrism. American character is in decline. And the most obvious national characteristic of the 1990s is not self-reliance. It is selfishness or self-indulgence.

The American hero of the seventeenth century was a rugged adventurer. In the eighteenth century, a pioneer settler or patriotic anti-British revolutionary. In the nineteenth century a cowboy. And now, in the late twentieth century, the American icon must surely be a therapist or lawyer, because the culture of the hero has given way to the culture of the victim. John Wayne is in tears as he trades in his guns and lies back on the psychiatrist's couch. Television screens are swamped by talk shows competing to parade victims rather than heroes, a dismal collection of unhappy voices calling out 'Don't Blame Me' for whatever has gone wrong in their lives. The anecdotal evidence of the rise of the culture of the victim is so compelling that I keep a special folder of news stories I call the 'Victims' File'.

Case One: Alison Wood, a police officer in Palm Beach, Florida, was dismissed for poor attendance and job performance. She sued, claiming that because she is an alcoholic she is legally disabled and, under the 1990 Americans with Disabilities Act, cannot be fired.

Case Two: Deborah Birdwell of Cookeville, Tennessee, who weighs 366 pounds. She sued a cinema chain for emotional suffering when they would not let her put a portable chair in a space reserved for wheelchairs. Ms Birdwell is so fat she cannot fit in ordinary seats.

Case Three: Rhode Island. Bonnie Cook weighs 320 pounds. She was refused a hospital job. She sued, claiming her weight was a 'disability'. The court awarded her the job plus $100,000, even though a doctor found her to be 'morbidly obese' with difficulty in walking, lifting, bending, stooping and kneeling.

Case Four: Albuquerque, New Mexico, and the notorious story of eighty-one-year-old Stella Liebeck who bought a coffee in McDonald's, stuck it between her legs while driving her car and spilled it, causing third-degree burns requiring eight days in hospital and extensive skin grafts. Damages were reduced from $2.7 million to a mere $600,000.

Case Five: Newport News, Virginia. Monika and Mark Skinner reached for their lawyers after their sixteen-year-old son died in a car crash. They sued just about everybody you can think of, including the supermarket which sold computer cleaning fluid to the car's driver. That boy and the Skinners' son sniffed the fluid to get high before the fatal crash. The Skinners also sued the two engineering firms that had designed the lake into which the car fell. And then they sued the company which had designed the road on which the car was travelling, claiming it was too close to the lake.

Case Six: August 1995, Anaheim, California. Billie Jean Matay, aged fifty-two, takes her three grandchildren to Disneyland and is robbed in the car park. The Disney people helped her to recover in a backstage area but Ms Matay sued. She was, quote, 'traumatized' when she saw Disney characters taking off their costumes. Her lawsuit claimed emotional distress because, among other things, the children were exposed 'to the reality that the Disney characters were make-believe'. The truth that dare not speak its name in 1990s America is that Mickey Mouse is – gasp! – *not* a real mouse. If you can be 'traumatized' by Mickey Mouse, what would be your reaction to the battle of Antietam, the massacre at Wounded Knee, the Alamo, the hardship of the Oregon trail, or those heart-stopping moments on Apollo 13?

It is almost a cliché to say that in our common Western culture we live in a post-heroic age. Heroes are raised up only to be debunked and humiliated later. With the possible exception of Nelson Mandela it is difficult to think of any recent hero who has withstood the corrosion of our critical news media and rapid historical revisionism.

Even heroes safely buried are not heroic for long. We now know more about the sex lives of John F. Kennedy and Franklin Roosevelt than most of their contemporaries did. Since Watergate, Americans have come to regard all political leaders as yesterday's hero and tomorrow's embarrassment. The debunking of heroes by aggressive reporters feeding an already suspicious public can be seen positively as a new American realism. Franklin Roosevelt's wheelchair was hidden from view by a complicit press. Surely we are better off now knowing the truth that he struggled to overcome his disability? Whether we are also better off knowing about the illicit love affairs of politicians is a matter of judgement. But what is far more serious than the death of the hero is the rise of the victim. To the intense anger of many Americans, instead of the self-reliance which built their country, all around they hear wailing self-pity.

This culture of victims, like most things American, is spreading to Europe and beyond. In one variant, what the art critic Robert

Hughes calls 'linguistic Lourdes', all pain is supposed to be healed by changing the words to soften the meaning. It begins innocently, with polite euphemisms. Jeff Woodward in Dayton said he was 'phased out' after a company take-over. Other workers said they were 'downsized' or 'rightsized'. People who were once 'handicapped' are now 'challenged', though their problems remain the same.[1]

This is the beginning of *Alice in Wonderland*-speak in which nothing is 'right' or 'wrong' any more, only 'appropriate' or 'inappropriate'. For example, in the University of Pennsylvania, in a case typical of 1990s linguistic and legalistic lunacy, a white male student was studying late at night when he was disturbed by the yelling of a group of students outside his window. He shouted out, 'Shut up you water buffalo!'

The rowdy students were female and black. They decided his words were a racist (and possibly sexist) slur, and so began a series of events somewhere between Buster Keaton and Franz Kafka. A moment's common sense would probably have led to the conclusion that students who disturb the study of others should be warned or disciplined. Yet the number-one fact about America's culture of victims is that it cannot possibly coexist with common sense.

All institutions have to act defensively and take seriously even the most ludicrous arguments when threatened by the prospect of a lawsuit in pursuit of 'rights'. In the hands of an aggressive lawyer the words 'water buffalo' could be an expletive, and a racist slur. But then so could almost any other phrase you can think of. After the story received nation-wide coverage, the rowdy students withdrew their charge and Hillary Clinton pleaded with universities not to stifle freedom of speech. But the culture of victims has become a virus of the character, a disease which has spread so far and so fast, most Americans fear some of their fellow citizens have gone insane. In Texas there was opposition to the name of a local stream: it was called 'Cripple Creek'. In Minnesota the legislature wanted to rename two lakes called 'Squaw Lake' and one 'Squaw Point'. The word 'squaw' is offensive to Indians. Or rather, perhaps I should say Native Americans. (You can *never* be defensive enough to cope with everyone who might take offence.) The word 'squaw' is apparently a French corruption of an Algonquin word to describe female genitals. Most Americans, not trilingual in French and Algonquin, strive not to cause offence, but find themselves irritated by the ever-changing need to tiptoe through a linguistic minefield.

During the 1993 siege of David Koresh's compound in Texas, I travelled to Waco airport to meet the family of a British member of Koresh's Branch Davidian cult. I knew that the father was flying to Texas in the hope of rescuing his son from the compound. I was told the man was middle-aged, black, and from the English Midlands, but I had no other description. While I stood at the airport with other British journalists waiting for the flight to arrive, a white American television reporter, who had also been tipped off about the incoming relative, sidled up to me.

'How will you recognize him?' she asked.

'Well, he is British and black,' I replied.

'Oh,' she said, 'he is African-American.'

It is now regarded as politically correct to refer to black Americans as 'African-Americans'. But this was a *British* man who happened to be black.

'No,' I protested, amused at the mistake. 'The man is *not* African-American. He is British.'

'But,' the reporter persisted, 'you *said* he was African-American.'

'No. I said he was British and black.'

There was an embarrassed silence as, slowly, the last glimmers of common sense tried to reassert themselves. The journalist was adrift in the new rules, desperate not to offend anyone, yet managing precisely the opposite.

'Well,' she wondered, 'could I say he is African-British?'

Before I could answer, behind me a British voice called sarcastically, 'Maybe you should try African-West Indian-British. Just to be on the safe side.'

This story, like that of the water buffalo, seems superficially trivial. Yet add together millions of stories like this in the lives of millions of Americans every day and you begin to smell the rot of a society at odds with itself beyond the familiar battlegrounds of race, immigration and abortion. Americans watch with alarm as the culture of victims seeps from universities and television talk shows to the local court house and even to the White House where President Clinton notoriously 'feels your pain'. But they see beyond mere political correctness into a moral abyss at the heart of their society.

A study conducted by the Center for National Policy in April 1996 talked to groups of voters from California, Texas and Ohio. It concluded that Americans were angry and disgusted by what they sensed to be a decay in national character and moral drift. 'There is a widespread feeling,' the study asserted, 'that "life is not as it should be", that America is "rudderless" and that people no longer know what America "stands for".'[2]

The sense was of a profound moral malaise, that the '*rules [of the] American way of life have broken down*'. (My italics.) The study found a loss of feeling about being a united society, a perception of a declining work ethic, irritation that 'selfishness is now the norm' amid an 'erosion of American ideals, values and beliefs'.

This is one of the most significant, pernicious, yet under-reported causes of American anger and anxiety in the 1990s. Daniel Yankelovich, chairman of a company which tracks social trends, summed up the anger and pessimism of the 1990s. The vast majority of Americans, almost nine out of ten according to Yankelovich (87 per cent), believed America's social morality 'to be in a state of decline and decay'. Those surveyed understood there was a link between this sense of moral decay and criminal behaviour. But they saw the increase in crime, especially violent crime, in the past thirty years not in isolation but as 'a symptom of a broader malady, a sickness *in the very soul of society* to which they cannot give a name'. (My italics.)

Yankelovich suggested that this social decay is so profound

that American optimism, which Europeans greatly admire, has been replaced by 'American cynicism, resignation and shoulder-shrugging' which might even surpass that of world-weary *fin de siècle* Europeans. The more Yankelovich examined the implications of this cynicism, the more he was forced to conclude that Americans in the 1990s thought of a 'good community' not in positive but in negative terms. People would describe a good community as being one in which they were not afraid to walk at night, or where there were 'low levels of child abuse'. The overall sense was of an America where the rules had changed and where *every* institution appeared to be fraying: family, neighbourhood, government, schools, universities, jobs.

'The American public is in a foul mood,' Yankelovich wrote in 1995, contemplating the stresses within an increasingly angry society. 'People are frustrated and angry. They are anxious and off balance. They are pessimistic about the future and cynical about all forms of leadership and government.'[3]

Yankelovich was so concerned that he feared the result would be class and generational warfare, exacerbated racial tensions, political instability and extremism. Every one of these trends has contributed to the Angry Society of 1990s America. Even President Clinton, in the traditional optimism of his 1997 Second Inaugural, fretted that the choice for America was 'Will we all come together, or come apart? . . . We cannot, we will not succumb to the dark impulses that lurk in the far regions of the soul, everywhere.'

In the 1990s movie, *Falling Down*, a patriotic defence worker – a typical hero of the old order of the past fifty years – plays by the rules, works conscientiously and, through no fault of his own, loses his job. Then he loses his mind. The rules have changed. He is a victim of corporate downsizing. He fought valiantly in the war against Communism, yet he ends up destroyed, running amok in a violent, lawless, changing society full of immigrants who speak no English and signs of decay from the idealized America of the old order.

Falling Down is a parable of white, middle-aged, middle-class anger at the prospect that the country's best years may have gone. But Hollywood, always a rough mirror to America's social concerns, reflects an even deeper cultural pessimism, that of the disconnecting of Americans from each other and the Balkanization or atomization of American society. Compare, for example, typical movies about the Second World War and Vietnam. In *The Dirty Dozen* the underlying theme is national cohesion in a great cause – the defeat of Nazi and Japanese totalitarianism. The plot centres on the US government forcing criminal misfits into military service to defend the arsenal of Democracy against the evil of Nazism. The misfits triumph. They become socialized soldiers, unlikely heroes – in a secular sense, born again. This is quintessential American optimism, the best of the American Creed, in which even the worst sinners can be saved. It is the optimism which stretches to the back of one cent coins with their hopeful Latin motto *E Pluribus Unum* – out of many, one America will be created. Out of the scum of the earth, it is still possible to believe in an American hero emerging in *The Dirty Dozen*. But not any more.

The typical post-Vietnam movie shows precisely the opposite. *Platoon, Hamburger Hill, Apocalypse Now* or, most strikingly, *Born on the Fourth of July* take normal, socialized individuals as the starting-point. The government presses these 'heroes' into military service in a lost war and they emerge emotionally, morally or physically crippled. And the 'heroes' end up, in one way or another, 'victims' of a society which sacrifices individual happiness for the self-serving interests of the governing élite. It is the perfect cinematic representation of a culture of victims.

Charles Sykes, in his book *A Nation of Victims*, finds plenty of other examples. He writes of an FBI agent who embezzled $2,000 and blew it in an afternoon gambling at Atlantic City. The agent was reinstated at work after a court ruled his gambling addiction was a 'handicap'. In Philadelphia, a school district employee was fired for consistently turning up late for work. He sued, alleging he was a victim of 'Chronic Lateness Syndrome' – the adult equivalent of saying the dog ate your homework.

Then there was the convicted murderer who argued he was the victim of foetal alcohol syndrome. (Your mother drinks, so you are *not* responsible if you murder people? Could anyone but a lawyer argue this without a sense of shame?) Or, there was the Washington DC Mayor, Marion Barry, videotaped smoking crack cocaine. He, naturally, was a victim of the FBI's determination to 'bring down' a black man in a position of power, though presumably the mayor of the capital city of the United States could have refused to smoke crack when offered it.

The anger of ordinary Americans towards this all-pervasive victim culture was summed up for me by the Sheriff of a small county in rural Mississippi who sees and hears it every day. If your prejudice about a Mississippi Sheriff is some overweight and under-educated redneck from *In the Heat of the Night*, then Martin Pace is a refreshing shock. He is thin, wiry, intelligent, well read and, above all, eloquently irritated by the excuse of victimhood for criminal or antisocial behaviour.

Martin Pace is Sheriff of Warren County, a pleasant agricultural area around the town of Vicksburg on the Mississippi river. As he drove me through the streets of the town and along the bluffs where Confederate troops held at bay the Union army in one of the most decisive encounters of the American Civil War, Sheriff Pace explained that most of the crime in the area was – like everywhere else in America – drugs-related. But those whom Sheriff Pace and his deputies arrested for burglaries, robberies and worse would claim their drug addiction as an *excuse* for committing the crime, when everyone knew it was really a *motive*. The common complaint was that 'I did the robbery because I was high on drugs'. The real story was, 'I did the robbery because I knew I needed more money to pay for my drug habit'.

'We do *not* have a drug problem in America,' Sheriff Pace insisted, with exemplary anger. 'We have a *people* problem.' By way of illustration he pointed to a corner of his office. 'If I put a ton of crack cocaine in this corner, it would not be a problem – until people decided what a great idea it was to get high or to sell it to others.'

This is the traditional, common-sense voice of America, in which 'liberty' means giving citizens the freedom to do their best, but to hold them responsible if they break the law. Yet in the distorted mirror of the culture of victims which Sheriff Pace sees every day, behaviour – getting drunk, smoking crack, stealing money – is no longer a mistaken, culpable personal choice. It is a disease and therefore blameless.

As Charles Sykes points out, the sense of shame formerly attached to the behaviour has been transferred into criticizing it. Try suggesting, for example, that a 'morbidly obese' person might lose a few pounds in weight and the full fury of the American culture of the victim descends upon your head, just as it did with the student at the University of Pennsylvania. The disease of victimhood is not just blameless but incurable. We are all victims now, and that means no one is responsible for anything.

Heroes take responsibility. Victims claim their rights. And the culture of the victim devalues those genuinely victimized by racism, real disease or handicap, because if *everybody* is a victim, then *nobody* is. This has led to an apparently absurd conclusion. Many ordinary Americans fear the disease has spread so rapidly that significant sections of their fellow countrymen *covet* the role of victim. How else can we explain the fact that America's competitive victimhood has thrown up the ultimate 1990s designer victim, the Angry White Male? As we have seen, white male anger is largely the legitimate discontent of working-class or middle-class people who believe they are falling behind in a booming economy. But there is something more unpleasant beneath the surface of this anger. Of all the 'groups' claiming 'rights' in the United States you might have thought that white males had the least to whine about. Every American president, vice-president and speaker of the House of Representatives has been a white male.

The white male – Washington, Jefferson, Paul Revere, Hawk-eye, John Wayne, Superman – used to be the archetypal hero. But now he competes to be just another victim. The swag-bellied middle-aged white men in combat fatigues who join anti-government militias claim they are victims of a government threatening to take away their assault rifles. The 1994 congressional elections, which amounted to an anti-Clinton landslide, were widely (though simplistically) interpreted as the 'revenge' of Angry White Males on the Clinton administration for policies stretching from affirmative action for minorities to softening opposition to homosexuals in the military. The central premiss of one of the most poisonous books ever published in America, the underground hit *The Turner Diaries*, captures precisely this sense of white victimhood. The book describes a bomb attack on FBI headquarters, similar to the Oklahoma City bomb. The novel's cover proudly boasts that the FBI calls *The Turner Diaries* 'the Bible of the racist Right'. It begins with the rounding-up of gun owners by the hated 'Equality Police', and ends with a race war in which white 'heroes' hang black people, Jews and white 'collaborators' from lamp-posts. The white gun owners are justified in launching the race war, the book argues, because they are really victims of a tyrannical US government trying to take away their guns.

America's angry society of the 1990s is clearly caught, in Robert Hughes's phrase, between the obtuse whining of the Left-leaning 'Politically Correct' and the desperate maunderings of the right-wing 'Patriotically Correct'. Both sides claim to be the victim of something. In the middle, the majority of Americans have every right to fear that their central heroic myth of being a can-do, hardy people is being ground into dust. Unless the culture of victims is reversed, America can never 'come together' as President Clinton wants. It can only come apart. Competing 'victim' groups are already reaching for their lawyers in pursuit of their 'rights', but never in defence of their 'responsibilities'.

Robert Samuelson, in *The Good Society and its Discontents*, hammers home the point. He suggests that Americans whine in the good times of the 1990s because they have come to feel a 'sense of entitlement' about their lives, that they *deserve* happiness. If they do not get it, then it must be someone else's fault. Society's fault. The government's fault.

The fault of the usual scapegoats — black people, welfare mothers, immigrants, foreigners, Jews, the rich, the poor, the ungodly, the liberals, the conservatives, the media. Let us sue somebody, and, whoever we blame, we must never blame our increasingly fragile selves. Bestseller book lists are full of culture of victims guides on how to shift responsibility and blame, how to allow your 'inner child' free rein. The rest of America, increasingly irritated, wonders when the inner child is going to *grow up* and start behaving as an outer adult. In the words of an Eagles hit song of the mid-1990s, *Get Over It*, many Americans would gladly take the victim's inner child and kick its little ass, though they might stop short at the song's Shakespearean exhortation to kill all the lawyers, kill them tonight. (As we will see in the next chapter, they might not.)

Back in North Carolina, at the heroic shrine at Kitty Hawk, eighteen-wheel juggernauts and pick-up tricks drive past carrying the banner of America's most revered victims, the Lost Cause, the Confederacy. North Carolina licence plates declare proudly 'First in Flight', but some also show Confederate flags with nostalgic references to the standard bearer of the Lost Cause, the Confederate President Jefferson Davis. 'Don't blame me,' one popular sticker says of America's current political problems, 'I voted for Jeff Davis.'

And it would all be humorous nostalgia except for the new culture of victims in which 'Don't Blame Me' is becoming America's motto to replace the increasingly outmoded *E Pluribus Unum*. The local North Carolina Senator, Jesse Helms, in his 1990 election against a black candidate Harvey Gantt, ruthlessly exploited white male anger. Helms's campaign ads showed a white man — a victim — crunching up a job rejection notice. The voice-over boomed portentously: 'You needed that job. And you were the best qualified. But they had to give it to a minority because of a racial quota. Is that really fair?'

The culture of victims has reached transcendent absurdity with this message. The idea is that black people, the real victims of generations of racial injustice, are now victimizing white folks.

Senator Helms has managed something quite remarkable. He panders to the delusions of victimhood while simultaneously pleading for a stronger America. It is a new but ugly American Beatitude: Blessed are the Victims, for they Shall Inherit the Earth − or at least the right to sue for a piece of the action.

The wind is picking up at Kitty Hawk. I walk along the sand trying to pace out the track of the first flight by a heavier-than-air machine, marvelling that 120 feet would hardly make up the length of one wing of a modern jet airliner. These bicycle men from Dayton somehow created the modern world with their nutty invention and took us from Kitty Hawk to Tranquillity Base on the moon in little over sixty years.

Alexis de Tocqueville may have got it right in the 1830s when he wrote that 'America is Great because America is Good'. But he was most certainly correct when he also observed that in America there is 'so much distinguished talent among the subjects and so little among the heads of government'. For this reason, and despite the prevailing culture of victims, I have an illogical confidence that American common sense will somehow prevail. The 'distinguished talent among the subjects' will probably find a way, though, as we will see in the next chapter, the explosion of lawyers and litigation in the United States may make overcoming the culture of victims a hopeless dream.

Yet there must still be heroic Wilburs and Orvilles − crazy, admirable people determined to live up to the American myths of pioneer, pilgrim, cowboy and astronaut. The problem is how to clear the runway. It is littered with lawyers, therapists, politicians and the rest of the Victim Police. They are screaming that flying should be banned because a morbidly obese person could not possibly squeeze into the cockpit. They want to feel your pain. But you keep going until the air takes your wings and, as you soar above them, you call back in anger, unleashing the vilest epithet of America entering the new millennium.

'Water buffaloes!' you scream at the Victim Police below. 'Water buffaloes! Water buffaloes!'

And they call back, 'If you crash, *Don't Blame Me or I'll Sue.*'

The Rule of Law and the Rule of Lawyers

'Come to Major Hopkins to get full satisfaction. I win nine-tenths of my cases. If you want to sue, if you have been sued, I'm the man to take your case. Embezzlement, highway robbery, felonious assault, arson and horse stealing don't amount to shucks if you have a good lawyer behind you. My strong point is weeping as I appeal to the jury, and I seldom fail to clear my man. Out of eleven murder cases last year I cleared nine of the murderers . . . Come early and avoid the rush.'

Advertisement for a nineteenth-century Arizona lawyer[1]

Little Rock, Arkansas

You know the rules have changed in America when a family doctor sticks a gun in your face and you realize that within a second he could blow your head off. He probably won't because you are standing in his front room and your blood would make a terrible mess of the furnishings. It was a small gun, a 9-millimetre semiautomatic pistol, a Beretta. It was so close to my nose that the muzzle blurred as I looked at it cross-eyed.

'I have this for protection,' the doctor was saying, waggling the pistol as I grinned vacantly, hoping that the safety catch was on. I was thinking that in Europe family doctors don't draw guns on people. They don't even *own* guns.

We were standing in the front room of Dr Jim's house, a pleasant ranch-style bungalow in a tiny farming town in Arkansas, where the Mississippi river pulls sluggish and brown through the flat cotton fields towards the delta and where, if

Huckleberry Finn turned up barefoot off a riverboat you would not entirely be surprised. They call it the 'New South', but it looks remarkably like the Old South – Confederate flags on car licence plates, drawling speech, magnolia trees, the sticky feel of your shirt on your back in the heat, and a slow and easy pace to time passing as the riverboats come and go. Dr Jim was talking about being a family physician for thirty-five years though now he was about to quit. 'The government,' he said, spitting out the word. '*Gummint*. Lawyers. The insurance industry. The paperwork.' He was mad as hell and he was not going to take it any more.

I had crossed the Mississippi at Memphis to find out what health care was like in President Clinton's Arkansas, wondering if it might offer clues about the state of health of America. It did, but in a way I could not have imagined. I started at the Lee County clinic, an overcrowded, friendly building in the middle of the cotton fields where poor folk, white and black, routinely travel forty or fifty miles to see a doctor who is affordable. The clinic director, John Eason, a dignified black man in his late fifties, confessed that for many of his patients the choice was often between buying medicine or food. 'Am I going to get my prescription,' he quoted them as saying, 'or am I going to eat?'

Over a lunch from the real Old South – fried catfish, French fries, spicy red beans and rice, a heart-attack-on-a-plate of a meal – he resolutely but politely insisted on the formality of calling me 'Mister', as he explained how hard it was to find doctors to work anywhere in the Mississippi delta. One of the best was leaving with no replacement in sight, causing real problems. Dr Jim. I decided to find him.

A few schoolkids, mostly black, were dawdling on their way home. A couple of people with nothing better to do sat on the stoops of their houses chatting and drinking and listening to crackly blues from a battered boom box. The catfish lay in my stomach like a brick, and I was sure I would never need to eat again as I walked along Main Street sucking in the general air of depression, the closed shops, the faded paint on the storefronts, the battered pick-up trucks, one with a broken exhaust that sputtered like a machine-gun. There was a poster in the window of the general store appealing for anyone who had medical training to apply for Dr Jim's job. It smacked of desperation, and I thought of a grim joke from a friend in the State Department in Washington: 'It's better to be poor abroad than poor in America, because if you are poor abroad you qualify for US aid.'

I got directions and drove out to Dr Jim's house. He was a wiry man in his early sixties with quick eyes and a slow Arkansas drawl — full of Southern hospitality. He told me to sit awhile, have a glass of iced tea. There are seventy-five counties in the State, he explained, and a third of them have no obstetrician. To deliver babies, a prudent doctor needs to pay at least $50,000 in insurance against malpractice lawsuits every year — which means you have to make fifty thousand before you earn a penny, and you can't do that in poor areas of the South. American doctors live in fear of being sued, having their time wasted, their energy directed into dealing with lawyers, their reputation torn apart in courtroom dramatics. Every patient is a potential litigant. The form-filling has become intolerable and the pressures drain the fun out of a small family practice. Dr Jim thought the whole system was going to hell, and he hated the *bureaucracy*, snarling at the word as if it were a Communist imposition.

I said, 'But you like practising medicine?'

'Sure. It's my life.'

'And people here need you?'

'The fun has gone,' he admitted, a little guilty at his decision to quit.

Fear of malpractice lawsuits, lawyers, insurance, bureaucracy, form-filling, government controls, *gummint*, meant Dr Jim would have to employ perhaps two clerical staff to do his paperwork. The day of the country doctor was over, he concluded, at least for him. In poor areas of the world's richest country doctors were needed. He was a doctor. But he was being forced to quit. Neither of us could make it add up. 'I'm going to work in a hospital emergency room instead,' he laughed. 'It's less stressful.'

Less stressful? To put together gunshot victims and road accident casualties? Sure, he explained. The hospital meant he could practise medicine, which he liked. It paid a reasonable salary, which he needed. But, most important of all, it looked after the bureaucratic nonsense leaving Jim free to do what he did best – treat patients. I blinked in amazement. Even in small towns on the Mississippi, gang violence was now so bad that hospital emergency rooms had become high-risk areas.

I had arranged to visit one Arkansas hospital which was being redesigned to include bulletproof windows and a security desk for an armed guard, following a shoot-out. The story was that a local gangster had been shot in the street and taken to the hospital while his gang-mates hung around to hear if he would survive. Then the opposing gang drove by and sprayed the emergency room with bullets, replacing the Shoot-out at the OK Corral with the Shoot-out in Hospital ER, like a bad joke: don't go to hospital, people die there. And Dr Jim thought that was *less* stressful than dealing with the paperwork mountain of the modern country doctor's practice? That's when I made my mistake.

'Isn't it dangerous to work in a hospital emergency room?' I wondered, and before I could blink Dr Jim stuck his hand in the back of his belt and drew out the gun. I almost bit the top off the iced tea glass.

'Not if you have one of these,' he replied.

Here was the country doctor of the 1990s, armed like a cop and drawing his gun like a cowboy. I can still see the pistol, motionless like a frozen frame from a video recording, stuck in my face. And I still have the memory of an educated, articulate, disconnected man, angry with his government, the legal system, his lot in life, with America's state of disunion, angry against the faceless, nameless system that was grinding him down, angry that the rules of his life had most certainly changed for the worse. Dr Jim was prepared to do the best he could to defend what he had and maintain his sanity.

Eventually he put the gun away. We shook hands and I started the long drive to the Arkansas State capital, Little Rock. It was getting dark as I reached the Interstate, flashing quickly across the heart of the south through flat cotton fields the colour of dried blood. There was the obvious paradox: Dr Jim was a healer dressed to kill. I had met it before, once, in Texas, on a shooting range outside Houston. An attractive thirty-year-old blonde woman in a blue nurse's uniform was blasting away at targets with a LadySmith – a Smith and Wesson .38 revolver specially adapted for the smaller hand of a woman. When she paused to reload we started talking and she said she was an emergency-room nurse who had treated many shooting victims. In a way she hated having a gun. 'But, you know . . .'

I said I did not know. She explained that she worked strange hours in the hospital. A couple of weeks before she had left at two o'clock in the morning to drive home when a truck pulled alongside. She speeded up. The truck driver speeded up. She slowed down. He slowed down. He started making sexually explicit signs to her as she, alone in her car, and he, in his giant truck, roared down the freeway side by side. What are you going to do? Two-thirty in the morning in the middle of nowhere?

'So I opened my purse,' she indicated the revolver. 'And pulled this out.'

She showed me how she pointed the LadySmith revolver at the man in the truck. He took the hint and disappeared into the night. Retelling the story she smiled at me sweetly, embarrassed. She was probably about five-feet-five tall, the LadySmith like a bazooka in her small hands. Everyone knew the crime statistics were supposed to be going down, but not for her. Violent crime had tripled between 1965 and 1980, and then continued to rise until – apparently – levelling off or dropping in the mid-1990s. But *fear* of crime was an undiminished American neurosis. The nurse repeated that she did not like guns and had seen too many victims of shootings to point a firearm at someone lightly.

'But, you know . . .'

Now I did know. But there was something else going on beyond the continuing suspicion that whatever the crime figures might suggest, daily life was still dangerous. I had come across too many Americans like Dr Jim, decent and talented and yet on the edge, fearful, anxious and angry that something nameless yet awful was going wrong in American society. I could see the lights of Little Rock and crossed the Arkansas River. It was almost midnight and I was desperate to get to my hotel, too exhausted to be hungry.

I checked in, went upstairs and opened my bedroom door. In the room something was missing. The bed. It was past midnight, I was sweaty and tired and now beginning to get angry.

'We're sorry, sir,' the front-desk clerk said as if I happened to be a stray imbecile spoiling his evening. 'Your room does not have a bed.'

'I can see that,' I spluttered. 'But I booked the room on my credit card, guaranteeing . . .'

'Ah,' he interrupted. 'You booked a *room*. You did not book a *bed*.'

It hit me that this was exactly what Dr Jim meant when he spat out the hated word *bureaucracy*, the sense that in the worst of America there lurked the soul of a lawyer. *Gummint*. Only in *Fawlty Towers* (or in an American courtroom) might you insist that booking a hotel room and reserving a bed were two different operations.

'That,' I replied, the vision of Dr Jim's pistol coming to mind, 'is rather like saying someone is going to shoot you with a gun, when in fact it would be a bullet that would do the damage.'

At least now I had his undivided attention. He called the night porter to find a roll-away bed and place it in my room. I sat staring at the lights down the Arkansas River wondering if there was something beyond this trivial kind of anger that was gnawing at America. It was certainly gnawing at me. Dr Jim feared the *legal* bureaucracy almost as much as the *governmental* bureaucracy. Yet the truth was they were the *same thing*. There were obvious clues. Guess which profession shows itself in the greatest numbers in Congress? Lawyers. The profession of Bill and Hillary Clinton? Yup. Both lawyers. Senator Bob Dole?

Lawyer. What happens when big-name politicians in the United States – James Baker, former Speaker Tom Foley, former Democratic Senate leader George Mitchell – retire from politics? They work in law firms.

Even the lawyer jokes on late-night TV and the anti-Congress jokes are the same. *Sample one*: I hear doctors have stopped using laboratory rats for medical research. They have switched to lawyers/members of Congress. Apparently you never get attached to lawyers/members of Congress. And there were some things the rats just would not do. *Sample two*: What do you call a bus load of lawyers/Congressmen going over a cliff? A good start.

The explosive growth in the number of lawyers in America in the last twenty years has run parallel with three of the phenomena that Americans despise most about their society in the 1990s: the growth in government bureaucracy, the sense of decline in American character and the rise of the culture of victims. All four signs point to serious and perhaps irreversible decay. All four are inextricably linked – parasitic lawyers feed off a parasitic bureaucracy, contribute to the decline in character and encourage the rise of a parasitic, whining culture.

In the late 1970s, for example, there were 'only' 250,000 lawyers in the United States. I can find no 1970s publications lamenting a shortage in the legal profession. Nevertheless, by 1991 that figure had tripled to 800,000. By the year 2000 there will be an estimated 1 million lawyers in the United States, more lawyers than serving soldiers in the US Army. Vice-President Dan Quayle, as part of a Bush–Quayle attack on the exploding number of lawsuits, asked the American Bar Association in 1991: 'Does America really need 70 per cent of the world's lawyers? Is it healthy for our economy to have 18 million new lawsuits coursing through the system annually?'

For comparison, in Britain in 1996 the Law Society reported roughly 70,000 practising solicitors. There has been a modest increase in the number of British lawyers in recent years – and an increase in the number of inventive lawsuits following the American model. But Britain remains singularly under-lawyered by comparison with the United States. In *The Litigation Explosion*, author Walter Olson points out that in the 1990s Americans assume they cannot enter into *any* important transaction without briefing a lawyer. Lawyers exercise a much more important role in business, medicine, sport, entertainment, government and the media than in any other country in the world – and a more intrusive role than at any time in American history. 'Prenuptial agreements', drawn up by lawyers, even manage to turn marriage from a romantic partnership into a company merger. In one 1996 case a New Mexico couple had their lawyers draw up a prenuptial agreement which specified, among other things, the frequency of sexual relations and the type of gasoline to be used in the family car. So much for wine and roses. There is even a television channel dedicated to the over-lawyering of America, Court TV.

The boom, as Dan Quayle rightly suggests, has been in lawyers suing over individual 'rights'. Disney patrons have the 'right' to expect Mickey Mouse to keep his mask on; there are special 'rights' for very fat people to sit in cinema aisles.

No lawyer ever made money asking whether alcoholics or morbidly obese people also have *responsibilities* not to drink or eat to excess. Such court cases inevitably, and rightly, convince Americans that something is seriously wrong with the moral and social fabric of their country, contributing to the fragmentation of the United States as new groups of victims demand special treatment under law.

Nowhere is the over-lawyering of America more apparent than in the capital city. The broad avenue of Washington's K Street N.W. is known as 'Gucci Gulch' after the expensive tasselled loafer shoes once favoured by the lawyers who work there. The suggestion that lawyers in Gucci Gulch are modern cowboys, hired guns, is not accidental. In 1950 there were fewer than 1,000 lawyers who claimed membership of the Washington DC bar. By 1975 that had exploded to 21,000. In 1993 that had grown yet again to 61,000. The total population of the City of Washington is 600,000. What kind of society can survive if one out of ten of its inhabitants is a lawyer?

Of course, many of those registered to practise in DC will live in the suburbs, or even far away. They have to register with the DC bar in order to practise in the capital. But evidence of a lawyer and litigation explosion is still clear. Has a sixty-old increase in registered lawyers made Washington a better city in the 1990s than the 1950s? Is it any coincidence that the capital is generally regarded as the worst run major city in the United States, a national and international joke for inefficiency, cupidity and a deadening bureaucracy which rivals pre-perestroika Russia?

In *The Litigation Explosion*, Walter Olson suggests that too many lawyers are chasing too little real business. Honest, careful citizens are now being sued on frivolous pretexts, not just the minority of negligent villains who inhabit any profession in any country. According to Mr Olson's figures, 70–80 per cent of obstetricians and *every* neurosurgeon registered in the District of Columbia have, at one time or another, been sued. That is like the old joke about a town too small to provide a living for one lawyer, but there was plenty of work for two and by the time three lawyers arrived they all became rich. Except this is no joke. And the figure is almost a million lawyers, not three.

The lawyer explosion has affected the American way of life as profoundly as the crime explosion in the past thirty years. Both mean that Americans are far less willing to take risks. Too many lawyers, like too many criminals, put the livelihoods of other people in jeopardy.

The tripling of violent crime in the United States between 1965 and 1980 has meant that most Americans live more defensively than ever before. They avoid certain areas. They think twice about walking or jogging after dark. They consider where to park cars, and perhaps drive with the doors locked. They avoid eye contact on certain city streets. They lock up property when once they might not have bothered. The same pattern is true of other countries — and especially in big cities, from London to Paris and Rome — though it is more serious in the United States.

But what is unique to the United States is the quadrupling of the number of lawyers, which has had a similar effect on American society as the crime explosion. Most Americans know someone who has been sued in a vexatious lawsuit, or have been sued themselves. We read scary stories about ludicrous lawsuits every day in newspapers or see them on the evening television news. Like tales of brutal criminal attacks, the constant repetition of such stories cannot but affect the way in which citizens go about their daily business. The result is that Americans, often without realizing it, live defensively to protect themselves from those 18 million lawsuits every year. And living defensively flies in the face of the traditional American ideals of personal responsibility, ruggedness and common sense. Every American has been affected by this. A few examples:

- By 1990, according to *The Litigation Explosion*, malpractice insurance for obstetricians with good records in New York had already reached $100,000 a year. Miami neurosurgeons were paying $220,000. Walter Olson quotes the case of a New York State doctor who was sued twenty years after the delivery of a child for problems allegedly resulting from the birth.
- In Washington DC some doctors were put off delivering babies altogether because there was no limit to the damages in malpractice cases. Dr Jim was not alone in his anger and despair. While patients, of course, should be free to exercise the right to sue, cutting both the numbers and the costs of medically inspired lawsuits would inevitably reduce American health care costs.
- The over-lawyering of America not only defies common sense, it also means it is no longer only doctors who have to pay enormous fees for malpractice insurance. Among the newer customers are nurses, accountants, sports umpires, veterinarians and hairdressers, all fearful of being sued. School counsellors, social workers and clergy are also reported as buying malpractice

insurance after being sued for 'wrongful advice'. In a delicious twist, even lawyers themselves have been buying malpractice insurance for, naturally, the same reason.

• Roughly one baby in four in the United States is born by Caesarean section – about twice the average in Britain and more than three times the rate of Sweden and Japan. The US Public Health Service notes the percentage of Caesareans has grown from 5.5 per cent in 1970 to just short of 25 per cent in the 1990s, while a more reasonable rate, they suggest, would be about 15 per cent. Doctors, lawyers, insurers, health professionals and patients all know that Caesarean sections are not always being performed to protect children or mothers. They are often being performed for the convenience or the protection of the doctors who fear being sued. Off the record, American doctors admit that no doctor was ever sued for choosing the most invasive and expensive procedure (in this case a Caesarean section). But doctors *have* been sued for more 'natural' births. Clinical diagnoses are being swayed by the possible legal consequences. American obstetricians recognize that Caesareans are over-prescribed, while lawyers in court argue that they are under-prescribed. Who would you believe? Walter Olson quotes a National Institute of Medicine study which claims such 'defensive medicine' has led to millions of unnecessary operations being performed on American women in childbirth. This is a national scandal. One result is that over the past few years it is estimated that at least one in five rural family doctors, like Dr Jim, have stopped delivering babies, citing fear of lawsuits.

• Hiring ski equipment at any American ski resort, or even having your skis serviced in a sports shop, demands that you fill out an incomprehensible small-print form explaining that skiing is dangerous. If you break a leg, the forms indicate, it is your own fault. This information is not to tell skiers something they do not know. It is to tell skiers' lawyers not to sue the ski equipment company. By the time there are two million lawyers in America skis will, no doubt, carry warnings that snow – in certain circumstances – can be cold.

• *The New York Times* reported in March 1997 that among the defensive product labelling by toy manufacturers was a notice on a child's 'Batman' cape indicating that it would not help the wearer to fly, and on plastic armour of the type worn by medieval knights indicating that it was not really a kind of protection.

• A friend fired an employee for embezzlement. Before the police could complete their inquiries into the criminal case, the ex-employee's lawyer threatened a civil suit alleging wrongful dismissal. Workers now sue for being dismissed, not being promoted and not being hired in the first place. There have been lawsuits aimed at employers who give bad references. One worker who refused to take a drug test was awarded $480,000 compensation.

• In January 1997 New Jersey Superior Court Judge Leonard Arnold, weighing the case of a jailed pregnant woman seeking an abortion ruled that her five-month-old foetus had the right to an attorney. 'I have decided that the unborn child requires representation,' the judge said in his ruling. The lawyer, Richard Collier, said that an abortion would be 'infanticide', and he promised 'I will vigorously represent my client'.

• At Washington's National Zoo – an American treasure – children were once encouraged to handle non-poisonous snakes under supervision from zoo-keepers. By 1996, after a child in another zoo contracted salmonella from touching a reptile, the policy was suspended for fear of lawsuits. By 1997 common sense surprisingly prevailed. Handling snakes was allowed provided children washed their hands afterwards.

• A Washington DC-sponsored children's co-operative was thrown into turmoil because the parents were advised by the District of Columbia they may be open to lawsuits if, when running each other's children backwards and forwards to events, they have an accident. The District of Columbia was obviously trying to protect itself from lawsuits. But the implication for America's sense of community and responsibility is odious. The safe thing to do is not to drive the children of your friends

95

anywhere, because your *friends* might sue you. Is it any surprise that Americans trust each other less than a generation ago?

And so on, *ad nauseam*.

American lawyers argue that their system of allowing 'contingency fees' – lawyers taking a percentage of the payments in a successful case and no fee for an unsuccessful case – means that many more middle-income Americans are able to afford lawsuits than their equivalent in Britain or Western Europe. They also claim that if there was no demand from the public, the United States could not possibly support a million lawyers. This may be true. But are we seriously to believe that 70–80 per cent of obstetricians in the Washington DC area are not always up to the job, as the litigation explosion figures would suggest? This is clearly nonsense. Even if obstetrics attracts an unusually high proportion of knaves and fools (which I doubt), common sense suggests that only a few per cent of such tort cases are really solidly based. The problem is that in the United States there is no penalty for making false, vexatious or money-grubbing allegations. There is no penalty, in other words, for pursuing your 'rights' by reaching for a lawyer, and no punishment for failing to act responsibly.

The obvious solution – obvious to everyone except American lawyers and their brothers and sisters in the lawyer-dominated Congress – is to penalize heavily vexatious or frivolous lawsuits by awarding costs against the plaintiff, and potentially against the lawyer for pursuing a case he or she knows to be without merit. If lawyers seek to have a percentage of the 'profits' from winning a case on a contingency fee basis, they should also be bound to share a percentage of the 'losses' when such a case is thrown out of court. Until this is done, America's lawyer explosion – and the decline in personal responsibility connected to it – will continue to multiply like a giant tapeworm. It is already eating up the best minds of a generation of Americans in expensive and often idiotic courtroom battles. From the vulture lawyers known as 'ambulance chasers' who hang around hospitals hoping to encourage accident victims to sue someone — anyone — to the very highest levels, American lawyers contrive to look ridiculous.

The televised confirmation of Supreme Court Justice Clarence Thomas, accused of sexual harassment by Anita Hill, turned on lurid stories of pubic hair on Coca-Cola cans and conversations about a porn movie entitled *Long Dong Silver*. This was not *Perry Mason*. It was barely *Monty Python*. It was more like *Benny Hill*. Or consider the two most watched criminal trials in America in the 1990s: those of O. J. Simpson and the Menendez brothers in California. The accused in both trials were 'victims', of course — of racism in Simpson's case; of sexual abuse in the case of the Menendez brothers. The fact that four people had been murdered was less important to the television spectacle than their highly paid lawyers arguing about the competitive victimhood of the accused.

The trials were as close as television technology can get to medieval bear-baiting or gladiators killing lions in the Roman Coliseum. In the aftermath of the bread and circuses entertainment of the Simpson and Menendez criminal trials, the highly respected Governor of Oklahoma, Frank Keating — a former FBI agent — confided to me that his principal worry about the Oklahoma bombing trial was that it would become yet another televised legal circus. He confirmed the view of many Americans that lawyers in the 1990s did not care about justice or the truth but only about winning. The over-lawyering of America is driving out morality as well as basic common sense. Lawyers are fond of asking *cui bono?* — who benefits? The answer in this case is only the lawyers themselves. In a hundred years' time historians may conclude that the decline of America was directly related to the unchecked growth of a parasitic legal and political culture which distorted every aspect of daily life, and reinforced the angry divisions within American society.

Compare, for example, the best-known document of America two hundred years ago with its counterpart today. The Declaration of Independence, whatever the input from the legal minds of the day, comes from a time when litigation was regarded, at best, as a necessary evil in a free society. The Declaration speaks clearly of the promise of 'life, liberty and the pursuit of happiness'. The right was to *pursue* happiness, not to *achieve* it. Somewhere in the legal explosion this distinction has been lost.

Two hundred years later the clarity of the Declaration of Independence is utterly unknown in public pronouncements. The best-known document of 1990s over-lawyered America is, probably, Income Tax Form 1040. This form, the product of the best tax lawyers and their *alter egos* in Congress, reads, in part: 'Line 36: If line 32 is $83,850 or less, multiply $2,450 by the total number of exemptions claimed on line 6a. If line 32 is over $83,850 see the worksheet on page 24 for the amount to enter.'

Only a lawyer could love it. It is difficult to believe that the Declaration of Independence and Form 1040, Line 36 come from the same culture. In fact they do not. One comes from a culture of idealism and personal responsibility with the potential for heroism. The other derives from a culture of legalism and defensive living where heroism seems impossible, and where litigation is yet another 'right' without any connected responsibility. This is a sign of demonstrable and significant decadence, the triumph of the culture of victims and the rule of lawyers. It is against the best American traditions. And, as we have seen, opinion polls note that every generation that has come of age in the United States since the 1950s is *less* trusting of friends, neighbours and society. That is hardly surprising when the culture of victims motto, 'Don't Blame Me', becomes the motto of the rule of lawyers, 'Or I'll Sue You For Every Penny'.

President Clinton, America's Lawyer-in-Chief, has faced such a legal barrage he hired a $475-an-hour lawyer to defend himself against the sexual harassment allegations of former Arkansas employee, Paula Jones. The legal bills for Mr and Mrs Clinton and their most loyal White House staff will be in the millions of dollars by the time he leaves office. The president's lawyer argued before the Supreme Court that the Paula Jones litigation could paralyse the presidency by opening up the president to a time-wasting inquiry. Whatever the merit of Ms Jones' allegations, it is a pity that President Clinton does not draw the obvious conclusion, and argue that the over-lawyering of America is having the same paralysing effect on the United States as a whole.

America in Black, White and Green

'The most formidable of all the ills that threaten the future of the Union arises from the presence of a black population upon its territory. The white and the black are placed in the situation of two foreign communities. These two races are fastened to each other without intermingling; and they are unable to separate entirely or to combine.'

Alexis de Tocqueville, Democracy in America

'People, I just want to say, you know, can we all get along? Can we get along . . . Please, we can get along here. We all can get along. I mean, we're all stuck here for a while. Let's try to work it out.'

Police beating victim, Rodney King, during the Los Angeles riots, 1992

Washington DC

Milton lives at one of Washington's most desirable addresses, a short walk from the White House. His home is opposite the Daughters of the American Revolution building, one of the grandest neo-classical façades in the United States. This icy winter night the building's white pillars are illuminated by spotlights, and Milton's home is surrounded by the floodlit glories of Imperial America – the huge marble finger of the Washington Monument and the Capitol dome which pokes its bald white pate into the night sky.

Milton's home has everything to recommend it, except this:

no roof, no walls, no heating (unless you count the steam from the grate on which he and his friends are lying draped in grey blankets handed out by welfare workers). Milton, a thickset middle-aged black man, sees the van carrying Dr Janelle Goetcheus arrive and stands up to greet her, moving towards a bench where they sit together. Dr Goetcheus, a bespectacled white woman, is wearing a knitted polo neck with a large Christian cross, a red anorak and a stethoscope. She lives in Christ House in north-west Washington along with thirty-eight homeless people who suffer the diseases of urban poverty – pneumonia, tuberculosis, diabetes and complications from the AIDS virus.

She gives Milton an open air medical examination and asks him about his leg. Like many homeless people, Milton has lost a limb. Frostbite, gangrene, every medical horror you can think of – and a few which are unthinkable – are common on the dark side of the gleaming monuments in the heart of the greatest city in the richest nation in history. His leg feels terrible, Milton responds. To keep warm he has to do a lot of walking and the stump aches. Dr Goetcheus checks his temperature for hypothermia and explains that small ulcers can become infected. She has had to amputate frostbitten toes in the harsh Washington winters.

'I've seen maggots in wounds,' she continues, her breath steaming in the air as she details forensically more than most of us want to know about treating the ragged homeless who beg for small change on the streets while the limousines of the most powerful politicians in the world glide by. Maybe the limousines' dark tinted windows prevent the politicians inside from seeing out clearly.

'I have been here since 1976 and I have only seen things get worse and worse,' Dr Goetcheus says, comparing practising medicine in Washington to her missionary work in the Third World. 'I saw tremendous poverty when I was in Zaire, but I still saw hope among the people. Here I don't see hope. I just see so much despair. We talk about our city being a *Fourth* World, meaning it's a city in the middle of a rich setting and so it's a poverty that pulls the spirit out of people.'[1]

Nothing has the capacity to ignite American anger at the condition of their society more quickly than the question of race, especially when combined, as it often is, with unconquerable poverty and fear of crime. In every conversation I have had about racial issues with Americans from all ethnic groups over the past few years I have heard, unanimously, a longing to fix this problem above all else. But, equally unanimously, Americans tend to describe race relations in the 1990s as 'bad' or 'worsening'. What is most obvious to an outsider is the unchanging nature of the core problem. More than 130 years after slavery was abolished and emancipation proclaimed, after all the bitter struggles of the civil rights movement plus a generation of 'affirmative action' (what the British call 'positive discrimination'), the words of Alexis de Tocqueville in the 1830s could have been written this week or, even worse, next week, next year, or next century: 'The danger of a conflict between the white and the black inhabitants perpetually haunts the imagination of the Americans like a painful dream.'

Where race relations have changed, it often seems as if it is for the worse. A few miles from where Milton sleeps, the Washington neighbourhood known as Shaw was the home of the jazz musician Duke Ellington. Think of Shaw today and the sound of music does not come to mind so much as the sound of gunfire. Shaw in the 1990s is a war zone, Bosnia within walking distance of the White House. During the worst of the period of segregation Shaw – like many black inner-city areas – perversely thrived. It was home to a black middle class of dentists, doctors, lawyers and intellectuals. Now successful blacks have fled from America's inner cities, leaving behind an ever more impoverished and desperate underclass in the empty centre of the doughnut. At Shaw's redbrick Shiloh Baptist Church a couple of dozen nine- and ten-year-old boys are playing basketball.

The church's windows are boarded up, staring blindly into a neighbourhood which the Reverend Barry Hargrove describes as 'living in poverty and fear'. He shows me around the church proudly, an island of sanity in an insane world. 'Ninety per cent of [the boys],' he says, 'come from single parent homes headed by their mothers . . . almost half of them live at or below the poverty level.'

Roughly two-thirds of babies born to black mothers in the United States are now illegitimate. In some poor areas, 90 per cent of children living only with a mother is not unusual. Having a father at home is an aberration. Since single parent homes are likely to be less well off, more than a quarter of America's black families live below the poverty line – compared to 7 per cent of white families. Median family income for black families in 1995 was $24,000. For whites, $42,000. Black unemployment is twice that of whites.

'I go to school in fear,' one of the church basketball players admits, as a sea of innocent children's faces starts to rock with stories of friends or relatives murdered on the streets. 'They are almost desensitized by the occurrence of violence,' the Reverend Barry explains after we had listened to their stories of gang shootings, drive-by shootings, accidental killings. 'A child came to me recently and told me, matter-of-factly, "I don't want to die".' The child was twelve years old, but making plans to die violently in adolescence is not unusual. White people, the Reverend Barry said without rancour, don't know what goes on in the real Washington. 'It's a very divided city.'

Like most American cities, Washington is split by an American apartheid which persists in practice in the 1990s even if it lacks the legal force of past segregation. The only black 'neighbour' I can think of in the corner of north-west Washington where I live is in a house two streets away. He is a diplomat from the Caribbean. The black faces in this area tend to belong to visitors, those who are delivering the mail, repairing telephone lines, carrying out maintenance or fixing the roads. There are some mixed areas, but in huge swathes of this mainly black city – and even in some of the more prosperous suburbs – the only *white* faces you may see will be the occasional police officer or journalist passing through what everyone knows is a 'black' neighbourhood like Shaw or Anacostia.

Rather as in Northern Ireland, everyone knows where the

invisible boundary lines are. And, just as in Northern Ireland, groups which do not live together or go to the same schools have a tendency to regard each other through mutual ignorance and distrust. Americans of different colours often behave like diners at separate tables in the same uneasy restaurant, not sure whether to make polite conversation or to stick with their own.

This chapter cannot give more than a glimpse of the angry face of race relations in 1990s America, and there are plenty of studies which offer more complete accounts. But for the purposes of a book tracing anger and anxiety within American society, three facts stand out. First, the consensus over how to address 'poverty and fear' in the inner cities has collapsed in the 1990s with the backlash against sixty years of welfare policies and thirty years of affirmative action. Second, issues of black and white also have to be seen in terms of green, the colour of dollar bills. Money has created a dividing line not just between blacks and whites, but between the majority of prospering black people and the minority of the increasingly hopeless or terrifying black 'underclass'. And third, as Alexis de Tocqueville recognized, whites and blacks have long had reason to fear each other's capacity for violence. What follows is an examination of the ways in which each of these interlinked issues is a source of the almost immutable anger at the heart of American race relations.

The rioting which began in South Central Los Angeles in 1992 was the worst civil disturbance in the United States this century. Despite the general goodwill most Americans bear towards those of other colours, the most widespread anxiety of the United States in the 1990s is that it persistently teeters one angry incident away from a terrible racial conflagration. Some black commentators insist on calling the LA riots an 'uprising'. It was almost a replay of the rioting that shook Watts a generation earlier, and perhaps that is the saddest observation of all. The angriest outbreaks of racial tension in the 1990s, in LA and in southern states where dozens of black churches were burned, contribute to a dismal sense of *déjà vu*.

Even the spark that ignited the 1992 riots, the acquittal of white police officers caught on videotape savagely beating a black motorist, Rodney King, had the feel of a rerun of a movie from the worst of the bad old days of the American South: an all-white jury which would not convict white police officers for brutality, black anger and violence, white fear, soldiers of the National Guard mobilized, the 1960s disturbances in Watts and Detroit and Selma, and the ghosts of Mississippi all over again.

Southern California gun shops grew busy selling weapons and ammunition to citizens who feared – correctly – that the police in Los Angeles could not protect them. Some black leaders, including Arthur Fletcher of Washington's Commission on Civil Rights, believed that the United States was again what he called 'a racial tinderbox'.

'We could have a Bosnia right here in this country,' Mr Fletcher said. 'It's that bad. One of the reasons the average white household is armed to the teeth is over the prospects of an explosive racial war.'[2]

There were equally cheerless words from opposite sides of the political spectrum. In his second Inaugural Address President Clinton called the divide of race 'America's constant curse'. As he was sworn in for his second term as House Speaker in January 1997, Newt Gingrich – the first Republican re-elected to that post for sixty-eight years – marked the occasion by challenging Americans on their failure to grapple with racial problems. 'Do we not need to rethink our whole approach to race?' he asked Congress. 'I don't believe any rational American can be comfortable with where we are on the issue of race.'

But where *is* America on race? The same issues, from crime and welfare to affirmative action, or the verdicts in the criminal and civil trials of O. J. Simpson, are repeatedly seen so differently by most whites and blacks, attempts at mutual understanding are constantly undermined by resentment and anger. The story of Milton, for example, has the capacity to irritate both blacks and whites for different reasons. Many white people resent affirmative action policies because they give preference to minority applicants for jobs, university places and some government contracts. To them the persistence of a black 'underclass' of the hopeless, helpless or homeless, is a symbol of the failure of 'unfair' 1960s social engineering.

To these people, affirmative action and welfare have helped create a 'culture of dependency', encouraging illegitimacy and shattering black families without helping people like Milton to live 'responsibly'. But to the majority of black Americans who have prospered greatly in the past thirty years, Milton's story may seem to be a racial stereotype. There are plenty of poor whites in America, and the country's most under-reported story is of black economic success.

During the riots in 1992 I was filming a BBC news report at a charity in South Central Los Angeles. They were accepting donations of food and giving hand-outs to poor people in an area in which the supermarkets had been looted. The looting was an equal-opportunity affair. The first looters I saw happened to be white and Hispanic, smashing windows on Hollywood Boulevard and carrying off everything from supermarket food and booze to exotic underwear. Then I saw black looters and Asian looters. Melting-pot lawlessness does not minimize the clear black–white and black–Korean polarizations in Los Angeles, but *rich* Americans were not rioting. Poorer Americans of all colours took the opportunity to break the law in a revolt of the Have-Nots against the Haves.

As tempers began to cool, an elegant black woman in an African style kente-cloth dress struck up a conversation with me at the food charity while volunteer workers stacked cans of meat, vegetables and beans. The woman was most definitely one of the Haves. Thinking I was from an American TV network she angrily began to upbraid me about what she said was the racially divisive nature of media coverage of the riots. When she learned I was from the BBC she continued her complaints – politely, but very firmly.

She said she resented the stereotypical way the media treated black people, the underlying and inaccurate assumption that those on welfare or receiving government hand-outs must have a black face. Most Americans on welfare are *white*, she insisted, because most Americans are white. Yet television portrayals of the welfare 'problem' showed mostly black people. As we talked I helped the woman carry bags of food she was donating from the back of her fashionable Jeep Cherokee car.

We said goodbye and she sank into the leather upholstery, driving off to her home miles away in the prosperous suburbs, a different America. It was a sign of what *has* changed for the better since the 1960s. About two-thirds of America's black citizens have seen their economic opportunities rise, often dramatically, like those of the lady in the Cherokee. The tragedy for black America is that the remaining third, dismissed as 'the underclass', appear to be as isolated from the mainstream of the American Dream as their forefathers were before the birth of the civil rights movement. The tragedy for white America is that it seems unable to recognize the difference between the prospering black middle class in their Jeep Cherokees and Milton or the poor kids left behind in Shaw.

Not long after the incident at the food charity, any illusions I may have had that the colour of skin did not count as much in 1990s America as the colour of money were quickly destroyed. I was taken on a tour of LA by two black American friends, Ben and Emmett, in their van. Ben was driving, Emmett sat beside him in the front and they decided to show me the tourist sights of Beverly Hills. We left the inner city and the neighbourhoods became richer and the people lighter skinned until, between the palm trees and the Porsches, you could see the kind of houses that represent 1990s American success.

Once in Beverly Hills, Ben stopped at a road junction to allow a rich-looking white woman to cross. She was in her sixties and wearing a leisure suit – a track suit for people who do not care much for exercise. She caught sight of Ben and Emmett in their van, two black faces. I was in the back seat and watched as her expression changed into what Ben later described as 'the Look' – the look that is given when a white person sees but does not *want* to see a black face. It was a mixture of fear and hostility, as if Ben was the murderer, thief, rapist and rioter of white America's nightmares. 'It's OK, lady,' Ben said laconically. 'We got a white guy in the back. He's even wearing a tie.'

We drove on. Ben is moderately prosperous, middle class, well educated, sophisticated and fun. But he is also a big black man in a culture terrified of big black men, however much money they might have in the bank. The white woman did not see Ben. She saw Willie Horton, the black pin-up poster villain of white racism. He featured in the most devastating televised political advertisement in American history. Horton had committed a brutal murder in Massachusetts and received a life sentence, but he was eventually allowed out of prison on a series of weekend passes. He absconded, kidnapped a young white couple, stabbed the man and raped his girlfriend. What put this nightmare on national television was the fact that the Governor of Massachusetts was Michael Dukakis and, in 1988, he was running for president, for a time well ahead in the polls.

Supporters of his Republican rival, Vice-President George Bush, ran a television advertisement exploiting the Horton case. The theme was that Dukakis was 'soft on crime'. The Horton ad was widely reviled as racist, but there is no doubt it was effective. Black voters, in general, would not support Bush anyway, and white voters were treated to the powerful suggestion that Dukakis was keen to release black rapists and murderers to terrorize the law-abiding population.

The Willie Horton ad played directly to de Tocqueville's 'painful dream' of racial conflict in America, the classic angry 'wedge' issue which was cynically exploited by the Bush campaign to divide communities and reinforce racial stereotypes. Bush won. Dukakis lost. And, more importantly, Ben and Emmett lost too. A white woman they had never met looked into their faces and saw Willie Horton. She did not see General Colin Powell or Dr Martin Luther King.

I could not believe 'the Look', though Ben dismissed it as a kind of unconscious response from unthinking white people; not especially significant. The woman, he was sure, would be resentful if you suggested she was a racist. But in the words of Dr King she was judging a man by the colour of his skin, not the content of his character – a simple, common, perhaps universal fault, and one which ensures race remains America's hair trigger of social anger.

In October 1995 on the Mall in Washington, not far from where Milton sleeps, and where Martin Luther King delivered his famous 'I have a Dream' speech on civil rights, hundreds of thousands of black American men gathered to pledge that they would take responsibility for their lives, families and neighbour-hoods. This was billed as a 'Million Man March'. Many white Americans regarded it as if it were an invasion of the nation's capital by a million Willie Hortons.

The most controversial of the organizers was the Nation of Islam leader, Minister Louis Farrakhan. Mr Farrakhan is one of the angriest public figures in 1990s America, a man who exploits racial animosities with every bit of the cynicism of the creators of the Willie Horton ad. He referred to Jews as 'bloodsuckers' and his anti-Semitism and homophobia is combined with what, to white ears, sounds like a black version of the Ku Klux Klan. Many marchers insisted they were able to separate a good message – atonement, taking responsibility – from a flawed messenger in Farrakhan, though this is self-delusion. It is like claiming attendance at a Nuremberg rally was not really an endorsement of Hitler. In one of the more odious excuses of the culture of victims, some black leaders argue that it is impossible for African-Americans like Farrakhan to be considered racist since they come from an oppressed people. There is, in fact, a fearful symmetry between the views of racist white and racist black Americans.

Most Americans will remember the first news reports on the LA riots showing the brutality of black youths who beat the white truck driver Reginald Denny almost to death at a road junction in South Central Los Angeles. The scene was captured on videotape by a camera in a helicopter. No amount of rhetoric about 'oppression' amounts to a licence to beat a defenceless man with a lump of concrete. (Though Americans should also recall the heroism of local black people who rescued Mr Denny and saved his life.)

In fact, much of the anger of the black street mobs during the LA riots was not directed against whites, who usually live far from the ghetto areas. The target was frequently Korean-Americans who had set up small businesses within or near black communities. The riots came after months of racial animosity between some black groups and Korean store owners.

A Korean working in a typical small business drew a gun and shot a teenage black girl called Latasha Harlins who, she believed, had been shoplifting. African-Americans protested that the Koreans were racists. The prices they charged in their corner stores were too high and they treated black people badly. One African-American man told me that Korean store personnel would take money from him but would always leave the change on the counter, fearful of touching his black skin.

In this atmosphere of ethnic distrust, black rioters deliberately set about attacking Korean businesses and at least one Korean store owner was shot dead, execution-style. Signs on black-owned businesses made clear the racial background of the owner so the mob would leave them alone. Korean-Americans formed armed vigilante patrols to protect their houses and homes.

Black animosity towards other races extends from the ghetto into academia. Leonard Jeffries is a controversial and eloquent black university lecturer. He draws a distinction between whites whom he calls 'ice people' – cold-hearted materialists – and the warm-hearted, caring 'sun people' with darker skin. Mr Jeffries' views are, in fact, the mirror image of white racist propaganda which refers to black Americans as 'mud people'. In both cases pseudo-links are claimed between skin colour and character or behaviour. Such intellectually vacuous ideas are no more defensible in the lectures of a black academic than from the mouth of a white redneck sheltering under the pointed hood of the Ku Klux Klan.

But – to the alarm of white Americans who fear he is a black racist – Minister Louis Farrakhan was able to call from all corners of the United States hundreds of thousands of young black men to Washington. It was undoubtedly the biggest single mass protest by black people in American history, and everything about the march was a metaphor for the appalling state of race relations in the United States.

Many white people in the Washington area were nervous that one spark could ignite a repeat of the LA riots in the heart of the capital. A few days before the march a white neighbour, knowing I would be reporting on the event, looked at me in astonishment and said: 'Surely you are not going to the march? Won't there be trouble?' A white American journalist told me he was prepared to report on the rally because his job depended on it. But he said he was leaving his wallet in his office just in case he was mugged.

A Latino friend, from Honduras, warned that there most certainly would be violence with, as he put it, 'a crowd like that'. He was thinking of taking the day off work. And a white woman friend was told by an organizer of her child's playgroup, 'I'm not a racist but maybe this is just a day when we need to stay at home.' The playgroup closed.

So did much of the business section of north-west Washington. It was the most deserted I have ever seen on a work day in years of driving through the capital. The message was obvious. To many white Americans this was not a gathering of hundreds of thousands of their fellow citizens anxious about the state of their communities, it was an 'invasion' of Washington by the scariest group in America – young black men, a million potential Willie Hortons, criminals on the rampage.

I walked through the rally and talked to many young black men who – despite the fears of my white neighbours – were mainly amiable, articulate and good humoured. The atmosphere was about as violent as a papal mass, and considerably less threatening than many a British soccer match.

But crime, fear of crime and who is to blame for crime are just as prominently issues for black America as white America, though they may begin from different viewpoints. Many of the black marchers discussed how they could 'take back' their often violent neighbourhoods from drug dealers and muggers, how they could prevent their wives, mothers, grandmothers and children from becoming the victims of crime. But a popular T-shirt on sale showed prison bars and the slogan: 'Justice? Just Us'. The reference was to a study by the Washington Sentencing Project which showed nearly one in three black men aged between twenty and twenty-nine was in jail, on parole, or otherwise under the supervision of the criminal justice system. If one in three *white* men was in similar circumstances, one of the study's authors, Marc Mauer, said America 'would declare a national emergency'.

In 1997 the Sentencing Project also reported that one in seven black men was barred from voting as a result of felony convictions. These men had no vote, no voice and no stake in American society. Mr Mauer and many marchers concluded that this 'emergency' gripping black America was ignored by white politicians as surely as they glide by the homeless Milton sleeping beneath the monuments. But that is wrong. The crime emergency is *not* ignored by white America. On the contrary, it is seen as convincing evidence that young black males are indeed potential Willie Hortons because the crimes which most scare and anger America are, obviously, crimes of violence. And such crimes do, disproportionately, have a black face. In 1992 FBI arrest statistics showed that, compared to the percentage of blacks in the population, blacks committed five times as many robberies, almost five times as many murders and more than five times as many rapes.[3]

But black Americans are also, disproportionately, the victims of such crimes. The black leader, the Reverend Jesse Jackson, once memorably lectured African-Americans that their real enemy was not so much the KKK as the BBB — no longer the Ku Klux Klan but the 'Bad Black Brother'. In December 1993 he confronted this sense of division within the black community between the Haves and Have-Nots, with a compelling anecdote of how he, a veteran of the civil rights struggle, feared being mugged: 'There is nothing more painful to me at this stage of my life than to walk down the street and hear footsteps and start thinking about robbery — then look around and see somebody white and feel relieved.'

It was a courageous statement for a black leader to make about legitimate fears of crime within his community. And some of the statistics are quite staggering. Black Americans make up 12 per cent of the population, 13 per cent of the estimated drug abusers, 35 per cent of narcotic arrests, 55 per cent of convictions and 74 per cent of those receiving prison sentences.

One criminologist, Jerome Miller, predicted that by the year 2010 as many as 50 per cent of adult black men under the age of forty will be in jail. If this projection seems absurd, it is worth remembering that predictions about illegitimacy rates in the black community made in the 1960s seemed equally absurd. Until they came true, in areas like Shaw.[4]

But do the crime statistics show 'Just Us' because black men are treated unfairly, have fewer opportunities to advance themselves, are arrested more often and sentenced to longer terms in prison than whites? Or is it 'Justice' because violent crime, disproportionately, has a black face? Like the question of the guilt or innocence of O. J. Simpson, your answer may well depend on the colour of your own face. And whatever your answer, where race, crime and poverty meet, every American has plenty of opportunity to get angry. By 1995 the United States had imprisoned 1.6 million adults — the same number of men and women as were then serving in all branches of the US military. This number had *tripled* since 1980, a breakdown at the core of American daily life every bit as astonishing as the ballooning illegitimacy rate. At least another 3.75 million were on probation or parole.

While there was evidence by the mid-1990s that these statistics had peaked, some criminologists – most volubly John DiIulio, professor at the Woodrow Wilson School of Public and International Affairs at Princeton – begged to suggest there would be more bad news to come. DiIulio claimed that even if the overall crime rate stabilized, the juvenile crime rate would continue to rise. That meant an increase in the type of crimes Americans most fear – the Willie Horton syndrome.

DiIulio coined a new term, 'super-predator', to describe the kind of amoral dysfunctional villain of our worst nightmares. Super-predators are young men who kill without compunction, *Lord of the Flies* in America's inner cities. Citizens of every American city and even small towns fear that disaffected, rootless, impoverished young men are preying on their community without any sense of remorse or moral values. Often, just as with the 'underclass', whites assume that such super-predators will be black or disproportionately black, and point to FBI statistics (and nightly local news reports of inner-city mayhem) in justification.

In Little Rock, Arkansas, I met 'Sweet Pea', who seemed to fit the image. He was nineteen years old, dangerous, and with little expectation of living to the age of twenty-five. He was a gang member who made a tidy living dealing drugs, an industry he had been involved in since he was thirteen. On each hand Sweet Pea wore four gold rings, expensive knuckledusters. He proudly showed me a yellow handkerchief, the colours of his black gang, the Vicelords.

He explained in bewildering detail how the Vicelords were big in Chicago and the mid-West, but were very different from the Bloods (red) and the Crips (blue). When we talked about street violence, Sweet Pea said he could get me a 9 millimetre semiautomatic pistol for $80 or a Kalashnikov rifle for $250. Little Rock police confirmed that these were reasonable street prices for Guns-to-Go (though inflation and tougher gun laws have subsequently pushed the prices up). Sweet Pea said he had been shot at twice in the previous week, though he refused to go into details. Did he report the shootings to the police? He looked bemused. No, of course not. Why not? Because, Sweet

Pea explained, with the patience of a man in conversation with the village idiot, he himself will 'take care of business'. Taking care of business in Little Rock in 1993 – a small town of 180,000 people – meant seventy-six murders.

For comparison, in Northern Ireland in the early 1990s with a population of 1,700,000 and in the middle of a terrorist emergency, there were about 100 murders a year. Translate a Little Rock level of violence to Belfast and you would expect roughly 800 murders a year. Every day in the United States approximately sixty Americans will die of gunshot wounds.

In almost any American city in the early 1990s you were between five and ten times more likely to be murdered than in Northern Ireland. These figures demonstrate how crime, and fear of crime, have come to distort what is considered 'normal' in American life. The Center for Disease Control in Atlanta – the organization which tracks the Ebola virus and AIDS – became so concerned by the epidemic of gun violence that it began tracking homicide as if it were a communicable disease. Perhaps it is. In the early 1990s homicide was the most frequent cause of death among American black males aged between fifteen and twenty-four, though by the mid-1990s there were signs that the murder rate was going down, especially in big cities like New York, as rivalries between teenage drug gangs eased and the drug market 'matured'.

At a black church group on the outskirts of Little Rock, I sat while the Reverend Hezekiah Stewart discussed crime and violence with a group of teenage boys and girls. All had been involved with gangs. On the lawn in front of the church there were white crosses, one for each of those who had been murdered in Little Rock the previous year. Inside, like Sweet Pea, members of the group had a grim sense of their own mortality. Many knew that they could soon be commemorated by a white cross on the grass outside.[5]

'Why get involved with gangs?' the preacher asked. Money, they all agreed. Even children as young as eight or nine could earn $50 acting as a look-out for a few hours. Easy money. A replacement for broken families, some suggested. Excitement. Something to do.

'Why not read a book?' the Reverend Hezekiah suggested, knowing the answer. There were guffaws and sniggers, and a few cries of incredulity.

'We'll wait till it comes out on video,' someone laughed.

'No, man! No, *man!*' Another protested. 'What do you think the chances are I'd read a book?'

The boys and girls treated the preacher with courtesy. These were not the faces of super-predators. They were children in trouble being helped by a remarkable black church leader. And yet these were potentially very dangerous children indeed, already a year or two down the hard road from innocence to grotesque experience. The Reverend Hezekiah Stewart feared many of them would die before they had ever really lived. In the group someone mentioned the story of Frankie Webb. Frankie allegedly walked into a fast-food restaurant and shot two rival gang members in November 1993. At the time he was already on bail for attempted murder. Charges in yet another case were dropped when the victim refused to testify. Frankie Webb, Little Rock's one-man crime wave, was fifteen years old. A super-predator? Perhaps. A child dangerous enough to scare us all? Of course.

Sweet Pea, the nineteen-year-old OG – Original Gangster in street talk – admitted he could see his fate clearly. He was not going to live to retire and collect Social Security. But his gang, 'my organization', is 'there for me' twenty-four hours a day. And then he smiled. Joining a gang, he said, 'is like committing suicide'. There are only two ways out: you go to the penitentiary; or you die. Sweet Pea had accepted his role as the throwaway debris of an unspeakable underclass full of dehumanized super-predators.

A Cornell University study, *The State of Americans*,[6] suggested that in the 1990s one-third of all black American children were living in 'deep poverty'. Among developed countries the United States had the highest percentage of children living in poverty

– one in five of those under the age of eighteen. In Britain the figure was more like one in fifteen.

The difference between rich families (top 10 per cent) and poor families (bottom 10 per cent) was greater in the United States than in any other industrialized country. And, perhaps most extraordinary of all, one of the studies quoted by the Cornell group indicates that for those Americans who do go to prison, on release they are more likely to end up back in jail than in a job.

So what can be done? Perhaps the worst feature of all race relations in the 1990s is that growing sense that nothing much can, or should, be done any more. Ever since the 1960s there has been a consensus that one way of improving race relations would be to offer preferential treatment to black Americans and other minority groups to try to stimulate a sense of racial equity.

Since the Kennedy administration Americans have called this 'affirmative action'. But in the 1990s the consensus behind affirmative action has more or less collapsed, though the pro-grammes stagger on. The original idea, eloquently defended by President Lyndon Johnson, was to increase opportunities for minorities (eventually including Hispanics, Native Americans and women as well as blacks) in a kind of atonement for past discrimination. As President Johnson told an audience of black students in Washington's Howard University in 1965, 'You do not take a person who for years has been hobbled by chains and liberate him, bring him up to the starting line and then say, "You are free to compete with all the others."'

There is not space here to compete with the many book-length studies of the arguments for and against affirmative action policies, though clearly they were introduced with an element of enlightened self-interest. Whites would help blacks get a hand up to atone for past misdeeds. Race rioting would stop and the inner cities would magically improve.

Obviously, the 1992 LA riots and the conditions in most inner cities in the 1990s have shown that affirmative action has not worked a general miracle. As a result, the policies have become a key source of anger within American society with many whites complaining they have 'failed' and are unfair.

In his study of race relations, *Two Nations*, Andrew Hacker gives some examples: the University of Virginia in the 1980s tried to increase black admissions by accepting more than half the black candidates who applied but only a quarter of the white candidates, even though test scores on the Scholastic Aptitude Test measured lower for the black group than the white. Government contracts have been 'set aside' for minority companies only. New York City set a lower passing grade for black police officers than white, and so on. Obviously such policies have helped the majority of black Americans prosper in the thirty years since the birth of the civil rights movement. But have they damaged white Americans? There are no reliable figures for the number of whites displaced by such preferences but, from time to time, better qualified whites sue, claiming the practice is unfair. In conversation, whites occasionally suggest that black Americans in coveted jobs are unqualified or less competent and only hold down the job to make up a racial 'quota'.

This white backlash against affirmative action is profound and deepening. It stretches from ballot initiatives against such preferences in states like California to the insistence by private employers that they want 'merit' to be the only criterion for employment, not skin colour. (Though the unspoken implication is that merit may be found mainly in those with a white skin.) Critics also argue that it makes no sense to offer preferential treatment to the children of rich black families (like, say, the children of General Colin Powell) over the children of a poor white family in the Appalachian mountains of Tennessee. A new kind of affirmative action based on *wealth* would, in this view, be fairer than that based on skin colour, and it would still disproportionately benefit the black community. It might also defuse some of the growing class anger in the United States and rebuild the consensus that something can be done for poorer black American children and those of other minorities, while not excluding help to poor whites. In *Two Nations*, Andrew

Hacker points out serious flaws in the way in which affirmative action has worked.

White women and black women have gained more than black men. And big employers planning to build new factories often seek sites with minimal black populations. In this way it is possible to reflect the racial balance of the local community with a largely white workforce. Toyota, for example, built an assembly plant in Harlan County, Kentucky, which is 95 per cent white. Honda built its plant in rural Ohio, 97 per cent white. The result is that many white Americans in the 1990s resent the principle of affirmative action because it 'unfairly' benefits black Americans *too much*. And black Americans defend the principle but often resent the practice because it benefits them *too little*. In both cases the Great Society of Lyndon Johnson never came to pass. It has been swamped by the competing fears of the Angry Society.

But before swallowing entirely the idea of two Americas, black and white, separate and unequal, on the brink of a race war, it is worth considering finally how much of the gap between the races is, as I have repeatedly suggested, most acutely a *class*-based gap between rich and poor. Those who point to an unbridgeable racial gulf widening in the 1990s, amid mutual anger and incomprehension, have plenty of familiar arguments on their side.

White people, in general, were absolutely astonished that the former football player O. J. Simpson was found not guilty of murdering his former wife and a friend in his criminal trial. Black people, in general, believed there was not enough proof of guilt, or rejoiced that a 'brother' had escaped a system of white justice that already locked up 'too many' black men. When Simpson was found guilty in the subsequent civil trial it seemed that the roles were reversed as America managed the impossible: a 'black' Simpson verdict and a 'white' Simpson verdict.

Research on television viewing habits indicates that black and white Americans are often tuned in to different programmes. *In Living Color*, for example, is a largely black comedy show, though it does attract some white viewers. There is a black TV network,

Black Entertainment Television. *Martin* is a sitcom aimed mostly at a black audience. *Murphy Brown* is the equivalent for a white audience. 'Urban' radio is a euphemism for a radio station directed at a mainly black audience. There is some overlap, but there are clear differences – to the point at which in 1996 it was suggested that black and white Americans might speak different languages.

The school board in Oakland, California declared that the speech of poor black ghettos should be glorified as a new language, 'Ebonics'. America's most powerful black playwright, August Wilson, suggested that the American theatre was little more than an instrument of white hegemony. Black Americans needed their own theatres to celebrate the lives they lead – separate but equal.

Yet for every example of this kind of divide, there is an equally potent opposing example. Years ago, basketball team owners wondered if white middle-America would watch mainly black stars on the court. They do. Ask any white American ten-year-old about his heroes and you will hear a list of successful black sportsmen and women. Oprah Winfrey's talk show popularity extends far beyond the black community – and beyond the United States. So does that of Wynton Marsalis. Or Toni Morrison. Bill Cosby's portrayal of the loving father, Cliff Huxtable, in *The Cosby Show* on NBC from 1984 to 1992 had a great impact on the image of black families, crossing racial lines. It represented precisely the kind of success of most African-Americans that is so under-reported in the United States. The tape which showed the black motorist Rodney King being beaten by Los Angeles police was every bit as shocking to most white people as to black people.

Ebonics was criticized as 'bad grammar' just as vehemently and almost unanimously by educated black people as well as white people. August Wilson's call for a 'separate but equal' black theatre was not popular among black actors, writers and directors. The two O. J. Simpson verdicts were more complicated than 'black' and 'white' justice: different evidence was permissible in each case, and there are lower standards of proof in a civil trial. Besides, if blacks and whites disagreed about the verdicts, was there any disagreement that police officer Mark Fuhrman was a racist?

By 1993 President Clinton was promising a cabinet that 'looks like America' and made strong efforts to find qualified blacks, Hispanics and women for his team. Above all, in 1996 a black man, General Colin Powell, was considered by most Americans to be capable of becoming president of the United States – a strong black leader who did not threaten white America. Something, surely, *has* changed in race relations for the better?

The State of Disunion survey shows that while many Americans consider race a powder-keg issue, most blacks and whites are desperate for tolerance and mutual understanding. In fact, 80 per cent of blacks and 82 per cent of whites believe cultural and ethnic diversity is good for America. Nine out of ten blacks and whites believe that treating people equally, regardless of race, is 'absolutely essential' or 'very important'. Whether they actually *do* so, of course, is another matter. But in a society which was once based on the God-given inferiority of 'lower races' the general acceptance of the desirability of equal treatment suggests the practice of equality can follow the principle. Even if Martin Luther King's Dream of toleration is a long way from being realized, most Americans still earnestly share that dream. My friends Ben and Emmett, or the elegant black woman in LA, earn enough money to get out of areas like Shaw, and don't come back. Ben and I have more in common than either of us does with homeless Milton. And the most patronizing myth of modern America is that black people as a group think or behave alike.

In another dangerous area of Washington near Shaw, Glennis Williams is general manager of a fast-food chain. Glennis is a twenty-nine-year-old, upwardly mobile black man who says he would not live in the inner city near his workplace because 'it is far too dangerous'. He began work as a sixteen-year-old on a minimum wage flipping hamburgers and has now risen to respectable middle-income America, $30,000 a year, a wife, two kids in the Washington suburbs, a new car, too many bills to pay, but economically stable.

Glennis proudly displays pictures of the restaurant when he took it over – dirty, encrusted with grease and food. It is now spotlessly clean, a model of civility and good service. But when he produces pictures of his two daughters aged four and ten months, he also emphasizes that the tension in aspiring black America is not just with whites, but within itself. Glennis is fearful about the future for himself and his children. One of the successful black majority, he recounted the stories of two armed robberies at his restaurant and innumerable break-ins – black criminals attacking black victims.

'There's drug dealers around here earning $800, $900 a day – a *day*!' Glennis says angrily. 'I work from 8 a.m. to 5 p.m. for $15 an hour. I am scared out of my mind bringing up kids in this society, black men killing black men.'

His words were a painful echo of the Reverend Jesse Jackson's fear of being confronted by a Bad Black Brother. Glennis is as scared of 'Sweet Pea' or 'Willie Horton' as any white American would be – and Glennis is *far* more likely to meet him. Black Americans are five times more likely to be murdered than white Americans. Among hard-working, often religious, ordinary black working people there is abiding anger at the lifestyles of the rich and dangerous within their community, at the easy money and immorality of the Bad Black Brother. Glennis, for example, told me his car costs $400 a month to lease. 'Drug dealers round here can go in and buy one,' he spits out in disgust, 'and pay in cash.'

According to a study quoted by Cornell University academics in their statistical compilation, *The State of Americans*, in two poor inner-city areas in the United States between half to two-thirds of the men under the age of forty-five were selling drugs. The traffickers earned at least three times what non-drug sellers earned in the same neighbourhoods. For young black men like Glennis it may seem that all the expectations are stacked towards failure. But Glennis does not look like a failure. He has ridden above the statistics by a combination of hard work and personal grit, virtues which white America should recognize and celebrate in its black neighbours.

And Glennis reserves his bitterness for those black people who resent his modest success. He does not speak 'Ebonics'. Consequently, some people in the neighbourhood complain he 'talks white' because he uses proper grammar, doesn't swear and avoids street slang. He acts and dresses like a Buppie, a black Yuppie, and there is even a condescending word for it – an 'Oreo', a popular American cookie which is black on the outside but white on the inside. This is the divide within black America coloured in green. It does not minimize the racism of the white woman glimpsing Ben's face in Beverly Hills, but it does suggest that living well may be black America's best revenge on the racists.

'Round here they play basketball,' Glennis says. 'I play tennis. They cuss and talk street slang. I don't. I work hard and better myself, moving out of the neighbourhood because I want to bring up my family right.' And then he laughs, a laughter which tells you that the gulf between black and white America is not unbridgeable, though that between rich and poor is deepening and the chasm between the underclass and the rest may prove unconquerable: two nations, separate and unequal, Haves and Have-Nots, divided by green and black and white.

'And when it comes five o'clock,' Glennis chuckles with satisfaction, 'I'm out of here. Gone to the suburbs.' He pauses and laughs again. 'Just like a white guy.' And just like Ben and Emmett and me, and the black woman in LA. But behind us, in the increasingly desperate cities, we have left Sweet Pea. And far, far behind, under the great monuments of Imperial Washington, Milton curses the pain in his leg and looks for his place to rest.

Pity the Poor Immigrants

New York City

The immigrant taxi driver sits tapping his hands on the steering wheel and gently blipping the accelerator with his Nike trainers. He is chewing gum and wearing a baseball cap, every inch an American until he opens his mouth.

'So, you're late,' he confirms in an accent which mixes Mother Russia and Brooklyn. 'So what can I tell ya? I work miracles. I'll get ya there.'

'There' is the other side of Manhattan, midsummer hot, a shimmering haze between the concrete skyscrapers in the eternal paralysis of crosstown traffic. The lights change to green and the driver's thigh stiffens. He clacks the gum in his mouth and jams his right foot to the metal. The tyres screech and spin when he makes the hundred-yard dash to the next red light, amused by his genius at the essential Manhattan survival skills: intimidation, wit, speed. He is fortyish, holding down two jobs to make ends meet, tired from working all night. Another green light, another pedal to the metal, another hundred-yard dash and more New York performance art as he swears and yells at a driver who, for a few seconds, would not get out of the way.

The Empire State Building is up ahead which means, with normal driving, I cannot get where I am going on time, but this immigrant has quickly assimilated the values of New York cabbies. There is no *normal* driving. The word which comes to mind is that he is 'strutting'. It is difficult to strut while sitting at the wheel of a cab, but he does it magnificently, brash and content, the meanest predator in the urban jungle. The cab lurches forward again as I sit gripping the seat with whitened knuckles, pretending this is the 'real' New York — which, of course, it is. The real New York is a city of perpetual motion and the constant optimism of immigrants who have come here in their millions, the city of social Darwinism where you survive or die. I am being driven by a survivor.

At the next light, disaster. The two lanes going west come down to just one lane fifty yards ahead. The driver curses the roadworks and then looks at his rival, a sleek BMW 700 series — a cheetah where his cab is a warthog.

He rolls down his window and knocks on the side of the BMW. The sticky Manhattan air smells of car fumes and unemptied trash cans. It hits like hot vaseline. The BMW driver, an angular middle-aged man in his shirt sleeves, reluctantly rolls down his car window.

'Hey,' my driver shouts at him, pure Brooklyn now. 'Dis *your* car?'

'Y-yes.'

'Well dis ain't *my* taxi,' the cabbie responds. 'So you better let me go foist.'

The lights change and we roar ahead. In Aesop's fable of New York, the clever warthog has just outrun the cheetah. He receives a big tip for his performance, another triumph for the immigrant ingenuity which built the United States.

At the southern tip of Manhattan, which is where we are heading, you can stare across the water towards Ellis Island and the Statue of Liberty, symbols of promise for the poor, huddled masses yearning to breathe free — or, just as likely, to make a few bucks and do better than they would in the old country. But by the mid-1990s this nation of immigrants was suffering from one of the strongest and most intolerant anti-immigrant back-lashes in its history. Immigration had again joined the angriest issues dividing Americans from each other, as divisive as race relations and with an explosive potential to bring about serious political dislocation. The core problem is numbers.

It is estimated that the new immigrant population of the

United States in the 1990s is the highest since the Second World War – twenty-three million people, about 9 per cent of total US residents. In *Divided We Fall*, author Haynes Johnson reported that the 1980s saw the largest flow of immigrants in US history, with nine million legal entrants and two million estimated illegal entrants – a rate of more than a million newcomers a year. Others claim the figure for illegals might be eight million, though by definition, of course, no one really knows. In February 1997 the Immigration and Naturalization Service (INS), the federal government agency which monitors immigration, estimated that there were five million illegal immigrants living in the United States, an increase of a million over four years, and 2 per cent of the total population. Whatever the precise figures, there is no doubt that in the closing two decades of the twentieth century the United States was under strain from one of the largest population movements in world history.

The full extent of the social dislocation posed by these waves of immigrants may not be fully felt until after the new millennium, but one statistic yields a clue to its enormity. By 1995 the Immigration and Naturalization Service could boast that legal immigration had fallen significantly – to a mere 720,461 new legal arrivals in one year. Illegal immigration was a further quarter of a million. Even in the most hospitable country in the world, a million foreigners arriving to seek work and a new life every year adds up to an impossible problem for an increasingly angry society. In sheer numbers, in the 1980s and 1990s the rate of legal immigration was more than double that of the glory days of Ellis Island from 1892 to 1924.

At its worst, immigration contributes to racial unease as well as cultural, social and economic difficulties. The character of American cities is changing, yet again, under the weight of the newcomers. There are significant Arab and Iranian populations around Washington, in the New York City area and in the industrial mid-West. Vietnamese, Laotians, Cambodians, Chinese, Indians, Somalis, Ethiopians and Russians have all flooded in and, like the Russian cab driver in Manhattan, they do what immigrants have always done. They work hard, often in jobs native Americans do not want. They pay taxes, learn the language, become citizens. But when Americans talk of the *problem* of immigration, most often they mean Hispanic immigration, legal and illegal, across the Mexican border. Hispanics – with their roots in more than twenty countries – are now the fastest growing ethnic group in the United States, twenty-seven million strong. The majority of illegal immigrants come from Mexico. The worst fear, sparking the toughest anti-immigrant backlash, is that Hispanics are becoming a new, entrenched Spanish-speaking underclass, an ethnic timebomb, unable to prosper or assimilate into mainstream culture and promising future chaos in America's inner cities. In consequence, America's traditional hospitality to immigrants is rapidly fading, a significant casualty of the angry society of the 1990s.

At the time of the American Revolution about nine out of ten of the white colonists were of English, Scots-Irish or German descent. From the 1830s onwards the mix changed. In Boston, now regarded as America's best-known Irish city, the first waves of impoverished Irish Catholics were greeted with great hostility by inhabitants of English stock.

Succeeding waves of Italians, Hungarians, Czechs, Poles, Russians and, in the West, Asian immigrants bore the burden of suspicion from those Americans who arrived earlier. Every few decades there would be a backlash. New laws would limit legal immigration. Politicians railed against the lack of patriotism of 'hyphenated' Americans – German-Americans or Chinese-Americans. During the Second World War Japanese-Americans were interned as potential enemies of the United States. In every generation there was always a nativist politician prepared to argue that the last good immigrant boat was the one which brought his people to the New World.

There were three rules to assimilating in the United States. Immigrants had to learn English. They had to accept a new American identity which valued liberty, the traditions of the Constitution and equality of opportunity. And, whatever their religious origin, they were expected to live by what used to be called the Protestant work ethic – work hard and prosper.

According to a writer on immigration issues, Peter D. Salins, ever since the 1960s these three rules, which derive from the white Anglo-Saxon Protestant origins of the country, have been under threat. Multiculturalism and bilingualism have allowed Spanish to thrive as America's unofficial second language. Historical revisionism has worked to discredit many American ideals as hypocritical myths which glorify white Anglo-Saxon Protestant males. And the welfare state has superseded the traditional risks and benefits of the American economy.[1]

In the 1990s anti-immigrant resentment is, therefore, following a familiar historical pattern, but it comes at an especially unsettled time. The waves of newcomers are arriving when many native-born Americans fear that the ideals which made the United States a great nation and which hold this diverse country together are under threat. It is a pincer movement: a softening of American traditions, plus an 'invasion' of foreigners.

White New Yorkers, Texans or southern Californians – states with large immigrant populations – will often remark that they increasingly feel like strangers in their own home, foreigners in their own country. Hispanic immigrants, in the words of one congressional staff member working on controlling immigration, are not playing by traditional rules.

This is dangerous for the future of the United States because by speaking Spanish, the congressional staff member claims, they are 'refusing to assimilate and [are] instead transplanting their culture to the United States'. Other anti-immigration campaigners speak of 'chain migration' – one immigrant brings his spouse, who brings her brother, who brings his family, in a never-ending series of links.

This cultural and racial tension means immigration is potentially an extremely dangerous cocktail for American society over the next twenty years. Three problems are especially worrying. First, there is a growing consensus that overall immigration – especially of poor and uneducated immigrants – is too high.

Second, uncontrolled illegal immigration makes many Americans view *all* immigrants with suspicion, and the US government as weak and ineffectual. And third, anti-immigrant campaigners fear the impact of what they see as an alien wedge disuniting the United States in the way Canada is torn between French and English speakers in Quebec. Fear of Spanish-based separatism within the United States may seem fanciful, but it is a real source of anxiety and anger.

There is virtual unanimity on one point: that the United States has to fix its illegal immigrant problem first. Feelings about illegal immigration are typically most angry along America's porous border with Mexico – in California, Texas and Arizona. It is estimated that 80 per cent of the babies born in California's San Diego County Hospital are children of illegal immigrants. Up to half the workforce of Los Angeles and neighbouring Orange County may be illegal, according to one estimate. And the 1986 Immigration Control and Reform Act – which made it a crime for American businesses to employ illegal immigrants – is widely seen as a sham.

Illegal immigrants typically work for less money and with fewer complaints than US citizens or legal immigrants. Businesses which want cheap labour 'contract out' the hiring to middlemen who provide the necessary documentation for the workers. The documentation may or may not be genuine. Nobody asks too many questions. Hypocrisy over employing illegals stretches from the vegetable fields of California to the upper levels of American society. In 1993 President Clinton's first two choices as Attorney-General, America's top law officer, were both women – Zoë Baird and Kimba Wood – with illegal immigrant nanny problems.

Both had to withdraw from consideration for the post. Zoë Baird was earning $500,000 a year as a corporate lawyer and her husband was a law professor at Yale University. Yet they did not pay Social Security taxes for their immigrant nanny. Kimba Wood, a New York federal judge, had a similarly embar-rassing story. It is no surprise the 1986 law does not work when those considered for the post of America's top law officer appear so unconcerned about employing what are tactfully called 'undocumented' aliens.

Perhaps it is a compliment to the magnetic pull of the United States that so many people are prepared to risk their lives to sail from Cuba and Haiti or to cross from Mexico illegally in order to share the American Dream. But a nation which is not in control of its own borders cannot fully function as a sovereign state. Ask anyone what government is for, and border control usually features high on the list. If it is not achievable in the United States then – yet again – the institution of government looks feeble, a gigantic Gulliver pinned down by hundreds of thousands of Lilliputian illegal immigrants. In Los Angeles, estimates speak of half a million resident illegal immigrants from El Salvador *alone*, and the social stresses extend far beyond traditional border areas. In small farming towns in Oregon or Washington State, there are neighbourhoods where the first language is Spanish, spoken with Mexican, Nicaraguan, Guatemalan, Colombian and Salvadoran accents. Many of these workers will be legal. Many will not be. The sense of doubt increases the backlash against *all* immigrants.

Illegal immigration is resented not just by whites but more deeply by inner-city minority groups. Young black men in South Central LA angrily told me during the 1992 riots that illegal immigrants from Mexico had pushed job opportunities for African-Americans even lower down the racial pecking order. The illegal immigrants undercut the job market for those black men seeking unskilled or semiskilled positions. Anti-immigrant resentment is fuelled by even the most mundane daily tasks, like getting money from a bank. In many areas of the United States when you try to obtain cash from automated teller machines, the first question on the computer screen does not ask for your code number or banking details but whether you wish to conduct the transaction in English or Spanish.

Some Americans, especially in Texas, California and Arizona, even suggest that Hispanic immigrants are in effect reversing the expansion of the United States in the early years of the nineteenth century, 'taking back' states which were once part of Mexico, 'recolonizing' them through immigration. If that seems fanciful, the backlash against immigration is intense and real. It has included repeated campaigns to re-establish the old rules for immigrants by enshrining English as the 'official' language; with legislation to deny public services (including education) to illegal immigrants or their children in California and elsewhere; and through congressional debates about tightening the rules and plugging the leaky Mexican border.

'Every three years enough *illegal* immigrants enter the country permanently to populate a city the size of Boston or Dallas or San Francisco,' Republican Congressman Lamar Smith of Texas told a congressional debate on immigration control. 'Classrooms bulge, welfare jumps, the crime rate soars.'[2]

Immigrants, of course, are an easy scapegoat for disappointing education standards, poverty and crime. But Congressman Smith, who advocated the hiring of 5,000 new Border Patrol agents over five years, points out that the United States is 'the only industrialized nation that cannot control its own borders. And if we cannot control *who* enters our country, such as illegal aliens, we cannot control *what* enters our country, such as illegal drugs.'

There is evidence that drug smugglers and illegal alien smugglers are the same people using the same routes. They are nicknamed 'coyotes' – unprincipled opportunists often attached to organized criminal gangs. Congressman Smith also points out that the foreign-born population of US federal prisons has soared from 4 per cent of the total in 1980 to 29 per cent, almost one prisoner in three, in 1995.

The backlash has spilled over from tackling illegal immigration to moves against *legal* immigrants too. Congressman Smith and others complain that there is a 'welfare magnet' drawing foreigners to the United States, that poor immigrants come not to work but to enjoy 'generous' welfare benefits.

The most significant part of that backlash came in 1996 when the Republican-dominated Congress pushed through one of the most controversial pieces of social legislation in decades. The Welfare Reform Law saves $55 billion by various means, but the biggest slice involves cutting $24 billion from payments made to *legal* immigrants. Some immigrants became so frightened by the changing atmosphere that they urgently sought American citizenship – which begs a central question. What is an American? What holds this country together? The English language? A respect for the Constitution, democratic government and the rule of law rooted in English common law? The Judaeo-Christian heritage? A set of values created by white Anglo-Saxon Protestants? Or is America simply an idea of freedom and an opportunity to prosper?

The straightforward answer is that an American is anyone born in the United States, or a legal immigrant who takes an oath of citizenship after living in the United States for five years, or three years if married to an American citizen. The newcomers take special citizenship classes. Typically for nine weeks, three hours a night, three times a week, immigrants sit in school classrooms learning the answers to questions about their adopted country. How many stripes are in the American flag? How many stars? Who were US allies in the Second World War? Who was the president at that time? Who was the first president? Pass the test, clear the other requirements, take an oath renouncing 'all allegiance and fidelity to any foreign prince, potentate, state or sovereignty' and then, officially, you can fall in line to pursue the American Dream.

In the anxious anti-immigrant atmosphere of 1996, in Los Angeles alone 10,000 legal immigrants a month became US citizens. In Brooklyn, New York, 1,200 immigrants a week were taking part in the same ceremony. Fear of the anti-immigrant backlash spread to those who had not in the past voted in presidential and congressional elections. Naturalized immigrants began to register and vote in surprisingly large numbers in 1996 – one of the few groups to overcome the national trend towards apathy. The votes of alarmed Hispanics even helped a Democratic candidate of Mexican-American stock defeat former Republican

presidential candidate, Congressmen Bob Dornan, in that supposed bastion of conservatism, California's Orange County.

But if the anti-immigrant backlash had the perverse effect of
pulling some immigrants into the mainstream of American life,
there were also nastier results. In New York State alone, according
to the Republican Governor George Pataki, the new welfare
law meant 80,000 *legal* immigrants would lose food stamps or
Supplemental Security Income. SSI is extra aid paid to poorer,
older Americans. About 450,000 legal immigrants were expected
to lose SSI nation-wide, according to the Congressional Budget
Office, which forecast savings of $13 billion.

America's immigration dilemma, therefore, is especially brutal
now. A further tightening of the rules is likely when one further
fear is explored: that many new immigrants are simply not what
the US economy needs for the twenty-first century. From the
seventeenth century onwards the first immigrants were mostly
farmers, opening up the West for settlement and exploitation.
Then a hundred years ago, at the peak of Ellis Island, there was
a new flood of cheap labour from southern and eastern Europe
to work in factories and mines as America industrialized. Now
the United States faces a third economic revolution, the information age. Does it require up to a million new, cheap,
non-English speaking manual labourers every year at a time
when industrial jobs are being lost? Those who answer that
question with a resounding 'No' point to 1995 Census Bureau
figures and the unpleasant suggestion that America is creating
a new Spanish-speaking underclass.

In 1995 median household income in the United States rose
modestly for every ethnic group – except Hispanics. In that year
the median income of Hispanic Americans *dropped* 5.1 per cent
in the middle of an economic boom. The poverty rate among
Hispanics was higher than that among black Americans. They
now amount to 24 per cent of the poor, up 8 per cent since 1985.[3]
The biggest part of the poverty trap for Hispanics is failure to
speak English. Often they are caught in low-paid, seasonal or
menial jobs: farm labourers, nannies, restaurant workers, cleaners.

In a United States preparing for the information age, many Hispanic immigrants have not yet made the leap from their rural Latin American backgrounds into the industrial age, and seem unlikely to do so.

The blue-collar industrial jobs in steel and lumber mills, coal mines and car factories which helped Russians, Poles, Italians and Czechs work their way up to middle-class America are precisely those jobs which have been most threatened by technological change. In poor Hispanic ghettos or *barrios* in east LA or New York, crime gangs inevitably flourish in these most desperate conditions. There have been outbreaks of relatively minor Hispanic rioting over the past few years, including in Washington DC, where there has been ill-feeling between Hispanics and the mainly black DC police.

It begins to sound like a familiar, potentially explosive story: poverty, race, crime, misunderstanding and resentment. The creation of a new Spanish-speaking underclass may well prove to be the nastiest social and racial time bomb for the United States in the early years of the twenty-first century. This will not be the separatism of another Quebec. It could instead be the street disturbances of 1992 in LA, repeated with a different disadvantaged minority. If many Hispanics feel there is no chance of prospering, that they face discrimination from whites and blacks, that the safety-valve of upward mobility is closed for them, then serious problems are inevitable and violence quite likely.

Yet the American immigrant represents the most idealized qualities of what it is to *be* an American – hard work, strong communities, optimism and family values. Julio from El Salvador works (legally) in a Washington DC sandwich shop from seven every morning until two-thirty in the afternoon every weekday. At three he changes his apron for sports clothes to begin his second job cleaning out a health club until eleven o'clock every night, five days a week – sixteen hours a day, eighty hours a week. His wife also works.

Michaela is a middle-aged Korean woman who runs a laundry

in a Washington office block by herself. Her English is so bad it might really be Korean. She was robbed twice in a year, once with a knife at her throat in broad daylight, the second time by two thugs who pushed her to the back of the laundry and might have killed her. You can tell she is still assimilating American values because she was visibly shocked when, after one attack, I told her she should buy a gun and shoot the next robber. She said she would pray for him.

Or there is Kadri, the hairdresser from Turkey who came to the United States in the 1980s with nothing more than a skill and a pair of scissors. He managed to save enough money by the 1990s to open his own hairdressing salon.

Or there are the migrant Mexican workers I met in a cotton gin near Como, Mississippi. The farmer who ran the gin said the men kept complaining he was not working them hard enough. They worked ninety-three hours a week during the cotton harvest, and wanted to work all day Sunday so they could send more money home.

Julio, Michaela, Kadri, the migrants in Mississippi and the crazy New York Russian cab driver individually sound like America's secret source of strength. But the dilemma remains. How many more low-skilled workers does the United States want with a population already exceeding 260 million? Drive south and west out of New York City, past Ellis Island, and you can find one answer.

This is the route tens of millions of immigrants took on the next step up the ladder towards the American Dream, a life in the suburbs. America's most remarkable suburb is called Levittown, Pennsylvania. What Henry Ford was to the automobile, William Levitt was to housing. Levitt brilliantly conceived the idea that America's postwar boom would create a new middle class. What turned immigrants into middle-class Americans, above all, was owning their own home. 'No man who owns his own house and lot can be a Communist,' Levitt famously said. 'He has too much to do.'

A Levitt home could be mass produced inexpensively for

working people on assembly-line principles. It was the American Dream in a box, ideal for immigrant families like the Munros. Alex Munro emigrated to New York as a teenager from Belfast in the 1940s. His wife Ruth emigrated from Norway around the same time. They met, married, worked hard, prospered, had children and grandchildren who live in and around Levittown, a new species of American created during the old order – Suburban Man. When he arrived from Belfast Alex was forcibly assimilated thanks to a draft notice which put him into uniform in the US Army at the time of the Korean war. He finished military service then easily found work as a carpenter in the post-war construction boom.

'I had a contract with Levitt,' Alex Munro says proudly, 'building 17,000 homes. We worked four months and then I decided to buy a house in Levittown. We've been thirty-eight years in the same house.' Alex has a handsome face much younger than his years and a thick head of wavy hair. You can hear his Northern Ireland accent break through every so often. Their brick bungalow is snug and his wife Ruth ladles out a thick soup and brews coffee while Alex reminisces about his life as an immigrant carpenter in the Promised Land.

'We were told you come to this country and you pick dollars off the sidewalk,' he laughs, then admits that he *did* find the American Dream. 'I think I got it. Not a millionaire, not a rich man, but rich in family.'

Ruth Munro, Alex's wife, is a good-humoured blonde woman who instructs aerobics in a local gym. These Norwegian and Irish immigrants became American citizens, never quite lost their old accents, and live surrounded by the descendants of East Europeans, Sicilians and Greeks. They produced four children and ten grandchildren who all live locally and who say they are most definitely *not* hyphenated Americans, not Norwegian-Americans or Irish-Americans, just plain hard-working *Americans*, proud of their backgrounds but even more proud of their new country. They followed the three rules for immigrants: speak English, love American traditions and work hard.

'I've been working twelve hours a day, seven days a week for twenty years,' Alex says. 'I have always been busy. I always made good money ... and loved it.' But when it came to 1990s immigration, there was a display of irritation. Some in the family complained about official forms printed in Spanish. There were Spanish signs in local shops, Hispanic food in the supermarket, the ATM machines asking if you spoke English or Spanish. Everyone knew about the boatloads of illegal immigrants trying to get in from Haiti and Cuba and China, plus innumerable Hispanics walking across the Mexican border.[4]

There were even homosexuals able to claim that they were 'refugees' because their sexuality made them liable to abuse in their native country. The sense, to use Margaret Thatcher's word, was that the United States was becoming 'swamped' by people from an alien culture. Ruth and Alex, the only two in the family not to be born in the United States, were strongly in favour of closing the door more tightly against the newcomers.

'I think it should be like it was in the 1950s,' Ruth said. 'It took Papa years for us to be able to come here. The church sponsored us, and boy, we really had to be healthy. Neighbours down the street from us had a boy who was just not the brightest and they wouldn't let him in. I think it should be stricter than it is now. I think we should have the jobs for our American people, and I don't think we should just let anyone in. I know they let people with AIDS in. And I don't think that's right. Now they don't seem to care.'

Ruth's Norwegian accent seemed most curious when she talked of 'jobs for our *American* people'. Yet there is nothing more American than being a proud immigrant with a foreign accent, living in a complex of houses that is so much part of America's old order that for the fiftieth anniversary of Levittown, in 1997, the Smithsonian Institution sought an unmodernized home to become a museum piece.

The Munros sum up America's difficult choice. Immigrants built the country just as the immigrant Alex Munro built Levittown. Immigration is, or always has been, as American as apple pie. But it seems America will inevitably close the door. Anti-immigrant sentiment is growing and assimilation for many poorer Hispanics is proving extremely difficult. The immigration economist George Borjas, himself a Cuban immigrant and Harvard University professor, wants sharply to curtail immigration for this reason. He believes the latest newcomers are less skilled, less educated and more likely to go on welfare than native Americans. In the information age they will, he claims, become a drain on the US economy, not a net boost.[5] In the heyday of Ellis Island, some immigrants believed the Statue of Liberty was the tomb of Christopher Columbus. Maybe it is. It is certainly a universally understood symbol of America's greatness, the world's children seeking freedom and filling the mostly empty continent.

Stepping off the boat to Ellis Island on a slippery gangplank in the rain it is easy to imagine the relief and shock of immigrants desperate not only to breathe free but also to stop being seasick after the crossing from Europe. In the museum they narrate touching and amusing stories of the welcoming America: the Russian immigrants who were deloused and bathed and then given bananas to eat, never having seen one before. They ate them, skin and all. Many recorded their shock that for the first time in their lives a stranger had given them food, but America and Americans have usually been kind to newcomers who stick to the rules.

The peak day was 17 April 1907, when Ellis Island processed 11,747 immigrants – enough to fill half of Levittown in one day. Doctors watched the newcomers walk off the boat and up stairs. Any who appeared breathless had an 'H' chalked on their clothes for heart problems. Any who limped had an 'L' for lame. One in fifty was sent back as unfit, and 3,000 committed suicide rather than return to the miseries of the Old World, their American Dreams ending on these few grim acres.

A tour guide from the National Park Service, which runs the island, summed up America's historic attitude to immigration, though she might just as easily have been talking about the 1996 Welfare Reform Law: 'If you could not work, this country did not want you,' she said. You were stamped 'LPC' for Likely to become Public Charges. This was America's Original Sin and the mark of Cain. It still is. America, like God, helps those who help themselves. And the Munros and most other citizens believe that in this, America, like God, is absolutely right. But you do not need a degree in economics to know that the vigour and optimism of immigrants has driven the American miracle, and America will lose something beyond price when, inevitably, it closes its borders more firmly. If you don't believe me, try a cross-town ride in Manhattan with an immigrant cab driver salivating for a big tip. He'll get ya there.

Snakes in Church

Newport, Tennessee

You hear the battered Ford pick-up truck before you see it. The sun is going down on a hot summer's evening near Newport, east Tennessee. At the lake the last of the kids jumps off a rock into the swimming hole, towels himself dry and wanders home. The forest rises and falls like a purple blanket over the hollows of the Great Smoky Mountains, shimmering in the haze as the sun drops even lower. The exhaust sputters as the pick-up creaks and bumps down a dirt track road, raising dust until it stops beside a white country church. The man inside steps out. He is wearing a neatly pressed white shirt and black jeans. He turns and lifts from the front seat a thick, black family Bible and a small metal box with a wire mesh grille. Inside the box are two rattlesnakes. Within the next few hours both the Bible and the snakes will, in a peculiarly American ritual, play a central part in the Christian church service which is about to begin.

The Tennessee mountain air is clean and warm, humming with cicadas. From somewhere in the trees the smell of meat grilling on a distant barbecue wafts through the hollow. In clearings on the sides of the dirt road you can see small, neat houses, most with satellite dishes in their backyards, big white discs pointing skywards sucking in ninety-nine TV channels or more. A dog barks in the distance and children are playing, enjoying the last moments of coolness before night falls. And, at the end of the track, Pastor Alfred Ball greets me at the Jesus Christ Apostolic Church.

Pastor Alfred is a wiry middle-aged man, hipless, slim to the point of being skinny. He shakes hands warmly, but I can tell he is suspicious, and with good reason. In an age of televangelists making money from people of faith, being exposed as hypocrites and occasionally going to jail for the dubious practice of religi-business, Pastor Alfred wants me to know he is a decent man. The church does not support him. He helps support it. He makes his money as a lumberjack, but he is so delicate I think he looks easier with a Bible in his small hands than a chainsaw. The hands are, however, very definitely, working man's hands – rough, calloused, with broken nails.

The church doubles as Pastor Alfred's home. He has a small living area and a couple of bedrooms downstairs. Upstairs there is an altar and benches to seat sixty. Behind the Bible-stand there are acoustic and electric guitars and two microphones for the singers. We sit down outside and I look at the black metal box Pastor Alfred has placed beside him. *He* knows I have come to this hollow in east Tennessee to find out why a Christian minister handles snakes in church. And *I* know there are poisonous snakes in the box. But neither of us talks about it for now. We are discussing the beauty of the Appalachian mountains, the weather, the kindliness of local people, country folks.

The Appalachian mountain range, of which the Smokys are a part, has for years been the home of America's poorest white people. President Lyndon Johnson was so shocked by poverty in Tennessee and Kentucky that he mobilized the federal government into what became his 'Great Society' programmes in the 'War on Poverty'. The coal-mines which dot Appalachia are run by small partnerships or private companies digging the Blue Gem seam. The seam is rich but typically only two feet high, and generations of Appalachian miners have carved it out in runs up to six miles deep into the mountain, crawling and scraping their way to a decent living. When times got tough you would catch a bus or drive your pick-up down one of the new roads LBJ built, and head out of the Appalachians forever.

Even now, in hard times, miners will steal coal. The cowboy miners find a place where the Blue Gem breaks through in the forest. Then they dig small gashes into the hillsides and run them as quickly as possible a few hundred yards inwards to rip out as much coal as they can before they get caught. There is never time for safety precautions. Every year the newspapers carry stories of Appalachian miners dying when the roof falls in. This part of the southern Bible Belt also used to be the home of illegal whiskey distilleries. Today nobody bothers with moonshine, though some counties are still in favour of prohibition – no bars, no liquor stores – so you have to drive to a neighbouring county to buy your bourbon or beer. Every so often the county puts its 'dry' policy to the popular vote.

'Round here,' a resident from a 'dry' county told me, 'we vote Dry.' And then he laughed. 'But we drink Wet.'

A waitress in a diner in Newport, noticing my foreign accent among the native Tennessee twangs, confided that if I wanted a beer there *was* a place, but it was difficult to find. I took down directions. Cross the main road, take a left, go down a side road for three miles, down a track, across a ford in a river and then along a forest dirt track road. 'You can't miss it.'

That evening I followed her instructions and, after fording a small river, there it stood. In a clearing in the forest in the middle of nowhere was a large drinking den, a secret bar, a giant boozy warehouse. Thirty or forty cars were parked outside and, like some B-movie about prohibition, when I rang the bell they slid back an eyehole to have a look at me. I gave the name of the waitress and they let me in.

Despite the existence of this bar in the Tennessee backwoods, there is no money in distilling moonshine any more. The most profitable Appalachian cash crop is now marijuana, 'Hillbilly Hemp'. It was one of the results of the Vietnam war. Local boys who were too poor or lacked the political connections to do what Bill Clinton did and avoid the draft, ended up in South-East Asia, where marijuana was the drug of choice. When they returned home they discovered that it is perfect for Appalachia – easy to grow and hide in the woods or among legitimate crops down on the farm. It seems an odd combination, a Bible Belt with traditions so strong you cannot legally buy a beer, and yet a place where marijuana is cultivated in the forest.

'Be careful,' one local lectured me. 'Some of the boys use fish hooks hanging from lines from the trees to protect their crop. An old idea from 'Nam. You have to watch your eyes.' He said they hang batches of fish hooks at face level on monofilament line near the growing marijuana, to catch the eyes of folks who should not be wandering around. I was not sure whether this was a true story or an Appalachian tall tale for the edification of strangers. But I decided I was not interested in finding out.

In his backyard, Pastor Alfred was warming up. I asked if I could watch the evening service in his church. He made no objection but warned that he could not promise that the snakes would ever come out of their boxes.

'Depends on the Lord,' he explained, though with the clear implication that listening to four hours of preaching would do my soul good anyway. More worshippers had begun to arrive at the Jesus Christ Apostolic Church. The congregation was all white. I had not seen any black faces since I arrived in town. They did not look prosperous. Pastor Alfred was the only one with a tie. No one wore a jacket. Most of the men wore blue or black jeans. The women had long hair and modest cotton skirts with sensible flat shoes. The men carried family Bibles, and about half had snake boxes. Pastor Alfred explained that throughout North Carolina, Georgia, West Virginia, Kentucky and Ohio, as well as Tennessee, there were what he called 'holiness churches'. Members of the congregations will pick up and hold venomous snakes or drink deadly poisons as part of the Christian act of worship.

'We do it,' he asserted, staring hard at me for any sign that I found this ridiculous, 'not to prove our *Faith*. But to confirm the *Word*.'

'The Word' in question comes from St Mark's Gospel, Chapter 16, verses 16–18. This is Mark's version of what happens to Jesus after the crucifixion and the resurrection, and immediately before he is received back into heaven. Since these are the last words spoken by Jesus on earth they obviously assume great significance for all Christians. Among snake-handling fundamentalists who believe in taking every word in the Bible literally, these are the most important words of their faith. Jesus says to the Apostles: 'He that believeth and is baptized shall be saved, but he that believeth not shall be damned. And these things shall follow them that believe. In my name they shall cast out devils; they shall speak with new tongues; they shall take up serpents; and if they drink any deadly thing, it shall not hurt them; they shall lay hands on the sick and they shall recover.'

I could feel my jaw drop slightly, and tried to meet Pastor Alfred's unrelenting stare. Rather like the growing of marijuana in the Bible Belt, it is never easy to cope with America's astonishing contradictions. We were sitting in the most technologically advanced country in the world, a country which in this century had invented flight, put a man on the moon and had arranged life so there was a satellite dish in the backyard of everyone who wanted it, even here in rural Tennessee. It was possible to watch live TV pictures of interviews with American and Russian astronauts orbiting the earth together. And yet this serious-minded, sombre man was talking about taking up serpents as a way of demonstrating the truth of the Word of God. I glanced at the black box at his feet. No sound. Nothing moving. Perhaps the rattlesnakes, or whatever they were, were sleeping before the evening service. Resting their fangs. A heretical thought crossed my mind. St Patrick cast the serpents out of Ireland. In Pastor Alfred's theology, did that mean the Irish were spiritually doomed because there were no serpents for them to take up? Or is Ireland already saved for the same reason? Was that why Tennessee was blessed with so many rattlesnakes? I decided to let the matter rest. Pastor Alfred was hot to preach.

'What kind of snakes do you pick up?' I wondered.

He lifted his box. 'Copperheads, cottonmouths, rattlesnakes.'

All deadly. Cottonmouths are known as 'water moccasins', and if you see one swimming in a lake in Tennessee you get out of the water as quickly as if it were an alligator. Pastor Alfred opened his box and took out a snake. It was a copperhead, about eighteen inches long and, as I rapidly calculated, about twelve inches from my knee. The snake tasted the air with its tongue and slowly wound its body round his wrist. Pastor Alfred started to explain that he handled serpents only about half a dozen times a year, 'when the Lord anoints me to do so'. Then he quickly threw the snake back into the metal box where I could see the coils of a second copperhead.

'The Lord told me I should not have done that,' he said, shutting the box securely.

'The Lord told me exactly the same thing,' I smiled back. Pastor Alfred smiled too, and we both started to relax.

'And what "deadly thing" might people drink?' I wondered. He listed those deadly things that had been tried by the Faithful intent on proving the Word. Potions containing strychnine and arsenic. Also carbon tetrachloride and car battery acid. I must have looked sceptical, or quite possibly amazed, because he started to tell me that not everybody was 'anointed' to do it, and that the children of the church were kept well away from any kind of danger. That word 'anointed' again. I pressed him on what he meant, and he found it difficult to explain.

'God placed enmity between the serpent and the seed of woman because of the Fall,' Pastor Alfred explained. 'By taking up serpents we confirm that in God's world such enmity will cease.' Anointing meant that God spoke to him and instructed Pastor Alfred that he 'shall have victory over the serpent'.

Suddenly Pastor Alfred stood up and grabbed his snake box, ready to preach, hopping from foot to foot like a small bird. We were facing each other, a yard apart. There was clearly something important he wanted to say to me before we proceeded. He started by insisting that the people in his church did not do dangerous things out of sinful pride or spiritual bravado. 'We are not proving our faith in God,' he repeated energetically, for about the tenth time. 'We are confirming that Christ's message to the Apostles is as alive today as it was yesterday and will be tomorrow.'

I said I understood, and he seemed satisfied. Pastor Alfred turned and left his snakes at the back door of the church, checking that the black box was locked. Then he went inside. I took it as a sign of approbation, and followed. It was now almost dark and moths fluttered around the lights at the back of the hall. The first of the country gospel singers was already beginning to play. For the next forty-five minutes, accompanied by guitars, anyone who wanted could come up and take a turn at the microphone. The songs were joyful. Whatever our fears of eternal damnation, this was a church which preached the redemptive power of the risen Christ.

Pastor Alfred started his sermon. He began by talking of people who had been healed by the Spirit, of devils cast out, of modern miracles. As he spoke, members of the congregation called out loudly 'tell it brother', or 'come-o-on', or 'A-men'.

At times his sermon became almost like a chant, deep breaths followed by a torrent of words that I could barely follow, a hypnotic stream of Christian consciousness. Then he asked those who needed prayer to come forward. A young woman said she thought she had cancer. Pastor Alfred shut his eyes tightly in prayer, his face twisted with concentration. God told him it was not cancer.

'It is *definitely* not cancer,' he repeated several times, laying his right hand on her head. A second woman said she felt sick. Nothing specific, just sick. A third had pains in her leg. A man crippled with arthritis so he was less than four feet tall, his back bent and twisted, asked for prayer. Many in the congregation laid hands on him as he swayed backwards and forwards to the rhythm of country gospel music. He moaned, making indecipherable noises, speaking with 'new tongues'.

In the 1930s the snake-handling Holiness churches of Tennessee and elsewhere in Appalachia came under pressure from the authorities after a number of deaths at church services. A law was passed making serpent-handling illegal. But, as Pastor Alfred put it: 'If the choice is between obeying God's law and man's law we'll obey God.' I had heard the same justification frequently in the United States – from anti-abortion protesters in Operation Rescue to David Koresh's cult followers at their sect headquarters outside Waco, Texas.

You hear the same words from members of armed militia groups who despise the US government and believe there is no law between themselves and God, or from the Posse Comitatus movement which claims there is no legitimate authority in the United States under God except the 'power of the county'. You even hear the same sentiments (somewhat differently expressed) in the speeches of the Nation of Islam leader, Louis Farrakhan. In each case such words represent the triumph of extreme belief over all reason, the decision not to render unto Caesar those things that are Caesar's. Yet unlike many of those other groups, Pastor Alfred risked hurting no one but himself. He admitted he had been bitten twice while handling snakes, once with no effect and once becoming very ill. In that instance he did not seek medical aid and did not die because 'my brothers and sisters prayed for me'.

Others have not been so lucky. One of Pastor Alfred's best friends, Pastor Jimmy Williams, died in 1973 after drinking strychnine. I challenged Pastor Alfred about this story, saying that Jesus did not intend us to tempt fate by drinking poison. The words quoted by St Mark suggested some blissful future state when mankind has embraced salvation. Handling snakes is a metaphor for conquering evil, not a literal exhortation. Jesus says they 'shall' take up serpents, but does not command that they 'will' take up serpents. It was an important distinction.

Pastor Alfred listened to my arguments but was clearly not a man for metaphors. When I finished he heatedly disagreed. He suggested that those who died mistook what God told them to do. Maybe they were anointed to take up serpents but not to drink strychnine in that particular case. The deaths of some believers proved that, like the early Christian martyrs, the possibility of death was real. The snakes had not been milked or de-fanged. The strychnine was fatal. And, he said, 'What better way to leave this life than in the process of confirming God's Word?'

I started to split hairs: 'But the Bible says "they shall take up serpents". It does not say *poisonous* serpents. Would a grass snake or a rat snake do as well as a copperhead?'

'Heck, no,' Pastor Alfred said, for the first time becoming extremely irritated by one of my questions. He looked appalled at the thought of using non-poisonous snakes. '*Anybody* could pick up a non-poisonous snake,' Pastor Alfred responded indignantly. 'How would that confirm God's Word?'

How indeed.

The singing, preaching and healing had gone on for three-and-a-half hours, but no one appeared to be tired or bored. It was completely dark outside, though I could see lights through the trees in the hollow. Inside their comfortable houses with the air-conditioning whirring, or sitting on their porches behind mosquito screens, I could imagine local people watching cable television, studying the news from halfway around the world beamed live by satellite. Or they were speaking by mobile car phones, surfing the Internet, sending e-mail or computer faxes to the other side of America and the other side of the planet. Here, as the United States made the uneasy transition on the cusp of a new millennium from the industrial age into the information age, Pastor Alfred was announcing that − tonight at least − he was *not* anointed to take up serpents. It would be foolish for him to do so under the circumstances. But if the shepherd was reluctant that night, others in the congregation had received different messages from God.

There was an air of general confusion as some of the men went to retrieve snake boxes from outside or under the pews. Clyde Ricker, in his forties, balding and red-faced from working in the sun, produced two copperheads. Behind him, two other men were doing the same thing. One had on a baseball cap which said 'Jesus Man' and bore a snake motif. The men were singing, Brother Clyde loudest of all, as he closed his eyes and swayed rhythmically.

'Jesus . . . Jeee-sus . . . I don' wanna be lo-ost . . .' The copperheads slithered around his fingers, confused in the bright light after the darkness of the snake box. 'Jesus . . . Jeee-sus . . . I don' wanna be lo-ost.'

With a rapid flick of his head sideways on to his shoulder, Clyde began speaking incomprehensibly, like a tape recording of a speech run backwards. He held the copperheads close to his chest and then next to his face. Beads of sweat washed his brow and his thinning hair was plastered wet on his head.

The snakes tasted the air with their tongues repeatedly, as if trying to make sense of what was happening. The tongues flickered and Clyde sang, his voice softer now at the climax of the evening. 'Jesus . . . Jeee-sus . . . I don' wanna be lo-ost.'

He put the snakes above his head, singing and sweating in the humid night as they twisted in his fingers and moths fluttered confused wings against the light overhead. Behind Clyde, Jesus Man and his companion were doing the same, again and again and again. 'It is *real*,' Brother Clyde pronounced. 'It is *real*. The spirit of God lives tonight.'

I left Tennessee early the next morning, as confused as ever about America crossing the bridge into the twenty-first century. There was the obvious clash between the old and the new – a lumberjack who used a motorized chain-saw and drove a modern car, yet who was also pastor of a peculiarly American branch of the Christian religion.

This is a poor area of the United States – but everybody seemed to own a car, and it was hardly poor by the standards of anywhere else in the world. Pastor Alfred, his congregation and dozens of other small Holiness churches were entitled to believe as they wished. He was a good-hearted, polite, decent man, but there was no point in arguing with him about snake-handling. You can never reason someone out of a position that they never reasoned themselves into in the first place, and – despite his protestations – there was a strong element of bravado in what took place in the church.

St Augustine had written that belief precedes understanding. Being a Christian demands a leap of faith. Pastor Alfred clearly had made the leap. But his belief did not *precede* understanding, it *replaced* understanding. He had no use for reason where snake handling was concerned. This, of itself, would be no more than a curiosity, far from the mainstream of American religion, but for one important point. All across the United States in the 1990s there are countless, far more troubling, examples of precisely the same phenomenon at the heart of the angriest people in America. The United States is riven by snake-handling politics, by those who believe without or beyond all reason, and who call upon their strong but irrational beliefs as justification for intimidating, terrorizing and even murdering those who do not agree with them.

The same belief untroubled by reason that guides Pastor Alfred also guides the extreme anti-government militia movement, the conspiracy theorists who see cabals of the Washington élite plotting to overthrow American democracy, the violent fringes of the abortion 'debate' and any discussion of gun control. To Europeans the most militant sections of the American gun lobby seem like gun worshippers rather than sportsmen, quoting the Constitution as if it were the Bible, conducting their pieties with the same enthusiasm as snake-handling in Tennessee, and equally impervious to argument. At their worst, America's believers without reason are prepared not merely to risk death, as Pastor Alfred does, but to kill, to bomb abortion clinics, shoot federal agents, burn the cult compound in Waco or bomb the Oklahoma federal building. Belief beyond all reason drives the anti-government militias in their assertion that the US government is the arm of the Devil, the beast whose name is 666, the 'Zionist Occupation Government' they call ZOG.

Belief without reason consumes the angriest snake-handling politics, that of the anti-abortion activists who argue that in the name of being 'pro-life' — that is, stopping abortions — it is perfectly permissible to murder abortion doctors. The same compulsion drives the conspiracy theorists attached to Nation of Islam leader, Louis Farrakhan. They angrily preach that there is a white racist plot to afflict black communities with drugs and

AIDS. Belief without reason drives fringe Christian millennial cults, like that of David Koresh, who stockpiled infantry weapons in preparation for what he believed was biblically predicted disorder about to engulf the United States in the time immediately preceding the second coming of Christ.

Millennial cult activity, with a capacity for violent disorder, will undoubtedly flourish over the next few years, stoked by preachers who believe the millennium may signal the coming to pass of the truth of the Book of Revelations. America is, after all, historically a credulous country prone to sudden panic attacks, from fear of the witches in Massachusetts in the seventeenth century to the 1990s millennial anxieties fomented by those like Dr Jack van Impe, a Michigan televangelist who preaches that Christ will return to earth shortly after the year 2000.

Above all, belief without reason helps explain why so many Americans – one in ten, according to *The State of Disunion* survey – are capable of believing the most outlandish conspiracy theories about their country and their society: that the United Nations is about to take over America; that the Freemasons, Jews, Trilateral Commission, Bilderberg Group and Council on Foreign Relations are part of a monumental conspiracy to destroy the United States. In each case the desire to believe drives out rational argument and polite civil discourse. These angriest and least rational Americans pursue extreme political beliefs with all the unreasoning faith of Pastor Alfred handling his copperheads – and without Pastor Alfred's good-hearted Christian charity.

For most Americans religion remains, as it has always been, the glue of a community, a tolerant guide, a moral compass and a consolation in troubled times. Roughly 80 per cent of Americans believe in God and about half of those go to church or synagogue regularly. In Western Europe the figures are much lower. In France or Britain, for example, only half the population say they believe in God and church attendance is 10 per cent and 14 per cent respectively. *The State of Disunion* report found that evangelical Christians made up around a quarter of the American population, including many black Americans. Those evangelicals who described themselves as conservative and politically active – the Christian Right – amounted to less than 5 per cent, a tiny minority. And yet by volume level, and degree of divisive political activity, the Christian Right has emerged as one of the most powerful forces of anger in American politics, frequently but incorrectly claiming to speak for the majority of American Christians (through organizations like 'The Moral Majority').

The Christian Right has led crusades on all the 'hot button' issues in which morality and belief meet politics: abortion, homosexuality, obscenity and pornography, plus the old battlegrounds of prayer in schools and the teaching of Darwinism and evolution in biology classes. In each case, these have become issues of snake-handling politics in which extreme beliefs have driven out reason in increasingly intolerant debates. As a result of such energetic activity, the Christian Right has emerged in the 1990s as the most significant pressure group within the Republican party, with a voice at the table of the most important politicians in the United States. It is a voice stridently against the Clinton administration, intolerant of all dissent, and unshakeable in pursuit of its obsessions.

Christian Right supporters are also the most angrily pessimistic Americans when asked about the future of the United States. Around 80 per cent believe the United States is in strong or moderate decline (compared to 51 per cent of the general population), and they are the most critical of government institutions. Four out of five Christian Right supporters have little or no confidence that the people who run the US government tell the truth.[1]

To understand how genuine Christian belief becomes, at the extremes, the angriest of intolerant snake-handling politics, it is worth examining the career of the best-known figure on the Christian Right, the Reverend Pat Robertson, in some detail. He is the most important Christian broadcaster, televangelist and religious entrepreneur in modern America. He is also a stirrer of the pot of anger in America's angry society, a propagator of the most bizarre conspiracy theories, involving freemasons and political cliques, to undermine the United States. The combination is the ultimate in snake-handling politics as Mr Robertson loudly and proudly represents extreme belief at the expense of all reason.

The Reverend Pat Robertson is the founder and leader of the Christian Coalition, the most prominent political organization of the Christian Right with, by the mid-1990s, an estimated 1.7 million members. He ran for the Republican nomination for the presidency in 1988, and came second, ahead of Vice-President George Bush, in the Iowa caucuses. But he rapidly realized he could wield more influence in the party if he never again tried to wear the crown, and constructed both a business empire and a powerful grass-roots organization of energetic, very conservative, Christian activists. In the year after the election of President Clinton the Christian Coalition claimed to be recruiting new members at the rate of 10,000 a week, helping make Mr Robertson a powerful behind-the-scenes kingmaker within the Republican party.

Christian Coalition activists are eagerly sought political workers. In support of conservative candidates and causes they knock on doors, run telephone banks and call up voters with evangelistic zeal. Unlike the apathetic majority of Americans, Christian Coalition activists can be counted upon to go to the polls and, consequently, have a disproportionate effect when turnout is low, as it frequently is. Mr Robertson's Christian Coalition conferences, therefore, always attract the top names in the Republican party, especially in an election year. In September 1996 the guest list at the Christian Coalition conference in Washington, called 'Road to Victory '96', read like the Republican party's top table: House Speaker Newt Gingrich was there; as was George Bush's former Education Secretary, William Bennett; House Majority Whip, Tom DeLay; House Majority Leader, Dick Armey; Oklahoma Congressman, J. C. Watts; House Judiciary Committee chairman, Congressman Henry Hyde; and Senate Foreign Relations Committee chairman, Senator Jesse Helms. The event also drew Reform party presidential candidate, Ross Perot; Colonel Oliver North; Arkansas Republican Governor,

Mike Huckabee; Republican Senator, John Ashcroft; and former presidential candidate, Congressman Bob Dorman. So what? Well, among Mr Robertson's strongly held beliefs is the idea that there is an anti-American conspiracy in everyone's pocket.

According to his 1991 book, *The New World Order*, if you pull out a dollar bill and look on the back you will see on the left-hand side the Great Seal of the United States, adopted by Congress in 1782. There is an American eagle with an olive branch of peace and thirteen arrows of war, but there is also a peculiar unfinished pyramid, above which Mr Robertson describes an eye set in a blaze of glory. The date at the base of the pyramid is that of the American Revolution, 1776. But over the pyramid is the Latin phrase '*Novo Ordo Seclorum*', which Mr Robertson translates from the poet Virgil as a 'new order of the ages' and then as a 'New World Order'. Mr Robertson links the Masonic symbols on the back of modern US currency with a centuries-old 'conspiracy' stretching from eighteenth-century Bavarian freemasons — the Illuminati — to the 1990s United Nations under the all-purpose hate figure of the paranoid American Right, former UN Secretary-General Boutros Boutros Ghali. Mr Robertson earnestly believes he has uncovered a sinister plot to force America under the domination of a 'One World Government'.

It is difficult for Europeans to understand that these views, and Pat Robertson, are taken seriously in American politics. The idea of 'One World Government' has been an obsession on the American far-Right ever since the end of the real threat of Communism. Those who believe in this invented threat do so with all the passion of snake-handling believers in Tennessee.

They argue that the United Nations, the World Trade Organization and the General Agreement of Tariffs and Trade are all part of a gigantic conspiracy to destroy American civilization. Those who believe in the conspiracy angrily declare that America's élite in Washington is prepared to sell out the United States to the United Nations, evil bankers, freemasons and others who are seeking world domination. It is impossible to write these words without assuming they are the product of mildly neurotic fiction sold to teenage boys. But Mr Robertson, in *The New World Order*, reveals that this conspiracy is, in fact, true.

The idea, he says, drawing on the engraving on the back of the dollar bill, was that under the watchful eye of Osiris the endeavour begun with the American Revolution in 1776 would, 'according to their secret Masonic rituals, bring forth a new world order ... Indeed it may well be that men of goodwill like Woodrow Wilson, Jimmy Carter and George Bush who sincerely want a larger community of nations living at peace in our world are in reality unknowingly and unwittingly carrying out the mission and mouthing the phrases of a tightly-knit cabal whose goal is nothing less than a new order for the human race under the domination of Lucifer and his followers.'

Pat Robertson, the man who can attract the Republican leadership to his Christian Coalition conferences, is no voice-in-the-wilderness, snake-handling preacher. *The New World Order* reached *The New York Times* bestseller list. My paperback copy boasts 'over half a million copies sold'. Mainstream Republicans who could publicly repudiate the notion of outlandish conspiracies involving former President George Bush instead suck up to Mr Robertson when they can, ignore his more bizarre assertions and capitalize where possible when his views stir up the fears of an excitable section of the American public.

'It is time we did battle against World Government,' Republican presidential candidate Pat Buchanan lectured an appreciative audience in New Hampshire in February 1995. There is no democracy in the world outside the United States in which such a sentence could be uttered by a serious politician without attracting ridicule. In Europe, battling 'World Government' ranks as an issue alongside preparing for war with Martians. But Mr Buchanan repeatedly promised that he would 'do battle' and end the practice of putting US troops under the UN flag and the 'command' of UN Secretary-General Boutrous Boutros Ghali. Senator Bob Dole made the same commitment repeatedly — even though the United States only extremely rarely puts tiny numbers of US troops under direct UN command.[2]

Even the Clinton administration did not directly challenge the 'One World Government' nonsense. Embarrassed by the débâcle of US troops on a UN-sanctioned peacekeeping mission in Somalia, the Clinton administration pandered to conspiracy-mongers by deciding during the 1996 election campaign that Boutros Boutros Ghali would have to be replaced as UN Secretary-General. Publicly it was claimed that he had not been aggressive enough in reforming the United Nations bureaucracy. But the Clinton administration was trying to defuse a potentially distracting issue before it gathered momentum. Every other UN Security Council member, including Britain, backed Mr Boutros Ghali.

However ludicrous Mr Robertson's conspiracy theories may seem to Europeans, and indeed to most Americans, they have a peculiar potency to enrage, energize and misinform. Unlike Pastor Alfred in his tiny Tennessee church, the Reverend Pat Robertson speaks from a billion-dollar electronic pulpit to millions of Americans every week. For many years he has been regarded as a source of news, interesting views and political, as well as moral, leadership. He founded the Christian Broadcasting Network in Norfolk, Virginia – America's first overwhelmingly religious broadcasting network. He is president of the United States Media Corporation and chairman of The Family Channel, which became the tenth largest cable network in the United States, available to at least fifty-eight million homes on 10,000 cable TV systems. He is the host of CBN's news show, the *700 Club*, which is regarded as 'the most watched evangelical programme in television history' by the Jewish Anti-Defamation League. That programme can be seen in more than eighty countries across the world.

The ADL monitors Mr Robertson as part of their continuing investigation of 'the assault on tolerance and pluralism in America'. The ADL's report, *The Religious Right*, lists Pat Robertson as one of those who bring 'to cultural disagreements a rhetoric of fear, suspicion, even hatred. The result is not surprising: real debate over the problems afflicting American society is eclipsed by the blare of grievance, blame and chauvinism, and the fragile structures of consensus are bulldozed by sectarian, absolutist declarations. In this way we proceed down the road to the "Christian nation" trumpeted by these prophets of rage.'

Pat Robertson, like Pat Buchanan and Louis Farrakhan, is indeed a prophet of rage. They are all masters of snake-handling politics, evangelists of extreme beliefs which drive out reason. Each man detects conspiracies and foments fear and anger. Each has the megaphone of constant publicity which ensures they are significant beyond the numbers who wholeheartedly endorse their extremist messages. Each claims to be on the side of God, or Allah. But Mr Robertson is by far the most influential. The ADL report says he controls the Standard News radio news network with at least 270 affiliated stations. He is chancellor of Regent University and involved in numerous charitable organizations, including the American Center for Law and Justice, America's leading evangelical legal organization. And yet, powerful as he is, the ADL investigation demonstrates that Pat Robertson believes Christians are part of America's culture of victims. Mr Robertson protests against 'anti-Christian bias' in the media and elsewhere:

Just like what Nazi Germany did to the Jews, so liberal America is now doing to evangelical Christians . . . It is the Democratic Congress, the liberal-biased media and the homosexuals who want to destroy all Christians. Wholesale abuse and discrimination and the worst bigotry directed toward any group in America today. *More terrible than anything suffered by any minority in our history.*' (My italics.)[3]

In Mr Robertson's universe, America's Christian Right is more persecuted than black slaves, an extraordinary assertion. But what is worrying is not Mr Robertson's Christianity. It is that his unreasonable 'blare of grievance', as the ADL puts it, does indeed unsettle all around him, fomenting angry disagreements and making consensus on difficult social issues, such as abortion, almost impossible. Mr Robertson's books, pamphlets and public statements contribute to a national mood of anger, pessimism and unease. In a 1992 fundraising letter Mr Robertson announced: 'The feminist agenda is not about equal rights for women. It is about a socialist, anti-family political movement that encourages women to leave their husbands, kill their children, practise witchcraft and become lesbians.' Feminism, like abortion and the United Nations, is part of a demonic agenda for America. Homosexuality is the same. Mr Robertson calls it 'a sickness' and concludes, 'Many of the people involved in Adolf Hitler [*sic*] were Satanists, many of them were homosexuals – the two things seem to go together.'

The moral and political issues which so divide modern American society – abortion, homosexual 'marriage', gay rights – cannot be solved or ameliorated by normal political methods when confronted with a significant section of the population which appears to believe that feminists fly around on broomsticks or that homosexuality has a satanic, Nazi connotation. This is not reasoned argument. It is intolerant abuse. Each of these 'issues' is argued by Mr Robertson and his followers with the enthusiasm of medieval disputations concerning the number of angels dancing on pinheads, or biblical commands that ye shall take up serpents. As the political historian Richard Hofstadter put it, commenting on what he called the 'paranoid style' in American politics of which Mr Robertson is merely the most potent 1990s example:

The distinguishing thing about the paranoid style is not that its exponents see conspiracy plots here and there in history, but that they regard a 'vast' or 'gigantic' conspiracy as the motive force in historical events. History *is* a conspiracy set in motion by demonic forces of almost transcendent power ... what is at stake is always a conflict between absolute good and absolute evil.[4]

In his 'non-fiction' and in his popular novel, *The End of the Age*, in which the world is virtually destroyed in preparation for the return of Jesus, Mr Robertson writes of social turmoil, political and spiritual unrest, a 'time of troubles' of biblical proportions leading up to 'the revelation of a new world order'. The Gulf war victory was one of the many signs of this because it was the first time since Babel that all the nations of the world acted in concert with one another in the land of the ancient city of Babel. Strange weather patterns, the spread of the AIDS virus, the explosion at Chernobyl, all point to a world on the brink of disintegration. Taken together, Mr Robertson's views amount to a deeply troubling political liturgy. Conspiracy-mongering plays to the worst fears of Americans at a time of considerable social upheaval. It makes normal politics a noisy circus of competing intolerant beliefs. One of the triumphs of the United States is that its Constitution allows religious belief to flourish without having any official role in the government.

A nation founded on reason *without* permitting religious belief risks the worst excesses of the French Revolution which elevated for worship the Goddess of Reason. Conversely, a nation founded on belief without insisting on reason or understanding, risks becoming a fanatical theocracy in which, one way or another, everyone will be forced to become snake-handlers. The Constitution permits belief but *demands* reason, a sublime product of educated eighteenth-century thinkers who conceived it as working like a Newtonian machine, exquisitely balanced between the branches of the American government – the Supreme Court, Congress and the presidency.

Yet belief without reason is perverting America's political system, throwing sand in the gears of the machine. The American political debate is being corroded by political snake-handlers, those who start from dubious premises and move with utter faith towards pernicious and angry conclusions. They have become worshippers of the Goddess of Unreason. At least the fangs of Pastor Alfred's copperheads pointed only at himself. America's worshippers of unreason regard their opponents as agents of the Devil. They are not winding the snakes round their own hands. They are pointing them at you and me.

Guns, God, Gays and Gynaecology

'Intolerance is a Beautiful Thing.'

T-shirt worn by anti-abortion protesters at the Republican Convention
in San Diego, August 1996

Minneapolis, Minnesota

The anti-abortion protester was very insistent. They always are.

'Take one,' he said with the grin of an unhappy flight attendant. 'A Vote for Bill Clinton is a Vote Against God', the pamphlet read.

'Are you sure about this?' I asked.

'You bet,' he smiled again, confident, in a world of changing rules, that the president of the United States was on the side of the Antichrist. Then he turned to hand out more pamphlets on the street outside an abortion clinic in Minneapolis. His T-shirt revealed another of the slogans of the anti-abortion movement, 'Intolerance is a Beautiful Thing'.

In the United States, abortion is the noisiest example of snake-handling politics. You either believe in it, or you do not. No amount of reasoning makes a difference. It has become one of the unsolvable 'issues' which have come to dominate, at least by volume level, much of the angriest public debate about the future of American society at the end of the twentieth century. Like the question of gun control versus the 'Constitutional right to bear arms', or the 'right' of homosexuals to serve in the US military or to 'marry' one another, or questions about whether evolution should be part of biology lessons in schools, belief does not precede understanding. It has replaced it.

Abortion, gun control, homosexual rights and the other angry issues are not 'problems' to be solved or issues to be debated. They are sets of beliefs to be trumpeted, shouting down opponents, who are demonized. This is quite literally true. On these issues, those who contradict true believers are treated as if they were servants of the Devil, compounding the sense that millions of Americans have of a pointless, uncivil public debate between extremes in which the views of ordinary, moderate, rational people are not welcome.

The result is that many Americans with better things to do, turn off completely from the hysterical screaming of the zealots. Anger and apathy go hand in hand. Complex social and moral issues guided by genuine religious faith are difficult to solve in any democratic society, but in the United States achieving reasonable consensus is impossible because each discussion is framed in the most polarizing terms. You either believe, in the end, that abortion is a kind of murder, or you do not. You either believe that homosexuals are born homosexual and as a group have 'rights', or that they 'have a choice' in the matter and pursue perversion because they are morally 'bad' and their lifestyle is 'an abomination'. And you either believe that the Constitution gives Americans the unrestricted right to bear arms – any gun, anywhere, any time – or alternatively it suggests something far more limited in the context of raising a local militia.

These are the issues which light up the anger of American social politics in the 1990s. They spill over into crime, since gun control is a central issue in trying to cut violent crime, and since doctors who perform abortions have been murdered for practising legal medicine. They spill into education, through debates about what to teach children about homosexuality and Darwinism, and also into the debate over the role of prayer in schools. Even the Pentagon is not immune from angry social politics, most obviously in the gays-in-the-military debate but also on the question of whether US government funds should pay for women soldiers to have abortions in military hospitals.

In each case the style, fury and importance of these debates in the United States sets the country apart from much of the rest of the world. No industrialized democracy debates guns, God, gays and gynaecology with such vigour and frequent hysteria. No issues have so directly contributed to the loss of civility in American public life with, for example, a leading member of the gun lobby, the executive vice-president of the National Rifle Association describing US government agents as 'jack-booted thugs', or the angry heat-without-light politics of America's 'abortion debate'.

In fact, the abortion debate is typical of all the others. It is a journalistic fiction. There is no debate. It is the 'Abortion Shout'. What follows is an examination of the mutual loathing between the rival camps over abortion which serves as a guide to the other intractable issues which make American society so angry. In each case the arguments vary, but the fury and incivility with which they are pursued does not.

I travelled to Minnesota to watch the more extreme wings of the Abortion Shout clash on the streets. The anti-abortion rights supporters of Operation Rescue tried mass picketing of clinics to stop women from entering to have an abortion. A group of pro-abortion rights supporters yelled back that they had the 'right' to 'abortion on demand'. In the early 1990s Operation Rescue – which describes the more than thirty million estimated legal abortions in the United States as a new 'Holocaust' – brought towns like Buffalo, New York and Wichita, Kansas almost to a standstill in violent confrontations with police at the gates of abortion clinics. Mainstream anti-abortion groups, including the leadership of the Catholic church, were embarrassed by the tactics of the extremists.

A string of new laws and judicial restraints, including the Clinton administration's threats to use anti-Mafia legislation against Operation Rescue and other militant groups, muted some of the protests. In consequence, Bill Clinton is hated among militant anti-abortionists. Not disliked. *Hated*.

'No rest for the Wicked', one of the pamphlets from

'Missionaries to the Pre-Born' reads. By the 'Wicked' they mean the president of the United States. 'On Wednesday night, May 22nd [1996], from 9.30 p.m. to 10.30 p.m.,' the pamphlet reads, 'Missionaries to the Pre-Born will gather outside the Pfister Hotel . . . in downtown Milwaukee where President Clinton will be spending the night. The missionaries will gather with bullhorns and large photos of pre-born babies murdered by abortion and will hold Bill Clinton accountable for his crimes against humanity, namely the helpless pre-born.'

'Crimes against humanity' – the phrase used to indict Nazi war criminals with genocide – was the charge levelled against the president of the United States. The pamphlet promised that anti-abortion activists would 'follow Clinton everywhere he goes'. It concluded with a quote from Pastor Matt Trewhella, founder of Missionaries to the Pre-Born. 'We will show the president the remains of people he has so ruthlessly oppressed by his vetoes and executive orders.'

At anti-abortion demonstrations protesters typically carry graphic photographs of aborted and bloody foetuses. In some cases they produce real aborted foetuses for inspection. But to understand this extreme political anger, you need to learn a new vocabulary. In the Abortion Shout, like most of the issues which disconnect America, the two sides do not even speak the same language. Abortion rights supporters always speak clinically, using words like 'foetus' or 'procedures' – even when the 'procedure' is horrific. One of the most controversial procedures is described by opponents as a 'partial birth abortion', while abortion rights supporters prefer to call it by the bland-sounding 'intact dilation and evacuation'. Whatever you call it, doctors bring the intact foetus down the birth canal and then crush the skull so that the head can be pulled out. As you might expect in a debate in which people cannot even agree on the simplest vocabulary, no one knows how many of these 'procedures' are performed every year in the United States.

In the middle of 1996 an attempt to outlaw partial birth abortions passed in the Republican-controlled Congress and was then vetoed by President Clinton, because it did not permit the procedure even when the mother's life was in danger. The supposed 'debate' involved those in favour of abortion rights arguing that banning this one procedure would be the beginning of the end for *all* abortion rights in the United States. No compromise with the enemy was possible, though one usually pro-abortion rights senator, the independent-minded Daniel Patrick Moynihan of New York, was moved to describe the 'procedure' as being 'as close to infanticide as anything I've come upon'.[1]

Even the terms pro- and anti-abortion rights groups use for themselves are suspect. The 'Pro-Choice' group offers a choice, but not, of course, to the foetus. The 'Pro-Life' group demands 'life', without significant sympathy for the reduction in the *quality* of life too many children or handicapped children may cause reluctant mothers. In fact, here at the meeting of Operation Rescue in Minnesota, there is no such thing as a 'foetus'. There are only 'pre-born babies'. This, of course, is a logical extension of a society in which everyone is a 'victim' with 'rights', now including those not yet born. The campaigners who bring Christ's word to the foetus in the womb are therefore 'ministering to the pre-born'. For the anti-abortion side a 'rescue', to continue the vocabulary-building lesson, means physically blocking abortion clinics or engaging in 'sidewalk counselling'.

This means yelling at any woman entering a clinic (on the assumption that she might be a patient) that abortion is murder and that God will never forgive her. Then there are 'stalkings'. Abortion clinic personnel are followed home from work, trailed around the supermarket or berated in the street as 'murderers' or 'baby killers'. The admitted objective is to humiliate them in front of their neighbours. The unspoken objective is to terrorize them and anyone in the pro-abortion rights community.

At a Pensacola, Florida abortion clinic Dr David Gunn was shot dead by an anti-abortion fanatic. He regularly performed abortions and the man arrested and finally convicted of his murder, Michael Griffin, was said to have yelled out 'Stop Killing

Babies' as he pulled the trigger. Griffin cited the Bible in his defence and had been a fixture on the extremes of the 'Right to Life' movement. Killing someone in defence of the 'Right to Life' is, of course, the ultimate, absurd triumph of unreason. It is a verbal Vietnam, in which South-East Asian villages were 'destroyed' in order to 'save' them from Communism. Now doctors are killed because they are not 'Pro-Life'.

Michael Griffin is not alone in his anger. There have been other murders and attempted murders, plus numerous petrol bombings and violence directed towards clinics and their personnel. In January 1997, abortion clinics in Oklahoma and Georgia were the targets of no-warning bombs. Some abortion doctors routinely wear bullet-proof vests and carry guns in order to go about their legal business. Operation Rescue publicly condemns such attacks, but the organization's Reverend Flip Benham, writing in a pamphlet handed out at anti-abortion rallies, speculated on why some anti-abortion supporters were prepared to kill for life:

They come from a church which will not stand to defend the defenceless, thus opening the door to vigilantism. They come from a culture in which the value of human life is cheapened . . . They come from a political system that imposes greater penalties for sitting in front of an abortion clinic than for dealing drugs or for theft.

I visited the Spiritual Life Church in Minneapolis. The church is a big, light, modern building and it was packed with several hundred worshippers. The music was as joyful as anything in Pastor Alfred's church in Tennessee, and much more professionally delivered. There was an expensive sound system, the harmonic clash of electric guitars and happy, well-rehearsed singers on the stage. Everyone seemed in a good mood. At the back of the hall they were selling 'Intolerance is a Beautiful Thing' T-shirts and giving away anti-abortion books and pamphlets. We were waiting expectantly for one of the big names in Operation Rescue, the Reverend Keith Tucci.

In the friendly way of all Christian churches, people would stop to talk to a stranger in the hall. A middle-aged man wearing a T-shirt and jeans told me he had joined Operation Rescue because his daughter had had an abortion and it disgusted him. He had been on the picket lines at clinics in Minneapolis but, like most otherwise law-abiding people, he was worried about being arrested for his acts of civil disobedience. The few nasty incidents during the time I spent in the city were provoked not by the anti-abortion protesters, as I had expected, but by young anarchists and militant feminists on the pro-abortion rights side. I suggested to the middle-aged man that the lesson of Dr Gunn's murder, and the pro-abortion rights militancy here, was that there were extremists on both sides.

'Yes,' he agreed at first reasonably. 'But the pro-aborts have dead eyes.' I thought I had misheard, until he repeated it. 'Look in their eyes. They are dead. They have no souls.' The conversation had taken a strange and sudden turn. I replied lightly that he made it sound as if those in favour of abortion rights were in the grip of satanic possession.

'Sure,' he answered, pleased that I had grasped the obvious point. His words tumbled out. Abortion was so evil, man could not have come up with the idea himself. It had to be satanic influence. What other explanation could there be? I swallowed hard. So what did that make abortion clinics? 'The Gates of Hell,' he answered matter-of-factly.

I wandered to the stalls selling or giving away anti-abortion books and pamphlets. One pointed out that abortion is the second most common surgical procedure in the United States after circumcision. The estimate was that more than 1.5 million abortions were performed in the United States every year, 80 per cent to unmarried women, 30 per cent to teenagers and 20 per cent on what a pamphlet called 'repeat customers'. If the statistics were appalling, the pictures were unspeakable. Mostly they showed aborted foetuses, almost indistinguishable from newborn babies, cast away in buckets or in the hands – 'the loving hands' as one pamphlet said – of anti-abortion activists. The titles give some idea of the contents: 'Abortion: the Hidden Holocaust'; 'RU486: A Human Pesticide' (RU486 is an abortifacient); 'Breast Cancer – the Deadly After-Effect of Abortion'.

And there was even a pamphlet suggesting that Planned Parenthood, founded by Margaret Sanger to educate American women about contraception and abortion, was fundamentally racist. 'We do not want word to go out that we want to exterminate the Negro population,' it quotes Sanger as saying, describing her as 'an avowed racist' and suggesting she promoted birth control as eugenics.

But the most interesting publications, in the context of America's angry society, were those which explained why it was permissible for Christians to break the law. One pamphlet by Randall Terry, Operation Rescue's founder, was entitled 'Higher Laws' and quoted from the Acts of the Apostles 5:29: 'We must obey God rather than men.'

The pamphlet was written in the America-is-doomed style favoured by the most angry citizens. 'By doing massive rescues, we could create the tension needed to turn the tide . . . On God's clock, time is running out for America . . . The very survival of America as we know it is at stake.' De Tocqueville again, turned on his head. The fear that America, ceasing to be good will also cease to be great.

I chatted to a few of the people looking over the pamphlets at the rear of the Spiritual Life Church. Whenever I mentioned the name of Bill Clinton it had the effect of making whomever I was talking to almost spit on the floor, a skunk at a dinner party. 'We believe in higher laws,' the Reverend Joseph Foreman, a 'minister to the pre-born' told me, in the same words and with the same enthusiasm I had heard from Pastor Alfred discussing snake-handling. 'The scripture commands us to obey God above man.'

Clinton was beneath contempt, a symbol of the evil which had infected the American political system. A womanizer. A draft dodger. A pot smoker. A man called by God to shock America back to righteousness. And as for his *wife* . . . Suddenly

Mr Foreman stopped speaking. There was a *frisson* of excitement as Keith Tucci appeared on stage. I walked back into the main part of the church for a better look. Tucci was a tall, lively, impressive-looking man in a neat light brown suit, shirt and tie. He has long, straw-coloured hair and a fixed even-toothed grin. He was most definitely the star of the show, and he knew it.

'There's gonna be a revival in the land,' he boomed in a sonorous voice. 'There's gonna be a revival in the land. From the north, the south, the east, the west. There's gonna be a revival in the land.' Mr Tucci smiled again, and then calmly delivered the most devastating phrases from Operation Rescue's gospel. 'Intolerance is a Beautiful Thing. There's gonna be a revival in the land. Thirty-one million children killed in the land. There's gonna be a revival in the land.'

The congregation was moving with him now, moving to the cadences of his voice. Then, abruptly, he stopped and called for the 'testimonies' of those who had protested outside the abortion clinics. A small group joined him on stage.

'We were at the Gates of Hell,' a woman called Judy declared proudly. 'The Gates of Hell.'

'It was really *awesome*,' a twelve-year-old girl called Katie said, tongue-tied in front of such a large audience.

'If we are obedient to what God calls us to do,' a woman called Karen lectured the congregation, 'it doesn't matter how we look to the rest of the world. We are the Warriors of God.'

The phrase and the unnatural shine on her face suggested the Shiite martyrs in the Middle East, the dedication of the young men of Baalbek or Beirut, Gaza or Tehran. But this was *Minneapolis*, one of the most delightful cities in north America. I looked around at the faces of the Warriors of God. If this was America's Hezbollah, it was comfortably overweight and middle class. Outside the church, tidy pick-ups and family sedans with bumper stickers – 'I'm Pro-Life and I Vote' – were parked neatly in rows on the car park. There were no Kalashnikovs discharged into the heavens. No men in black balaclava masks. Just Ford Explorers,

Dodge Caravans and Pontiac Bonnevilles with infant seats carefully belted in the back.

Yet this, indeed, was the party of God which put the fear of God into abortion clinic workers. One after another speakers talked of the struggle which they were 'destined to win' against the 'pro-aborts'. They preached the 'humanity of the pre-born child', and the inhumanity of the 'Baby Killers'. They organized a rendezvous the following day at a clinic which was 'the largest killer of pre-born babies in the state of Minnesota'. The audience was now truly getting wound up, and Pastor Keith Tucci strode back to take charge.

'When we see the enemy raged,' he declaimed, 'what we're doing must be working.' He began reading from the Bible, Jeremiah Chapter 19 – hardly the happiest of lessons from proverbially the least cheerful of the biblical prophets. He boomed out the Old Testament verses and the story of God's power and vengeance. At one point, as if to ram home his exposition, Mr Tucci yelled, 'God is *not* Tiny Tim! He's God!'

Then came the climax: 'Child killing is *not* a social problem. It is a Demonic Agenda.' Only the Devil, Mr Tucci concluded – and I could see the middle-aged man with the white T-shirt nodding in appreciation – only the Devil could come up with a scheme so . . . *diabolical* as the murder of children. The 'pro-aborts' have 'filled this place with the blood of innocents'. They have worshipped the Devil Baal. And God, Pastor Tucci returned to Jeremiah, 'will bring evil upon this place the which whosoever heareth, his ears will tingle'.

My ears tingled. I walked out into the cool air of the car park, surrounded by members of the congregation, ordinary, tax-paying, clean, decent, working folk. I knew that the ubiquitous opinion polls showed that most Minnesotans – 58 per cent – believed abortion was wrong. But 70 per cent also believed it was up to the woman to choose. It was a common-sense compromise reflecting a natural ambivalence. Nobody much liked the idea of abortion, but in President Clinton's words, most Americans wanted it 'safe, legal, and rare'. Logic suggests this could be achievable. Both sides have an interest in reducing the shameful numbers of abortions conducted in the United States, and aspiring towards making abortion an emergency procedure rather than a form of birth control. But logic does not fit with snake-handling politics and the worship of unreason.

Those who call themselves 'Pro-Choice' dare not give an inch, fearing that all abortions will be outlawed if they compromise on any issue with those they regard as religious fanatics. The 'Pro-Life' side will not give an inch either, regarding their enemies as morally no better than Nazis following Hitler's orders to set up extermination camps. In such a poisonous atmosphere of mutual loathing, it is not surprising that there have been attacks on abortion clinics. What is surprising is how few people have been murdered. But the perverted debate means both sides are utterly fixated on an unreasonable war over the *supply* of abortions. America's real problem is the *demand*. A reasonable way forward would be to cut demand by promoting all forms of birth control, including abstinence, plus an energetic campaign directed at sex education of teenagers and especially those 'repeat customers'. But political problems cannot be solved when one side thinks the other is possessed by the Devil. And what is true of the unreasonable abortion debate is true of all the other examples of snake-handling politics: homosexual rights, gun control, the place of religion in schools.

It is no coincidence that another leader of Operation Rescue, Randall Terry, turned his enthusiasm away from the anti-abortion mission into a new mission on the sins of homosexuals. Nor is it a coincidence – though to Europeans it will seem utterly bizarre – that those most vehemently against abortion, like former presidential candidate Pat Buchanan, are equally vehemently against gun control and in favour of the death penalty. For Pat Buchanan and his supporters, the high priests of unreasonable politics, the right to life ends at birth.

In each case President Clinton has become the lightning conductor for the hatred of the most angry voices in America's uncivil social debate. He unwisely made the first days of his presidency in 1993 'Gays in the Military Week', causing those who were angry with him over abortion to become incandescent with outrage over homosexuality.

Dr James Kennedy, a conservative Presbyterian minister from Florida who presents his own television and radio shows from the Coral Ridge Ministry, captured this sense of anger on the Christian Right. Just three days after his inauguration, Dr Kennedy says, Clinton signed executive orders expressing his desire to lift the ban on homosexuals serving in US military forces, to approve the use of the French abortion drug RU486, to allow the bodies of aborted infants to be used in foetal tissue research, to allow abortions at US military hospitals and to end the ban on abortion counselling in government-funded health clinics. On top of that, Dr Kennedy asserts, President Clinton appointed more than two dozen homosexuals to high office.[2]

On such issues Mr Clinton and his wife have become targets for the United States of Anger because – as we will examine in detail in Part Four – they represent a new generation which has apparently betrayed the morality of the old order of the past fifty years. In Speaker Newt Gingrich's astounding phrase, the Clintons and their allies are 'the enemy of normal Americans . . . antithetical to their values, their pocketbook and their future'.[3] Hatred, disgust or vilification of President Clinton among a section of the US population became one of the strongest emotional undercurrents in American politics in the 1990s. Such hatred was fanned by the emotive and unreasonable tone of the attacks from the Christian Right, attacks frequently lacking Christian charity or civility.

The angry politics of unreason contributed to the fear that Mr Clinton – the man who inherited some of the mantle of the Kennedys – is a target for assassination. One bumper sticker, popular at gun shows, made the unspeakable link with previous assassinations: 'Lincoln. Kennedy . . . Clinton?'

For those who detest him, Bill Clinton represents the counter-culture of the 1960s which has come to power in the 1990s but never really grown up. As Dr James Kennedy puts it, the subversive ideologies of the 1960s had, by the 1990s, become a mission to overturn America's moral conventions and destroy traditional Judaeo-Christian culture. Republican presidential candidate Pat Buchanan was even more brutal. Speaking at the 1992 Republican Convention in Houston, Texas, he electrified his audience by claiming that such issues as abortion, homosexual rights, obscenity and gun control meant there was 'a religious war going on in our country for the soul of America. It is a cultural war, as critical to the kind of nation we will one day be as the cold war itself.'

In Pat Buchanan's cultural jihad the Clintons were, of course, on the enemy side, leading the troops of the infidel to destroy the United States. Buchanan claimed they represented 'the most pro-lesbian and pro-gay ticket in history . . . Hillary believes that twelve-year-olds should have the right to sue their parents, and she has compared marriage as an institution to slavery and life on an Indian reservation . . . Friends, this is radical feminism . . . abortion on demand . . . homosexual rights . . .'

It is the ultimate in angry politics when a presidential candidate can declare on prime-time television a cultural and religious war to replace the cold war, and suggest that his adversaries are morally the equivalent of the former Communist enemy. For the majority of the American electorate, Buchanan's speech was an outrage. It helped Bill Clinton win the 1992 presidential election as a voice of moderation. Roughly 60 per cent of Americans view the Christian Right leadership unfavourably, specifically Pat Robertson and Pat Buchanan. But that leaves 40 per cent — about 100 million Americans — who do *not* view Mr Robertson or Mr Buchanan unfavourably.

At their convention in 1996, Republican party managers were worried Mr Buchanan would again scare away moderate voters, so they made sure he was sidelined in a fringe meeting. But, however unfortunate Buchanan's 1992 statements were politically, as cultural commentary they were absolutely on target. One result of the end of fifty years of struggle against Communism has been the search for an equivalent enemy. Where none exists, for some politicians, enemies have to be invented. The most recent supposed enemies within, out to destroy the American way of life, include the 'pro-aborts', homosexuals, those who would control the supply of guns and even the bureaucrats in the US federal government itself.

One of the opening skirmishes of the cultural jihad was over the photographer Robert Mapplethorpe, a homosexual who died of AIDS. As with abortion, the merits of the arguments on both sides were drowned out by the unreasoning tone with which they were advanced. Mapplethorpe's work is as popular on the Christian Right as Salman Rushdie is in Tehran. Police raided a Mapplethorpe exhibition in Cincinnati in 1990, pursuing charges of obscenity. Dennis Barrie, the director of the Cincinnati Contemporary Arts Centre, was arrested. Demonstrators shouted 'We'd be better off in East Germany. There's more freedom there.'

The National Endowment for the Arts, since the 1960s America's most important government organization for chan- nelling money to artists, became embroiled in the angry skir- mishing of the cultural war, since the NEA had helped to fund a few exhibitions the Christian Right decided were obscene. 'It's not art if a monkey could do it,' Republican Congressman Dana Rohrabacher, one of the NEA's strongest critics, told me. 'And a lot of things that the NEA has sponsored wouldn't pass the monkey test.'

Congressman Rohrabacher imaginatively defined art with a clarity that had eluded Western thinkers from Aristotle to Keats. But to those on the opposite side of the issue, the Christian Right and their supporters were trying to censor artists, bleed funds from the NEA and dictate what their fellow Americans should see, read, watch or hear. 'There is a disturbing pattern of repression by the far Right,' Dennis Barrie, who staged the Cincinnati exhibition complained, 'in search of a new political agenda.'

'It is like the McCarthy period of forty years ago,' veteran Democratic Congressman and arts supporter Sidney Yates said.

'Only now the targets are artists and the NEA. The bogeyman isn't Communism. It's obscenity.'

That was one of the few points on which both sides seemed to agree. To the religious Right, cultural and social pollution, aided by the Washington 'élite', was subverting the American way of life in just the same way as Communism once did. As North Carolina Republican Senator Jesse Helms characterized it, things were bad enough when artists scrawled obscenities on toilet walls without the taxpayers being asked to pay for the crayons.

The key feature of all these most angry issues is not merely that they can lead to violence. It is that they are essentially unsolvable. No mechanism of the United States Constitution – a document based on reason – can ever quite cope with the politics of unreason, just as no rational argument will persuade Pastor Alfred to forbid the handling of serpents in his church in Tennessee.

The best the Constitution guarantees is the right to disagree, within the law. Even that is difficult enough. In 1994 four people were left dead and six wounded in the abortion wars. And the parallel with the equally heated debate on gun control is obvious. Just as anti-abortion campaigners quote the Bible as justification for their acts, those against all gun control quote the US Constitution as if it, too, had the force of holy writ.

The Second Amendment to the Constitution of the United States, in its entirety, reads as follows: 'A well-regulated militia, being necessary to the security of a free state, the right of the people to keep and bear arms shall not be infringed.'

President Clinton supported and helped guide into law the Brady Bill, which demands background checks on all Americans trying to buy handguns, slowing up the purchasing process for a few days, and denying guns to convicted felons. He also supported a ban on nineteen different types of assault weapons – Kalashnikov rifles and the like. The resulting fury against Mr Clinton was the same in tone as the anger over abortion and homosexuality, though on gun control he did have important Republican allies.

The Brady Bill was named after President Ronald Reagan's press secretary James Brady, who was seriously wounded in 1981 in the assassination attempt on President Reagan outside the Hilton Hotel in Washington DC. Sarah Brady, Jim's wife, made one of the most powerful speeches at the Democratic National Convention in Chicago on 26 August 1996 with her account of the day her husband was shot, beginning her long struggle to bring reason to the argument on gun control. Jim nearly died, she said.

'All it took was one gun, one bullet, and one man who should never have owned a gun.' She quoted statistics showing that adding up all murders, suicides and accidents, 'every year in this country nearly 40,000 Americans are killed with firearms. More than 100,000 are wounded. Every two hours another child is killed with a gun.' The original version of the Brady Bill, introduced in 1987, was killed in Congress even though nine out of ten Americans supported it. 'The National Rifle Association said that seven days, or seven hours, was just too long to wait to buy a handgun,' Sarah Brady told the Democratic Convention. 'It was an *inconvenience*. Well, our family can tell the gun lobby something about *inconvenience*.'

Since the Brady law went into effect on 28 February 1994 it has stopped more than 100,000 convicted felons and other prohibited purchasers from buying handguns. Every day that means eighty-five felons are stopped from buying a weapon – though, of course, that only applies to legal purchases. (And, as my conversation with the gang member 'Sweet Pea' in Arkansas demonstrated, it is not difficult to buy guns legally or illegally in the United States, ban or no ban.) But this 'debate' is constructed exactly like the ones on abortion, homosexuality or arts funding. It generates heat and rarely light, anger not clarity. The language of both sides is, yet again, utterly disconnected. Those in favour of gun control quote the *first* half of the Second Amendment – 'a well regulated militia'. Who should regulate the militia, if not the government? That means government *regulation of guns* in America. And the Amendment does not say that outside of a 'militia' anyone can own any weapon, though custom and practice in the United States has dictated otherwise. Meanwhile, the NRA and its supporters quote the *second* part of the sentence – that no one shall 'infringe' their 'right to bear arms'.[4]

Yet gradual changes in the law on abortion, homosexuality and gun control suggest the Buchanan side may slowly be losing the cultural war. The National Rifle Association is deeply riven by internal feuds. The NRA outraged some gun owners with its failure to see the difference between a duck gun and a Kalashnikov, and angered many more by its disparaging comments about law enforcement organizations. After agents from the Bureau of Alcohol, Tobacco and Firearms tried to storm the compound of David Koresh's Branch Davidian cult to confiscate illegal weapons, the FBI was called in to handle what became a lengthy siege at Waco. It ended when the FBI sent a tank towards the compound to pump tear-gas inside. Koresh's supporters refused to surrender and set fire to the compound, immolating themselves and their children.

Most Americans were horrified and upset by the errors and incompetence of government agents. But they were even more upset by an infamous letter sent by Wayne LaPierre, executive vice-president of the National Rifle Association, to NRA members in May 1995. In the letter Mr LaPierre worried about 'jack-booted government thugs' – meaning the BATF and FBI – being given 'more power to take away our Constitutional rights, break in our doors, seize our guns, destroy our property and even injure or kill us'. This uncivil talk was well beyond the rowdy arguments usual in the gun control debate. Former president George Bush resigned from the NRA as a result. The NRA's image now, even among gun owners, is not what it was ten years ago. But, as the bombing of abortion clinics has shown, the more ground intolerant groups lose in America's social and cultural wars, the more likely their angriest members are to resort to violence. America's love affair with guns will continue for the foreseeable future.

Where else but the United States could drivers happily put

bumper stickers on their cars bearing the boast: 'An Armed Society is a Polite Society'? It takes a peculiar type of unreasoned belief to see the world this way. Armed societies which come immediately to mind include the Taliban-dominated Afghanistan, Lebanon in the 1980s and Somalia in the 1990s. These are not polite societies. They are intolerant and dangerous societies.

America is moving in the same direction, growing more impolite and intolerant as a result of the anger of divisive zealots who speak of their fellow American citizens as 'the enemy', and 'possessed by the Devil'. Traditional American politics look impotently bereft of solutions when confronted with the angry society of guns, God, gays and gynaecology. Well-organized groups have destroyed civilized debate by insisting that they alone possess the word of God or a hotline to the drafters of the Constitution. This is an intensely depressing prospect. It implies that the Constitution, which guarantees the right of free speech does not also suggest the responsibility to use reason in applying it. The result is that America tolerates intolerance too much. Often only the loudest voices are being heard in the cacophony of America's new disorder, the braying of discontent from unreasonable people utterly resolute in the pursuit of divisive causes.

There is, however, an American solution to the American problem of the politics of unreason. It comes from the poet T. S. Eliot. It is impossible to kill for life, worship half a sentence in the Constitution, handle poisonous snakes in a Christian ceremony or declare a religious and cultural war on your fellow citizens if you bear in mind Eliot's analysis of the place of religious belief in a reasonable world: It is not the quality of the faith which is important, Eliot wrote. It is the quality of the doubt.[5]

PART THREE
ANGRY POLITICS

'There will always be dissident voices . . . perceiving gloom on every side and seeking influence without responsibility. But today other voices are heard in the land – voices preaching doctrines wholly unrelated to reality . . . They fear [the] supposed hordes of civil servants far more than the actual hordes of opposing armies. We cannot expect that everyone . . . will talk sense to the American people. But we can hope that fewer people will listen to nonsense.'

President John F. Kennedy. From the speech he was planning to give on the day of his assassination in Dallas, Texas, November 1963

'Head shots! Head shots! Kill the sons of bitches.'

Popular radio talk show host G. Gordon Liddy on how to deal with government agents entering homes of citizens

'We must stand up and speak against reckless speech that can push fragile people over the edge beyond the bounds of civilized conduct and take this country into a dark place.'

President Bill Clinton, five days after the bombing of Oklahoma City

'Clinton's ordering the bombing of the [Oklahoma federal] building is exactly parallel to Adolf Hitler's secretly-ordered burning of the Reichstag in 1933 to foment hysteria and institute draconian martial law to stop terrorism.'

American Patriot Fax Network communication alleging President Clinton was behind the Oklahoma bombing conspiracy

State of Apathy

Memphis, Tennessee

October is cotton picking time on the Mississippi River. In small, sleepy farming towns like Como and Crenshaw mongrel dogs sit warming on the road in the morning sun, reluctantly getting up and moving aside to let cars pass. Everything happens without hurry. Even the cotton harvest. A few men in blue denim bib overalls stop for coffee and cigarettes then head out to the fields leading down to the river. The cotton is high, the fields filled with wispy white tufts waiting for the machines to shake them loose. They will have to wait a little longer. Labourers hose down the harvesting machines while the farm owner checks the cotton by hand. Dew glistens like glass beads on the cotton fluffs and runs through his fingers as he squeezes, calculating how long it will take before the sun rises enough to ensure that the traditional crop of the Old South is dry enough for picking.

There has been a splash of rain overnight, so it is eleven o'clock before the sun has done its work. One more squeeze of the cotton. The farmer wipes his hand on his shirt then signals that it is ready. The machines are loosed. They sweep down the rows cutting, shaking then spraying the cotton like white feathers into huge mesh cages at the back of each harvester. The white feathers are compressed and sent off to the cotton gins to have the seeds extracted and squeezed for cottonseed oil. The finished cream-coloured bales, 500 pounds in weight, are put on trucks heading to the warehouses of the great southern city where cotton will always be king – Memphis, Tennessee.

The bales used to go by riverboat, but not any more. Memphis became Cotton Capital thanks to its position on a great bend in the river where Arkansas, Mississippi and Tennessee meet. At the railhead south of town, Neely Mallory's cotton warehouse is large, cool and empty, waiting for the peak of the harvest to hit so the cotton can be graded like fine wines, weighed then shipped in boxcars to the mill towns of North and South Carolina and beyond. Elvis Presley, the country boy from Tupelo, Mississippi, made Memphis his home, living and dying in Graceland, where every year hundreds of thousands of fans arrive in tour buses to gawp and weep at his grave.

Memphis also claims to have invented the Blues, turning the rasping, moaning melodies from the slaves in the cotton fields into America's original music, spreading from Beale Street in the centre of Memphis up the Mississippi north to Chicago and around the world. Today you can smell and hear Beale Street before you see it. The barbecue rib joints pump spicy fumes into the night air, as you follow your ears towards the wailing guitars of B. B. King and Buddy Guy, or their impersonators. Walk one way from Beale Street and you come upon a grand watering hole of the Old South where they boast that 'the Mississippi delta begins at the doors of the Peabody Hotel'. But walk the other way and you come to one of the most surprising historical monuments in the United States.

At first sight, the Lorraine Motel is unprepossessing, the kind of low-rise, cheap and characterless place you would most certainly avoid if the Peabody had room. Yet the Lorraine is a symbol of America's greatest domestic struggle of the twentieth century. While the Peabody catered for the great white farmers of the cotton plantations, the Lorraine, which opened in 1925, prospered as one of the few hotels in this part of the segregated South in which black Americans were allowed to stay. Cab Calloway, Aretha Franklin, Count Basie and Nat King Cole were among the guests. Not much more than a generation ago, the colour of their skin meant they were not considered good enough to mix with white folks in the Peabody. The civil rights leader, the Reverend Martin Luther King Jr., also stayed at the Lorraine.

And he stays forever. On a balcony outside room 306 on a Tennessee spring day, 4 April 1968, Dr King was shot dead. His assassination provoked race riots all across the country, though it is a testament to the extraordinary resilience of the United States that it survived the darkest forces unleashed by the troubled politics of the 1960s and 70s.

Those years, usually lumped together as 'the Sixties', began with idealism and hope for positive change. They ended with cynicism about government, distrust of politicians, violence and suspicion that dark conspiracies were at work behind closed doors in Washington. The legacy of the worst of the Sixties hangs over American politics a generation later. It was not just Vietnam and Watergate, in which the government repeatedly lied to the American people, but also the assassinations, which have never been fully or convincingly explained, of President Kennedy, his brother Bobby, Martin Luther King and Malcolm X.

Those who survived and were politically active during those years of domestic turmoil find it easy to believe these dreadful historical events were connected, linked by a conspiracy against every progressive element in the United States. On a sunny autumn day less than a month before the 1996 presidential election, Maxine Smith, a dignified black woman who has been part of the struggle for civil rights in Tennessee for decades, is standing at the Lorraine Motel, blinking in the sunshine, showing me around. She has recently had a cataract operation and her eyes are weeping. But with the idealistic fire of a favourite grandmother who has something really important to say about the history she has lived, Mrs Smith insists on leading me to where the gunman waited for Dr King. She takes off her dark glasses and blinks at the sun as she points out that the trees have grown now, obscuring the view. The roof where the killer lay is so close to where the civil rights leader fell that even a modest shot with a modern rifle could barely miss.

Mrs Smith said she was two blocks away when the gunman fired. She was supposed to have dinner with Dr King that night almost thirty years ago. Instead she prepared for his funeral. She puts on her dark glasses again, speaking slowly and reverentially as one does about the death of a hero. Her words run out as she remembers the chaos at the scene, Dr King's body on the balcony above us, his aides trying hopelessly to stop his blood oozing away, the end of a dream. A young white lawyer who had been helping black civil rights workers file lawsuits against Memphis police for brutality was arrested at the scene.

'He was *arrested*,' Mrs Smith says with thirty years of indignant disbelief in her voice at the outrage. 'Our *lawyer* was arrested! While the killer got away! Can you believe it?' Of course you can believe it. After a while the white civil rights lawyer was freed by the Memphis police. The alleged assassin, James Earl Ray, was eventually arrested and pleaded guilty to murder, though he later claimed he did not do it.

But James Earl Ray's initially successful escape from Memphis, the fact that the allegations against him were never aired in a trial, the possibility that he did not act alone, the handling of the investigation by the police and the FBI, and the pattern of political assassinations in those grim years of turmoil, have contributed to the abiding acceptance that political conspiracies lie behind the worst in American life. What did the government know and when did it know it? The FBI, at the prompting of J. Edgar Hoover, had been watching Dr King – not, of course, to safeguard him, but because he was considered a 'subversive'. How much did they know? Why were they looking for subversion in the wrong place?

At the spot where a wreath has been laid to Dr King we are joined by another black woman, a generation younger in the civil rights struggle, Mrs Johnnie Turner. She speaks with pride at the way in which this modest, dull hotel has become the National Civil Rights Museum, transformed by Dr King's blood sacrifice into a holy site, a place of pilgrimage. Buses draw up bringing tourists from all over the United States, and the rest of the world, to celebrate the most dramatic and vital struggle in America's recent history. This was where *all* Americans secured the right to vote, the right to be treated equally. But in the 1990s that struggle has died, fossilized like a bit of forgotten, ancient history.

We are talking together because Mrs Smith and Mrs Turner are political activists, anxious that young black voters go to the polls to re-elect President Clinton. The two women know that black community leaders have less than four weeks to convince people that this November 1996 presidential election is important. Instead they fear there will be a historically low turnout. President Clinton keeps saying this election of the last president of the twentieth century and the first of the twenty-first is important as a 'bridge to the twenty-first century'. But it is obvious to Mrs Smith and Mrs Turner that for most voters it is a bridge too far. Unlike the generation of political activists in the Sixties, their children and grandchildren in the 1990s are a hotbed of apathy. Centuries of struggle, sacrifice and occasionally death to secure the right to vote have ended with more than half the black population — especially younger black Americans — not voting. The irony is not lost on either woman.

'I guess we didn't pass on to them,' Maxine Smith says, shaking her head in irritation at the apathy of the young, 'the fire that kept us motivated. Things are taken for granted now. What difference does it make? That's the kind of question we hear from young black people. When I came along as a young black woman we had *nothing*. The political process is one of our main sources of relief from the drudgery of discrimination.'

The Civil Rights Movement did not die here on the balcony of the Lorraine hotel. It was killed by its own success, once the central grievance about the right to vote had been addressed. 'We do have apathy,' Mrs Smith admits. 'It's across the board, not limited to race. We are doing all we can to inspire our folks to vote.'

She speaks fondly of the days when she and her workers could get out 75 per cent of the black vote, knowing that 95 per cent of them would vote together. In the primary election in Memphis in early 1996, for comparison, she puts the turnout at 35 per cent — which is high by 1990s American standards of apathy. Drugs, crime, violence, illegitimacy and what she and Johnnie Turner call 'societal breakdowns' mean that many African-Americans are either too busy or too disillusioned to take an interest in politics. It is like the old music hall joke that there is no point in voting because whatever you do the government gets elected.

'We had our eyes strictly on the prize in the early '60s, the late '50s,' Maxine Smith says firmly. At that time there were fewer than 10,000 black people registered to vote in Memphis and the surrounding Shelby County. Now the figure is about 200,000. 'We've worked all the way. It wasn't easy. We didn't have postcard registration. We had to go from door to door, pick them up in a car, take them downtown. There was a *fire* that burned in people then that somehow has been smothered.'

Maybe, I suggest, the loyalty of black voters to the Democratic party means Democrats take the black vote for granted and Republicans ignore you. 'I'd rather be taken for granted than ignored,' she admits. 'But I don't feel taken for granted.' She speaks of President Clinton with the old idealism of someone who thinks this is another Kennedy in the White House, the lost younger brother to JFK and RFK.

But Mrs Smith is old enough to remember when blacks in the South were excluded by the old Democrat machine and instead looked to the Republican party as the vehicle of the Great Emancipator, Abraham Lincoln. 'In Memphis, in Tennessee, people still vote primarily on the basis of race. The old Democratic party was the party of the racists. When I was a little girl my daddy was a Republican because that's what black folks were.' Black Americans, she says, 'have no permanent enemies or permanent friends'. But they do have permanent interests. And that means they have to get out to vote.

But, I persist, maybe people are too *content* to vote. How else can you explain the apathy which, in one generation, has consigned Martin Luther King's heroic struggle to the museum of the Lorraine Motel? Mrs Smith blinks thoughtfully in the light. 'It's a changing time,' she says slowly, and the changes affect whites as well as blacks. But she thinks it is exactly the *opposite* of contentment which is stopping people from voting. 'The breakdown in society. A change in morals. A change in emphasis.'

Johnnie Turner believes it is something even worse. The brutal assassinations of great heroes of the 1960s like Dr King have been replaced by the *character* assassination of political leaders of the 1990s. What used to be done with bullets is now carried out by leaks, sleazy stories and innuendo. Mrs Turner is enthusiastic about re-electing Bill Clinton so he can be shown to have risen above the sleaze fomented by newspaper and television reporters who, she thinks, are accomplices in the crime of character assassination. They circulate stories which either have no merit, are irrelevant, or are inspired by the enemies of progressive people like the Clintons.

Does anybody really care whether Mr Clinton had an affair? Does it matter to his performance as president? Does anyone understand the Whitewater land deal of almost twenty years ago? For her, helping Clinton get re-elected despite the hail of unpleasant revelations has become a crusade, like helping President Kennedy or Dr King avoid the assassins' bullets.

Surely some of the allegations are true, I suggest. She nods. But Americans, Mrs Turner argues strongly, hear *so much* sleaze about politicians, people have become disillusioned and dispirited about democracy itself. 'Those [leaders] that voters have the greatest hopes for have not lived up to expectations,' she thinks. 'Every day you pick up the paper there's negative news about politicians on the local, state, national level.' The implication is that *every* politician is corrupt, stupid, lying or all of these things. 'That's fed to you for so long you believe it, unless you are smart enough to sift through the fast talk.'

Prominent Americans like General Colin Powell refuse to run for high political office because it involves volunteering to be showered with sewage in an increasingly toxic political culture which despises heroes and so destroys them. 'You'd be crazy to run for president,' Johnnie believes, saying that in the current media climate if you sneezed on someone as an infant in playschool it could be exposed and held against you thirty years later. 'It's come down to that.'

Her words have echoes all across the United States and in the extreme mood swings of American voters. Tennessee, after all, has been a reliable bell-wether in the 1990s. Like America, the state voted for Clinton in 1992. Then in November 1994 – again like the rest of the country – it rejected him overwhelmingly in the mid-term elections by throwing out both Democratic senators and electing two Republicans instead. In 1996 Tennesseans, once more in step with the national mood, switched back to Clinton.

'Why can't people here make up their minds?' I wondered. 'Why does the United States switch parties and leaders every two years in the 1990s? Why are voters so restless?'

'They are looking for the Answer,' Johnnie answered sombrely. 'And each time they put their faith in a certain political party, expectations were not lived up to. So they exercise their right to change their minds.'

And still end up disappointed. I left Johnnie Turner and Maxine Smith to organize the best possible turnout for President Clinton. I wanted to see if white voters in Memphis shared their sense that in the 1996 presidential election the clear winner would be apathy.

South of town I reached Neely Mallory's cotton warehouse where 500-pound bales of cotton from the new harvest were being graded, priced and put on fork-lift trucks for loading. Mr Mallory, a big friendly bear of a man with a warm handshake and a strong Tennessee drawl, is part of a long-time cotton family in Memphis. 'The headquarters of the three biggest cotton corporations in the USA – and the *world* – happen to be in Memphis,' Mr Mallory told me proudly as we walked around his warehouse complex. This year will be a good harvest. 'The cotton business is doing *exceedingly* well. In 1984–5 US textile mills processed five-and-a-half billion bales of cotton. In 1996 it will be eleven billion bales.'

Doubling the use of a single commodity in a decade is an extraordinary success. Cotton is the Comeback Kid of textiles, replacing the synthetic fabrics that once threatened the industry. 'Cotton is the *fabric of our lives*,' Neely Mallory joked, repeating the familiar slogan from American cotton commercials on TV. But the excitement in the warehouse at the prospect of the new harvest is not matched by excitement over the political future of the country. Mr Mallory laughed when I asked if he was happy with the choice confronting him in the election. 'No, I'm not happy with either one of them.'

He said Bill Clinton was not trustworthy and Senator Bob Dole was bound to lose. The system for electing candidates seemed so flawed, uninteresting or uninviting that even a well-educated businessman like Neely Mallory felt he was an impotent citizen in electoral politics. 'People are soured on politicians and politics. They see too many things done by politicians . . . to get re-elected as opposed to solving some problems.'

Keith Lord, one of the cotton warehouse supervisors, joined our conversation. He shifted his baseball cap to the back of his head and pulled at his beard when I asked him what he thought of politicians. He said he intended to vote, and to vote for Clinton.

'Do you trust him?' I asked.

'As much as you do any politician.'

'Which is how much?'

'About that much,' he replied, holding his thumb and forefinger an inch apart.

I decided to try one other familiar site of pilgrimage in Memphis. It is not as glorious as the Lorraine Hotel, but Elvis Presley's home at Graceland does indeed draw pilgrims from all over the United States and beyond. At his grave, Elvis fans shuffle around or stand in knots gazing at the tomb while a fountain dances behind them. Overweight white-haired grandmothers in bulging polyester suits place flowers at the grave and shed silent tears for a man who would now qualify for a retirement pension. Yet at Graceland he is forever young. You do not see images of the fat Elvis of later years, bloated by drugs and overeating, the man who died ingloriously on his toilet seat in 1977. Instead this is a shrine to the handsome, sexy, pelvic gyrator who helped bring rock and roll to white America and who was part of the cult of youth which pushed from the 1950s into the rebellions of the 1960s and ended with Bill Clinton – once nicknamed 'Elvis' – in the White House.

Every five minutes a shuttle bus brings sixteen new tourists to the mansion, 700,000 people a year. On the night of 15 August there is a candlelit vigil. A selected pair of fans march up the driveway and light torches from the eternal flame at Elvis's grave, then return and spread the flame to others. One of the 700,000 visitors a year, Rick Edmondson, is in his twenties. He walked away with a bagful of Elvis souvenirs. When I asked him about politics he said that when voting in America 'you are picking between the worst of two evils'. Clinton? 'He's a draft dodger. My father died in Vietnam, so it hits a sore spot with me.' How about Bob Dole and his running mate, the former football star Jack Kemp? Rick makes a sound like air hissing from a balloon. He remembers that a few years ago Dole suggested Kemp was such a blow-dried idiot, the best Kemp could achieve politically would be to lower the tax on hair spray. 'Now they are doing everything but make love to each other on TV.' He spat at the hypocrisy of politicians.

How about Ross Perot, the third party candidate? I suggested. 'You might as well throw away your vote.'

That about covered it. Thank you Rick Edmondson, Heartbeat of America. A man and woman in their thirties joined the conversation.

'In America,' the man said, 'we *expect* our politicians to be at least somewhat dishonest. There's an accepted amount of dishonesty. It's gotten to the point where we are past being disillusioned. We're very accepting of it. That's why all the mudslinging doesn't have much effect on how people vote. People just roll their eyes at it.'

The woman interjected. 'Everyone knows that the politicians are a little corrupt. Everyone is taking a little bit under the table. We've just got to figure out who is doing the best for us.'

At that time President Clinton was staggering towards his

1996 victory, knowing that America was disgusted by politics and politicians. 'This is a real important election,' Mr Clinton insisted, almost plaintively, in his first televised debate with Senator Bob Dole. 'The world is changing dramatically in how we work and how we live and how we relate to each other. Huge changes. And the decisions we make will have enormous practical consequences.'

Then he turned directly to the camera to address the voters – Rick Edmondson and the other tourists at Graceland, Neely Mallory and his workers, the young black men and women who have inherited what Martin Luther King and Maxine Smith fought for, and *who could not care less*. 'I want to talk about *your* responsibility,' the president said. 'Your responsibility is to show up on November fifth.'

Half the electorate were not listening or did not hear. In the 1992 presidential election Bill Clinton had been elected with 43 per cent of the vote. But only 55 per cent of those who could have voted did so. That meant that the most powerful elected leader in the world entered the White House with the approval of only 23 per cent of those eligible to go to the polls, fewer than one voter in four. In 1996 he received a slightly greater share of the votes in a lower percentage poll. These are signs of a sick democracy in which apathy and anger have become the two most prominent symptoms. Left unchecked these trends mean we are witnessing an unhappy sequel to Alexis de Tocqueville's book, *Democracy in America*. It is the withering of democracy in America, though there is another paradox. Americans love their country, but not the way it is governed. They remain patriotically supportive of the ideal of American democracy while increasingly cynical about and disconnected from the way it works in practice.

Only a third of all Americans admit to having a great deal or quite a lot of confidence in the US federal government. Local government is not rated much better. Nine out of ten believe that government wastes their tax money and eight out of ten believe America's political leaders are more concerned with their personal images than in solving serious national problems.[1]

It is not that the apathetic majority of voters no longer care about the future direction of the United States. Quite the contrary. But they believe that exchanging one group of flawed politicians for another will have little effect on their daily lives. Despite the extreme wings of both parties, party labels often seem irrelevant. Bill Clinton has swallowed entire sections of the Republican agenda. In the often-used phrases 'moderate Republicans' or 'conservative Democrats', the words 'moderate' and 'conservative' are far more indicative of the character of the politician than the party affiliations. Above all, many voters have become convinced that their vote does not matter. The politicians will do what they want to do, and the voters are angry at being cast as impotent citizens in what is supposed to be a participative democracy. Perhaps we should not be surprised at this decadence. In a country in which rights have precedence over responsibilities, why should voting be any different? The civil rights struggle guaranteed the right to vote. Who cares about the responsibility to do so?

But the consequences are dismal. The act of voting confers legitimacy on the institutions of democratic government. Even if we complain about the result, taking part in the process indicates we accept the verdict. The people have spoken. But when the people resolutely refuse to speak or mumble inconsequentially, as they have done throughout the 1990s, resounding apathy delegitimizes American government. It is a dangerous time for American democracy when, as we will examine in detail in the next chapter, 100 million potential voters will not go to the polls. Those who do not vote need take only a short step further towards failing to accept the moral authority of a government they did not endorse. It is one step beyond that to the position of the angriest Americans in the anti-government militia movement who do not accept the US government's legal authority either.

Such apathy, cynicism and anger are the most pernicious trends in American politics – far more of a scandal and ultimately far more damaging to democracy than Whitewater, the Iran-Contra affair or even Watergate. The British grumble about the quality of their leaders and the flaws in their political system. But most of those Britons who can vote in general elections choose to endorse the democratic system by doing so. In Britain the problem is not, as in America, that the party machines are too weak, but that they are too strong, often reducing the role of a back-bench member of parliament to that of an automaton, lobby fodder, whipped in to vote the party line. Traditionally, the wide ideological gulf between the Left and Right in Britain and western Europe has encouraged voters to go to the polls if for no other reason than to prevent the other side from winning. Perhaps one unintended consequence of New Labour jockeying for the centre ground in Britain will be to encourage apathy. If Britain follows the American model, then the smaller the ideological choice between the parties the more voting becomes a matter of choosing between personalities rather than radically different political approaches. When policies converge, the ugliest personal flaws of politicians become as significant as those of contestants in beauty contests. But for now, majority apathy remains the American political disease, with no obvious signs of a cure.

As I left Memphis I thought of the sunshine that brought a tear to Maxine Smith's eye as we sat in front of room 306 at the Lorraine Motel, of all the marches, picketing, demonstrating and rioting, of the resonating voice of Dr King proclaiming 'I have a Dream today', and of the struggle that finally achieved democracy in America for all its people just a generation ago in the 1960s. And I thought of the simple brass plaque behind Mrs Smith at the spot of Dr King's assassination.

On it is inscribed a biblical quotation, from Genesis 37:19–20. 'They said to one another, "Behold, here cometh the Dreamer. Let us slay him." . . . And we shall see what will become of his Dreams.'

The United States of Apathy

'The best lack all conviction, while the worst
Are full of passionate intensity.'

W. B. Yeats, '*The Second Coming*'

On the campaign trail in Louisiana, Iowa, Michigan and Virginia

The ferry takes just a few minutes to cut across the mud-brown Mississippi River from New Orleans to Algiers point. A February sleet whipped up by strong northerly winds appeared to fall sideways across the Big Easy where the Mississippi bends like a kink in a hose, and river barges slow down to negotiate the 180-degree turn.

In the French Quarter, tourists had been driven away from the bars and strip joints on Decatur and Bourbon Streets by the threat of an ice storm. Ice had already closed the main Interstate highways and the first frozen blasts left the barkers standing outside the girlie bars and burlesque shows wrapped up in puffy anoraks and thick wool coats. They stamped their feet and hissed steam into the air like horses after a race, yelling unconvincingly about the delights of the naked dancers inside. A sign in a strip club window read, 'Wash the girl of your choice at your table.'

'*Watch* the girl of your choice?' I wondered aloud as I hurried past a barker in a black coat and woollen hat.

'No,' the club barker called after me. 'Not *watch*. It's *wash* the girl of your choice at your table. C'mon. You don't *know* until you *try*!'

I passed by, heading towards the other side of the river, bowing my head to the ice wind. It was just a few days before the first vote of the 1996 presidential election season, which, unusually, was to begin in Louisiana. The creaking machine by which presidential candidates are chosen was about to crank itself into gear, an ancient, arthritic Godzilla about to beat voters into record apathy. Election primaries were supposed to find a credible Republican challenger to President Clinton. Louisiana was first – the earliest hardened artery of an increasingly sclerotic system, a foretaste of a much more serious illness to come.

In February 1996 New Orleans, the Big Easy, was indeed preparing for a momentous event, but it was not the contest to find a new leader for the new millennium. *Nobody* cared about that. N'yawlins was getting ready for *Mardi Gras*. Since I had failed to find any voters interested in discussing presidential politics on the icy streets of the French Quarter, I crossed the river to Algiers where *Mardi Gras* carnival floats were being prepared in massive warehouses bedecked with gigantic statues of cowboys and jesters. It is called 'Blaine Kern's Mardi Gras World', one of the unnatural wonders of the world, a freakshow so astonishing it amounts to an even greater collection of eccentric and wonderful Americana than the presidential election itself. The sensation is like walking into a Superman comic. Superheroes *Ka-Pow! Crash! Ka-boom!* from all sides. Everything is bigger and better and more heroic than real life, warehouses stuffed with enormous, eerie American icons. A gigantic moulded likeness of Jimi Hendrix in gaudy pink flared trousers stands ready to mangle the Star Spangled Banner on his guitar. Superman, pectoral muscles rippling, towers overhead, rescuing Metropolis. Ten-feet tall Fred Flintstone and Mickey Mouse smile inanely down at a sea of oversized cowboys, Pocahontas and American Indians, pool tables, football and baseball games, Coca-Cola bottles, Disney characters. It is the American Dream on acid. In a back room I found an artist, Tony van de Walle painting a Wheel of Fortune float with dollar signs under the Himalayan-sized breasts of the glamorous game show hostess, Vanna White.

Tony wiped the paint from his hands on a rag as he stepped away from the twelve-feet tall Vanna. When I asked him about the presidential election he made a sound of disgust that I was beginning to recognize as the common American response to reporters daring to speak about politics. *Ptttoooeh!* Tony described himself as a patriotic liberal Democrat, but complained of his disconnection from the entire political system. 'I have a sense of shame,' he said, speaking emotionally of government and politics. 'I am angry and frustrated. We are *all* angry and frustrated. We are all bitchin' and moanin' and desperate for change.'

Like most Americans, Tony had no sense that however he voted, he could transform Washington politics or the real lives of ordinary people. 'It's just continuing the ever more divisive spiral in the American political process. You're eliminating every-body in the middle and what you're left with are the most extreme ends of the spectrum. It's a choice between shooting yourself in the foot or shooting yourself in the head when you vote.'

The key to the crisis of American democracy in the 1990s is to understand that Tony *does* care passionately about his country. Yet, as with the voters in Memphis, he cannot see the political system as a way to bring his passions to life. He returned to painting dollar signs under Vanna's bust, convinced with outraged impotence that the system for governing the United States was in serious disrepair, and that there was nothing he could do about it.

Outside, the sleet had stopped but the air was prickly cold. I stood at the bow of the ferry as it cut back across the Mississippi, thinking that I had met scores of Tony van de Walles all across the United States – those who demonstrate, in Yeats's words, that the best lack all conviction while the worst are full of passionate intensity. It was hardly surprising that the turnout for the Republican primary a few days later would be just 5 per cent of registered Republican voters.[1] Nor was there any surprise that the most extreme candidate of all, Pat Buchanan, claimed victory. Buchanan – despite being one of the most unpopular political figures in the United States – was strongly backed by Christian Coalition and anti-abortion activists, whose enthusiasm among the apathetic majority give America the kind of politics it suffers, or deserves, in the 1990s.[2]

Two weeks after the sleet and ice storms of Louisiana came the frozen wastes of Iowa, the real start of the process. The presidential election and media caravan hit a mid-West about as different from Louisiana as Scotland is from Sicily. With one exception: apathy and anger at the political process prevailed everywhere in Iowa – except, of course, in the minds of the candidates and the eternally enthusiastic media.

In Iowa's picturesque Madison County, Clint Eastwood and Meryl Streep filmed their romantic movie *The Bridges of Madison County*. In the county seat of Winterset, a pleasant farming town, you can sit in the North Side Café, where Clint had breakfast, and eat enough bacon, eggs and pancakes to keep out the winter chill.

Or you can warm your heart by driving to the rust-red Roseman Bridge which featured prominently in the film. On the inside, pinned to the walls, are dozens of passionate love letters left by fans, spicy hot as they flap in the winter wind. A few miles further on, you reach the Hollingsworth family farm alongside a snow-dusted dirt road.

Mark Hollingsworth proudly showed me around his 3,000 acres, from the pens where pigs and beef cattle were being fattened, to the computer room where he has an on-line link to the commodity prices at the Chicago Board of Trade. At a click of his computer Mark can check soybean or grain prices in Iowa and Kansas, the weather reports for mid-West farmers, and all the instant facts you might expect from a high-tech businessman leaping into the information age with enthusiasm.

The Hollingsworths are conservative Christian Republicans. Their house is dotted with religious texts on the walls and perfumed with the sweet smell of flowers. At just about every level the Hollingsworths' Iowa could not appear more different from Tony van de Walle's Louisiana. Except for this: in both cases strong patriotism for American ideals is mixed with deep suspicion of the reality of politics and politicians. Mark's wife Brenda poured coffee and confided that in a farming lifestyle you either fix things yourself or they stay broken. But the family had little optimism that politicians could fix anything at all. The assumption was that the political system would stay broken.

'We are weary of politicians in this country,' Brenda said simply. 'Not all of them are corrupt and immoral but a good many of them are. I don't feel that I am always represented in Washington.'

In every state I visited during the 1996 elections – more than twenty – I heard the words of Tony van de Walle and Brenda Hollingsworth repeated over and over from Democrats, Republicans, Independents, Don't Knows and Don't Cares. In all America's diversity there seems virtual unanimity from thinking voters who care about their country but who fear that the two-party political system is broken, or stinks like rotting fish, or both, and that it cannot address the economic, social and moral challenges that make so many Americans anxious and angry.

The parties, Democrats and Republicans, are not alternatives, many people said. They are mirror images, indistinguishable Demublicans and Repocrats. The University of Michigan's National Elections Center showed voters abandoning the two parties since 1952, when 23 per cent called themselves Independents. By the 1990s that was 37 per cent.

The search for a third party, an independent force or 'anyone but a politician' is another echo of American politics of a century ago, though it has led voters into eccentric blind alleys. In 1992 one voter in five backed the Texas billionaire Ross Perot for president despite – or rather because of – his utter lack of political experience. By 1996 Mr Perot set up his Reform party to run for the presidency a second time, though after the robust inspection of Mr Perot by the American media he was revealed as less credible as a candidate. As Tony van de Walle put it to me, American voters have become so desperate to change their political system they are like tourists at *Mardi Gras*. They 'always like the shiny new things' on the floats passing by, until they examine them closely and discover dull plastic behind the shine.

Non-politicians, the shiny new things, were eagerly sought as presidential candidates throughout the 1990s, though the most admired, General Colin Powell, refused to be considered for public office in 1996. Rich non-politicians were less reticent. One of these, the multimillionaire publisher Steve Forbes, ran a campaign for the Republican nomination which demonstrated the absurdities of a crumbling, expensive and unloved system.

In just one state, Arizona, candidate Forbes spent $4 million, mostly on TV advertising. He secured 100,000 votes. In the most rotten English borough or the worst of Boss Tweed's machine politicking, $40 a vote would not seem much of a bargain. By the end of the New Hampshire primary the nine Republicans had spent $40 million. In Iowa alone they spent $10 million – and only 100,000 Iowans voted in their Republican caucus system. This works out at $100 per voter – an even worse bargain than Mr Forbes managed in Arizona. The Iowa turnout was only 17 per cent of registered Republicans. And Iowa, remember, is one of the states in which the media find the presidential primaries most *exciting*.

Steve Forbes's 'popularity' – buoyed up by the saturation bombing of his 'air war' television advertisements – points to the seriousness of America's political sickness. Like Ross Perot, he had never held political power at any level, and never run for any office. The biggest challenge in his life appeared to be inheriting millions of dollars from his father. And yet he was seriously considered for the presidency as if it were an entry-level political position. No American would have his teeth fixed by someone who was not a dentist. Nor would they fly in an aircraft with someone who had never been a pilot. But the search for anyone-but-a-politician means a significant number of American voters in the 1990s are willing to entrust the most complicated democratic political system in the world to political novices like

Steve Forbes and Ross Perot, because those who have political experience are routinely regarded as tainted.

This is not like summoning Cincinnatus from the plough to save Rome from the barbarians. At least Cincinnatus had military talent and a record of leadership. Neither is it democracy. It is desperation. And the only consolation Americans may take is that at least their elections cannot be bought by those with enormous personal fortunes. The millionaires and billionaires lost.

The author Martin Gross, in *The Political Racket* (the source of some of these cash and turnout figures), calls the American election system a 'crazy quilt' – corrupt, extraordinarily expensive, off-putting to voters and designed to perpetuate a clique of permanent politicians who end up with jobs for life.[3] For instance, in California, *only* registered Republicans can vote in the Republican primary to choose their 'nominee' for the November election. Sensible, you might think. But in other states, including New Hampshire, it is not just Republicans who can vote in the Republican primary. Independents can as well. And in Wisconsin and still other states there is an 'open primary' in which *anyone* from *any* party can vote in *any* primary. Democrats could vote for the Republican candidate they think is most likely to lose. On top of that, some states divide the vote proportionately for each candidate. Others work a winner-take-all system. Any state can decide to change its primary date, but traditionally Iowa and New Hampshire set the pace. There is no good reason for this.

It means the primary election season is usually 'over' before any big state has voted, because hopeless candidates (with the exception of the super rich) cannot raise any more money. After Iowa and New Hampshire, the less favoured challengers drop out, allowing the media – not the voters – to anoint the winner.[4] No wonder journalists find the circus so exciting while voters do not. The European equivalent would be choosing a Euro-president based on the preferences of Scotland and Sicily, but ignoring Germany, Italy and France until after the decision had been taken. It is irrational, undemocratic, expensive, over-long, biased against thoughtful candidates and absolutely guaranteed to turn off most voters. It turns them off with relentless success.

This haphazard system grew from sensible motives. In a country the size of the United States a long campaign allows talented local politicians — state governors with executive experience like Reagan in California or Carter in Georgia — to travel the country and see if their message 'resonates'. But in the era of twenty-four-hour news, CNN and C-SPAN, hundreds of channels of cable TV, thousands of radio stations, 'electronic town meetings', instantaneous reports by satellite and the huge resource of the Internet, America has retained horse-drawn politics in the information age. The method of choosing a president bears as much relation to 1990s American society as churning butter by hand, sailing the Atlantic in a clipper ship or hunting with a flintlock musket.

One obvious solution would be to hold four or five regional, rather than state, primaries in quick succession. A better idea, suggested by Martin Gross, might be to hold one national primary election on one day in the spring of the election year. But the most important reform would be to squeeze money out of the system by finding a way to regulate political advertising on television. American politics is sleazy and off-putting largely because candidates have to raise millions, sometimes tens of millions of dollars. They need the money to buy TV advertising so they can market themselves like baked beans and, more importantly, attack their opponents.

Limiting paid-for political advertising by candidates and offering a ration of free television and radio airtime instead would transform American politics. Candidates would not need to raise so much money by hobnobbing with business people and pressure groups hoping for juicy favours.

Moreover, if each free TV and radio slot were to be five or ten minutes long, the whole tone of a campaign would have to change. A thirty-second or one-minute attack ad can destroy its target. But it is impossible to construct five or ten minutes of attack advertising without sounding ridiculously negative.

Candidates would therefore be forced to talk positively about themselves rather than negatively about their opponents.

The problem with this suggestion is that it will never happen. It incenses the powerful TV companies who regard their use of the airwaves in the United States as a 'right' to make money without any special public responsibility. It would cost them money in lost advertising. And it would require a constitutional amendment, since banning political advertising would be a First Amendment 'freedom of speech' issue. It is not, therefore, likely, even if it would be desirable. The best that can be expected is that, as in 1996, TV networks in the future will voluntarily offer small portions of free airtime to candidates. But that will not stop the rot. We live in the age of political hyper-inflation as candidates recognize the way to win is to spend much more on television commercials than your opponent. That, obviously, means raising more, and doing it any way you can. And doing it again for the next election. And again. Politicians are not stupid. They know the current system, awash with sleazy money, is constantly off-putting to voters, but they respond like alcoholics determined to get sober after just one more drink of booze.

Republican pollster Frank Luntz has been tracking voter anger and desperation at the political system for several years. 'There's a frustration in American politics now that is unheard of,' he told me early in 1996. 'It's even greater than it was in 1994. There's an anger that the status quo doesn't work, that the leadership isn't listening to them.'

While scepticism about government is America's most noble tradition and vital for any truly free society, Dr Luntz and most serious pollsters concluded this depth of anger and disconnection was something quite new in the mid-1990s. It was beyond scepticism or cynicism, and it threatened the very legitimacy of the institutions of American government. If you really want to listen to the heartbeat of Angry America, Dr Luntz counselled me, you should try Macomb County, Michigan.

Macomb County is the middle of Middle America. Unlike Iowa, New Hampshire or Louisiana, it is representative of the kind of average America vital in presidential elections. It is to politics what the drosophila fruit fly is to biology: one of the most studied areas for the best researchers. 'As Macomb County goes,' one seventy-year-old resident explained, 'so goes the election.'

The county — a flat, unremarkable piece of the industrial mid-West — is made from the sprawling suburbs near Motown, the motor city, Detroit. Dr Luntz for the Republicans and Clinton pollsters like Stan Greenberg combed through Macomb as a guide to the disconnection between government and the governed in 1990s America, even though the statistics suggest it should be a bastion of contentment. The car industry, which is as important here as it is in Dayton and Cleveland, bounced back in the 1990s. By 1996 it was booming. Michigan's election year unemployment was around 5 per cent and in Macomb it was even lower — 4 per cent.

After many visits, I was never able to figure out where the heart of it all might be. Unmemorable shopping malls give way to long stretches of neat bungalows with barbecues in the yard, well-cut grass and middle-income, mostly white residents who abandoned Detroit after the race riots of the 1960s. On the shores of Lake St Clair you can sit on a beach and gaze at oil tankers on the horizon or look for the towers of Detroit skyscrapers in the mist to the south, but the suburbs mysteriously continue without any real sense of an 'urbs'.

Politically it was once solidly Democrat. But Macomb voters switched to Ronald Reagan in the 1980s and were nicknamed 'Reagan Democrats'. By 1992 they returned to Clinton. And again in 1996. Maybe they are now 'Clinton Republicans'.

At the county seat in Mount Clemens, fifty-five-year-old Bill Visnaw is typical of tens of millions of middle-income Americans fed up with politics and politicians. He runs a busy barber's shop and is a longtime Republican. Bill believes the two-party system is corrupt beyond reform. In 1992 he switched to the independent candidate, Ross Perot, as a protest vote.

'I don't think there's a defining line between Republicans and

Democrats any more,' Bill told me, weary resignation in his voice. 'Republicans are supposed to be for big business. Democrats are for the little guy. Clinton was in Detroit recently at a $1,000-a-plate fundraising dinner. So *who* is for the little guy?'

Nobody, Bill suggests. Such is the desperation of many 'little guys' like Bill that he assumes a multi-billionaire Texas non-politician like Ross Perot might be closer to his interests, and less corrupt, than any representative from either traditional party. At least, Bill pointed out with grim humour, Ross Perot's $4 billion bank account suggests he cannot be bought. He concluded sadly that the American public 'does not have any control' of a sterile political culture which dodges real issues and substitutes phoney ones like abortion, homosexual rights and other matters of personal morality, all the unsolvable issues of an angry society. The 'real' issues – the ageing of America, medical assistance for older Americans (Medicare), the fact that the Social Security system of retirement benefits may collapse by the time Bill needs it, the corrosive effect of the budget and trade deficits, spiralling tax rates and a bureaucracy that is out of control – were not part of a proper public debate.

In Britain, however slippery politicians may appear to be in ducking the issues, the parliamentary system usually ensures they cannot duck them forever. The prime minister endures the ordeal of prime minister's questions, robustly interrogated by his opponents. Other ministers face similar grillings. It is difficult to imagine the presidency of Ronald Reagan surviving if Mr Reagan had faced repeated public questioning by his opponents the way Mrs Thatcher did. Moreover, the media tradition in the United Kingdom is very different from that in the United States. Radio and television interviewers are much more aggressive in Britain. So is the endless pursuit of issues on television pro-grammes like *Channel Four News*, *Newsnight* and the *Today* programme. Occasionally this gives British election coverage the texture of All Bran – eat it because it is good for you – but voters cannot complain, as Bill Visnaw and many other Americans do, that they never hear enough about the issues at stake.

In 1996 Bill Visnaw voted as he had in 1992, for Ross Perot. And Perot, he admitted, was a wasted vote. 'But I have no other means of getting my feelings [that the two-party system is broken] to Washington. My only other alternative is not to vote.' Bill's anger, like that of America, is a hair's breadth away from apathy.

In nearby Warren, at the side of one of the long, featureless, fast roads that bisect Macomb County, Ken Johnson runs The Office Deli on the ground floor of a block filled with banks and insurance brokers. Ken, balding with a moustache, is wearing a fashionable no-collar shirt and cleans the deli while two of his employees prepare sandwiches. Office workers come and go, picking up bagels and coffees. Ken is thirty-eight years old with two young children. He is another disconnected American, a Michigan version of Choo Choo Caron, the New Hampshire café owner.

'I don't think in Washington they have a clue about what's going on in the country,' Ken says. He 'can't stand to look at' President Clinton, 'because I know he's lying'. The lying is 'blatant' on everything from tax cuts to the Whitewater scandal, and so Ken decided he will vote for Bob Dole solely to get Clinton out of the White House. I ask if he trusts Dole, and Ken thinks for a few moments before admitting that Senator Dole is 'pretty lame'. In fact Ken, a longtime Republican, says he does not believe in the centrepiece of Dole's agenda, to cut income tax by 15 per cent. Nobody believes it, he says. So Dole is lying too, but not as much as Clinton. 'I feel sorry for the guy,' Ken admits eventually, shaking his head. 'Because everything he touches turns into a pile of dung.'

Politicians are the hollow men of American life. As the Diagnosing Voter Discontent survey, published by the Center for National Policy in 1996, put it: 'Voters want leadership, but they clearly want a change in the type of leadership.'[5]

Voters also want the corruption of money raising taken out of politics. The 1996 election turned up a series of scandals of foreign contributions to the Democratic party, funny money from Indonesia, fund-raising at a Buddhist temple, convicted felons with alleged organized crime connections having coffee at the White House in exchange for campaign contributions, and President Clinton admitting lamely that 'most' of the time the fundraising was legal.

During the campaign it was revealed that big donors, $100,000 or more, could 'contribute' their way – the word used to be 'bribe' – to dinner with the president, or a night in the Lincoln bedroom at the White House. Smaller donors could meet the president over coffee, or attend receptions with the vice-president or first lady. Republicans played similar games, hosting meals with candidate Bob Dole. Congressional elections were also awash in loot. One senator admits his game plan was to raise $40,000 a week *every week* for two years for his election efforts in 1994. That is $4 million – a modest sum by Senate standards, but you could not rob banks quickly enough to raise that much money. At least the senator only has to concentrate his fundraising on his re-election efforts every six years. Members of the lower House of Representatives face re-election every two years. Their lives are an impossible struggle to do a little business of leadership in the perpetual scramble for funds for the next election. Newt Gingrich spent $5 million on his 1996 re-election. His opponent spent $3 million. Since congressional elections are held every two years in the lower House, Mr Gingrich's fundraising over that period amounted to approximately $7,000 a day, every day. And as soon as the dust settled on the 1996 race, Mr Gingrich had to think about raising a similar sum for 1998. Then again for 2000.

The question is not why so many American politicians are corrupt, it is how *any* of them can remain honest facing such financial pressures to raise money to pay for TV ads. Congress, therefore, like the presidential races, often attracts millionaires who do not have to demean themselves by putting around the begging bowl. In 1994, senate candidate Michael Huffington spent $28 million of his personal fortune in California. He lost. In 1996, aspiring Virginia Senator Mark Warner spent $11 million. He lost too. The total spending in all congressional races in 1996 was a record $626.4 million. In American politics, as the comedian Will Rogers once observed, it takes a heck of a lot of money just to get beat.[6]

Why do they do it? Many, probably most, American politicians undoubtedly enter public service to offer leadership to a country they love. Some nakedly pursue power. Others, to judge from the no-hopers who enter every presidential election, are consumed by an enormous degree of personal vanity.

Bill Clinton has been running for the presidency, one way or another, since his teenage years when he was photographed at the White House with President John F. Kennedy. Notoriously, he tried to avoid military service in Vietnam but – as he put it in a letter at the time – only in a way which would maintain his 'political viability'. There is something truly unpleasant about this single-mindedness in pursuit of power. It is rather like the selection of infant athletes in Communist countries to be intensively trained as Olympic gold medal winners. But whatever propels the political urge – public service, lust for power, personal vanity – financing campaigns has become the Catch-22 of American democracy.

What kind of perverse people would be willing to spend so much time raising money for their election campaigns? Precisely the kind of people who should *not* be allowed to go into any office of public trust. And which 'benefactors' would give away thousands of dollars to elect members of Congress? Precisely the kind of special interest groups – tobacco companies, trial lawyers, trades unions, banks, insurance companies, big business conglomerates all looking for favours – who should *not* be allowed to influence any democratic political system by dangling cash in front of desperate politicians.

In 1994, according to the Centre for Responsive Politics, the average winner of a seat in the lower House of Representatives spent $516,126 on his or her election. The job pays $133,000 a year. There must be some reason why it makes sense to spend half a million dollars for a job which pays $133,000, but most Americans cannot imagine what that reason could be. Author

Martin Gross describes it as the most convoluted, piously corrupt political system in history. According to Mr Gross, about $200 million a year of 'soft money' – that is, the money which slips through the 'hard' rules for individual candidates – is spent by the political parties on what the law defines as 'party building' and 'getting out the vote'. Yet, curiously, the more money spent on party building in the past forty years, the less enthusiasm Americans show for these parties. And the more money spent on 'getting out the vote', the more Americans stay away from the polls. Voters sense that the system stinks. They know American democracy is far from dead, but it is weakening fast under the obscene weight of its own corruption.

Cincinnatus, that great hero of Jeffersonian democracy, could never be called from the plough to save the American Republic. He would first have to organize a fundraising dinner, while the barbarians sacked the city.

The result is that American politics increasingly resembles thoroughbred horse-racing. It is fun for the élite, an exciting and expensive game for a tiny minority who can afford to take part, those whose business interests dictate they have to pay money to politicians for access, and those of us in the media who are allowed to watch the spectacle from front row seats. American democracy has become a distortion of what Lincoln promised – not government of the people, by the people, for the people, but by the rich, for the rich, orchestrated by an exclusive group of businesses and lobbyists, politicians and the media. Roughly eight out of ten Americans agree with this dismal point of view.[7]

The disconnection of the American people from the way in which they choose their leaders has become a truly vicious circle: fewer people participate in elections because they do not feel there is any point in being part of the electoral process. That means the political system becomes more unrepresentative of the American people. In consequence, even more people are turned off. The system does not – indeed cannot – represent them. The turnout in the 1996 presidential elections, at around

48 per cent, was the lowest in modern US history, completing a trend of almost steady decline since the Second World War.

A few optimistic commentators argue, bizarrely, that apathy is a sign that all is well in the Republic. Voters apparently did not see any issue compelling enough to make them want to vote, and must therefore be considered content. It is like arguing a department store is so successful no one shops there. Or a joke is so funny no one laughs at it. The number of Americans of voting age in 1996 was 196.5 million. About 93 million actually voted. More than 100 million did not. You have to go back to 1924 – when Calvin Coolidge was elected – to find such a previously poor showing. Those who look on the bright side say the 1920s were economic boom times like the 1990s. Apathy in 1996, like 1924, is therefore to be seen as a symptom of a happy country. This is dangerous nonsense.

The 1924 election turnout figure was 43.8 per cent of all eligible voters, distorted because that was a year in which newly enfranchised women were unfamiliar with voting and regis-tration procedures. In 1924, America was still expanding its democracy, and it took almost another fifty years before all black Americans were entitled to vote in all areas. But in 1996, American democracy is contracting despite efforts to make voter registration easier and an estimated five million new voters.[8]

Rather than being content, the electorate in 1996 was dulled by the constant drumbeat of more than 200 national opinion polls which had predicted a Clinton win all year. The media had anointed the winner. The result was a formality. The obvious crisis of confidence in American political life is recognized by almost every thinking voter in the United States, except those within the political and journalistic élite who are so enamoured of the horse-race they confuse apathy with contentment. Simply put, when more and more people don't participate, you cease to be a democracy.

The politics of 'change' that Bill Clinton had boasted about in 1992 has come to mean that most Americans flick the remote control to change television channels when a politician appears.

By 1996, 'made for TV' Republican and Democratic Conventions gave the American TV networks their lowest prime-time ratings in history. The networks concluded that to keep the attention of butterfly-brained viewers the average 'soundbite' from a presidential candidate – the amount of speech or interview used in a TV report – had to be cut drastically.

In 1968, candidate soundbites on network news reports averaged forty-three seconds of uninterrupted speech. That is about 120 words, or a paragraph. By 1988 it was around ten seconds – a sentence. By 1992, which journalists called the most exciting election for a generation, it dropped again to seven seconds. That is the length of a slogan, little more than a verbal belch. Newspaper quotes were also often clipped. And many candidates have learned to speak in soundbites, turning speeches into bumper-sticker philosophizing because that is apparently what TV journalism 'wants'. Whatever the precise cause, the effect is always the same. Churchill and Roosevelt cut to seven seconds sound like Bugs Bunny. Democracy, which used to be a great drama, is now a series of cartoons punctuated by verbal belching rather than thoughtful commentary. And still the viewers and voters switch off.

Even the 'Republican Revolution' of 1994 was a sham. A mere 38 per cent of those who could have voted in the November 1994 congressional elections did so. Newt Gingrich's 'mandate' for change was even slimmer than Bill Clinton's in 1992. His was a 'landslide' in which few rocks actually fell. An unbelievable 62 per cent of voters stayed away from the polls. If you were hosting a dinner party, a rejection rate of three out of five would signal social disaster. But if you are a political party it is apparently a mandate for a 'Revolution'. Reporters, hot for the big story of Newt's Revolution, missed the really big story: the disconnection between Americans and their political system in the 1990s is so profound it may prove irreversible.

In a democracy everybody has the right to be ignorant and to refuse to take part in the process. But the 1996 study by the Center for National Policy, 'Diagnosing Voter Discontent', demonstrated that apathy, anger and ignorance were the linked and worsening symptoms of America's diseased politics.

'The American political system has been experiencing a level of cynicism and public dissatisfaction that is unusual by historic standards,' the study concluded. Except for citizens who have deep political commitments, many Americans hate politics, cannot be bothered with it, or both. Typically, these voters angrily blame politicians for being unable to fix what ails America, or practise what the report calls 'protective withdrawal' in a 'vicious American cycle whereby feelings of control within one's own personal sphere contrast with feelings of external chaos or lack of control'.

That means America, a can-do country, is finally getting fed up with a can't-do political system. If democracy is to survive, change will have to come at every level, from the way candidates are chosen, the construction of primary elections, the way money is raised and spent, right down to the complicated voting forms, the lack of postal voting and the long queues at some polling stations.

The dreary war of political attrition which began in the ice storm in Louisiana in February ended, at last, at long last, on election day, 5 November 1996. Outside a polling station in Arlington, Virginia, on the other side of the Potomac River from Washington, voters were waiting in a 200-yard-long line to vote. They were desperate to exercise their democratic rights, otherwise they would have joined the 100 million of their fellow countrymen who did not make the effort. But even at this last stage, America's faltering democracy continues to erect barriers to stop voters from participating. This was merely the last off-putting hurdle.

The line moved so slowly everyone was forced to wait for more than an hour to vote, on a workday, in a society which values hard work above all. It reminded me of polling stations in Latin America, the long queues of voters in Nicaragua in 1990, ready to overthrow the Sandinistas. In Arlington, that most modern Washington suburb in this most modern nation, the slow Third World shuffle of voters was a fitting end to a journey through a disillusioned America which had begun in the horizontal sleet of an apathetic Louisiana.

The Arlington crowd was patient and polite, many voters reading books brought for the occasion. A family friend said she waited for more than an hour and then left without voting because she had to pick up her children. Others told of horrific problems of working through the entire gargantuan ballot paper, spending twenty minutes in the voting booth, in some areas electing everyone from the president and senator to members of Congress, governors, local representatives, county commissioners, sheriffs, judges and dogcatchers. Disenchantment with such a system is not surprising. Being satisfied with the system would, in fact, be irrational.

Voters are angry, like the woman tourist in Sanibel Island. They see clearly the threat from the alligator in the pond, yet no one can, or will, do anything about it. Squeezing money out of politics would help. So would postal voting. So would free TV coverage. So would realistic journalism, in which reporters refuse to be sucked into the excitement of a campaign which the American people clearly find boring or repulsive. American anger at the political system is the outrage of impotence in the face of a great beast.

It results in the United States of apathy, but also in the most dangerous belief of the politics of unreason in the 1990s: that the American government has become a conspiracy against the best interests of the American people. The result has been bloodshed.

The Wilburns and the Oklahoma Bombing Conspiracy

Oklahoma City, Oklahoma

The first thing you find difficult to believe about Kathy Wilburn is that she is a grandmother. Kathy is in her early forties with flame red hair and the looks of Jane Fonda. The second thing you find difficult to believe is her assertion that the United States federal government may be part of a conspiracy to murder her grandsons. However much American citizens dislike or despise their government in the 1990s, the idea of officials in a democracy being complicit in the murders of infants seems too much to swallow. But you listen to Kathy and her husband Glenn because their grief demands to be heard.[1]

The Wilburn home is in one of the neat middle-class housing estates that sprawl around Oklahoma City. It is Easter, sunny and cool, just like the day the boys died. Outside the house on a patch of grass a tiny shrine of angels and flowers glints in the sunshine. Glenn is one of those robust gardeners who likes everything manicured and regimented. The lawn is good enough to be a putting green. The hedge is clipped ramrod straight like a row of infantrymen at attention. A weed would not even *think* about poking its head through the soil without written permission.

Kathy opens the door, in jeans and a T-shirt, barefoot. Before visitors sit down they are taken on a tour of the home, in what has become a ritual of grief. The walls are covered with tastefully framed black-and-white publicity photographs and autographs of Kathy's favourite movie stars. There are numerous likenesses of Marilyn Monroe pouting and vamping and dipping to show her cleavage to best advantage. In one of the rooms two full-sized tailor's dummies, a man in formal wear, the woman dressed in white, smile like a display from a bridal shop. I ask Kathy if she makes bridal wear for a living and she laughs. No. It is just part of the decoration. Then I notice more angels, angels everywhere: in the shrine on the grass outside; on the mantelshelf, where two angels made out of painted wood are praying; to the left there is another pair in white plaster, kissing; down below there are still more. And more. And more.

On the wall there is a large painting of two blond-haired angels with white wings. The little one on the left is holding what appears to be the world in his right hand. The bigger one is kissing him, and there is an inscription 'Edye's Angels'. Edye is the Wilburns' daughter, Edye Smith, who lives with them but is not at home today. Edye is twenty-three years old and in photographs looks like her mother's younger sister, flame red hair and high cheekbones. The 'Angels' are Edye's dead sons, Chase, aged three, and Colton, two. Colton was so big you might almost think they were twins.

'And this was their bedroom,' Kathy says. The beds are made neatly as if prepared for their imminent return. Teddy bears and Easter bunnies sit expectantly. Everything, Kathy says, is exactly as they left it on the morning they died. The sound of music suddenly fills the room. Kathy has turned on a tiny carousel in the corner. Multicoloured horses dance up and down to jangling circus music as the carousel, another one of the boys' toys, rotates and plays. The jovial tune makes the room seem eerie, like watching a clown crying in a circus tent.

'This is Colton's last diaper,' Kathy says, pointing to something on a shelf. The diaper urine is dried up and preserved, mummified. 'And these are Chase's skivvies,' she starts to say, nervously unfolding then folding again tiny sets of underwear. Her hands are trembling and Kathy starts to break down, but she quickly regains control, saying it happens three or four times every day. The tour of her home seems as much for her benefit as it is for mine. She wants to talk through her grief, give things names, touch mementoes of Edye's children, play the carousel, in the hope that she will be able to find meaning in the purposeless death of innocents.

In the closet, the boys' clothes are hanging neatly, ready to be worn. The toys are packed, waiting for the grasp of a child's hand. The neatness of the room becomes unbearable without the messiness of children. It is a year since the bombing, and Kathy says that while she has to mourn every day, it will not destroy her. Nothing has been forgotten. Nothing has been thrown away. And nothing about their murder will ever be forgiven. We walk back into the main room, and sit down to talk about the Oklahoma City bombing in which the toddlers and a total of 168 people, including nineteen children, died. There is a kind of escape in such facts. Once you put numbers and names to the horror, you begin to establish order from chaos.

The tons of home-made explosives placed outside the Alfred P. Murrah federal building in downtown Oklahoma City on 19 April 1995 produced the worst domestic terrorist incident in American history. The bomb was so destructive no one is exactly sure how many people were killed – 168 or 167 as some reports suggested, or perhaps even more if there were people at the seat of the explosion who were blown into unrecoverable fragments.

Kathy and her daughter Edye worked together for the US federal government, in the IRS, or Internal Revenue Service, which collects income tax. The IRS office is five blocks from the Alfred P. Murrah federal building. In a country in which taxes are loathed, people pretend it is a swear-word, the 'T' word. The IRS represents for many Americans the worst of the US federal government in Washington, the hand of Big Brother in your pocket. But it is impossible to imagine any rational person thinking IRS workers like Kathy or Edye are enemies of the people with sufficient brutality to want to murder them. The Wilburns are the folks next door. The neighbours you would be glad to have.

On the day of the bombing, a Wednesday, Edye did not want to go to work. She had taken the Monday and Tuesday off with a sore throat and a bad cold. On Wednesday she woke up still feeling lousy, but decided to go to work because that was the day her colleagues in the office had planned to celebrate her birthday. There is a long pause in Kathy's narrative. The unspoken thought is that if Edye had followed her instincts and taken that Wednesday off, her kids would still be alive. Like most of us, Kathy and Edye would have watched the Oklahoma bombing on television, and I would not be sitting in the family's front room discussing the deaths of the two little boys. Kathy starts talking again.

Every morning Chase and Colton were dropped off at the Oklahoma federal building. The children's day care centre inside took the worst of the blast. At 9.02 a.m., when the bomb exploded, government workers could be expected to be at their desks. Among those killed were agents from the US Secret Service, the Drug Enforcement Agency, military recruiters and routine clerks in Social Security or veterans' affairs.

The children were non-combatants in America's cultural, social and religious war, and yet they were killed in the worst act of anger in an increasingly anti-government decade. The little broken bodies of Chase and Colton were found in the rubble, and Kathy, Glenn and Edye have been trying to console themselves by saying that in dying together, 'Chase will watch over his younger brother forever'. There is another long pause while everyone pretends to have something in their eyes.

Eventually Kathy switches on the TV. In one corner of the Wilburns' front room there is a massive screen, the size you see in sports bars for watching baseball games. Kathy sorts through videos of the boys as Glenn fidgets on the couch. They have watched the videos a thousand times, searching for the clue to America's heart of darkness.

'On the news,' Kathy says, 'we saw the pictures of one of their little shoes.' She almost breaks down again, but not quite. She pops a video in the machine as Glenn, who is sitting with his foot resting on his knee, pulls nervously at the toe of his training shoes. He's grey haired, mid-forties, thickset and fit. Not your typical grandfather. He pulls his toe again, stares grimly at the pictures, sucks in his cheeks. You wonder if any of this helps a man to avoid crying.

'That's just before Christmas,' Kathy says, pointing to some fun she videoed with Edye and the boys. Glenn sucks in his cheeks again. His face is white. The tape is running.

'Oh, I didn't did I?' one of the women's voices says on the video in the middle of an unexplained conversation. Either Kathy or Edye is talking on the tape. They sound so alike it is difficult to tell. 'It's December twenty-second. Colton is fixing his hair . . .' The boys brush their teeth, comb their hair or play in an old cardboard box, hiding from the camera, laughing. Kathy pops in another video, and then another until the mind begins to reel. Finally we get to the worst of all, just a few days before the bombing. Chase and Colton have little baskets in their hands. They are running excitedly around the manicured back garden hunting for Easter eggs. The boys are not statistics in the Oklahoma bombing now, not collateral damage in the worst mass murder in American history. They are two flesh-and-blood kids who will never grow up because someone killed them.

Glenn has turned sideways and I cannot see his eyes, but his cheeks are sucked way in and he is pulling hard on his toes. When the video ends, everybody in the room exhales deeply as if we all simultaneously come up for air. Kathy fixes glasses of iced tea and Glenn starts to talk about their crusade. They have begun their own investigation to find out who murdered the boys because they do not trust the FBI, the police and the US federal government to tell them the truth about the bombing. It is one of the most extraordinary ironies of America at the end of the twentieth century. The Oklahoma bombing was an attack on the US federal government by those who despise it and believe Washington is becoming increasingly tyrannical. But such is the distrust of government by ordinary citizens like the Wilburns, that even the victims of the bombing, government workers themselves, do not believe the US government is capable of telling them the truth.

It is the pathology of a country which is sick at heart, the utter disconnection of the government from the governed. It is the cynicism of a rogue worker in George Orwell's Ministry of Truth, or of a communist apparatchik who knows *Pravda* and Tass always distort the figures for the grain harvest. Unchecked, this kind of distrust will conclude with the destruction of the United States, though, in the case of the Wilburns, it has led to an investigation of the cause of the bombing to find out the truth, a logical way of coping with grief.

'People will talk to me,' Glenn says pulling on his toe again, explaining how he has amassed a filing cabinet of information plus a stack of tape recordings of eye-witness accounts of the bombing. 'And if they won't talk to me, they'll talk to Kathy.' He smiles grimly as he admits he has used moral blackmail to try to get at the truth. 'I tell 'em that two of the boys killed in the bombing are my grandsons, and folks just sort of open up.' That is undoubtedly true. After an hour with the Wilburns you would be inclined to tell them your deepest secrets. Kathy hands out the tea and says that any time a family has their children murdered, most people want to help. You demand answers. 'And we're gonna get them,' she says defiantly.

Edye has gone to New York to appear on a television programme for the anniversary of the bombing, to publicize the fact that many questions remain unanswered. The Wilburns laugh when they remember how for months no one wanted to know about the inconsistencies they have found in the government case, but now journalists and talk shows frequently call. They have a rule always to talk to everyone. It is part therapy, part self-interest. They have become a clearing house for the latest information, gossip and strange conspiracy theories about the bombing, passing on information and asking journalists and inquirers in turn to let them know if they uncover anything of interest. This is Conspiracy Central.

The bomb plot involved neo-Nazis, one conspiracy theory says. There was a German, the son of an important politician back home in Germany, living in a religious compound in

Oklahoma called Elohim City. After the bombing he returned to Germany. Then there was a Great Wizard or Grand Dragon of the Ku Klux Klan . . . White Supremacists. Then there is the story of a warning before the bomb went off. Agents from the Bureau of Alcohol Tobacco and Firearms were alerted by their personal pagers not to go into work that morning. The innocent kids were killed but the BATF agents were not. Or how about the story that the Oklahoma City police bomb squad had been mobilized for an all-night operation, but they were stood down before the bombing took place? The conspiracy theories come so thick and fast from Glenn that I cannot write them all down quickly enough.

Kathy switches on another video of Edye being interviewed by CNN shortly after the bombing. Edye is asking why agents from the Bureau of Alcohol Tobacco and Firearms were not killed or injured in the blast. 'Where was the ATF? All fifteen employees survived. They were on the ninth floor . . .' Edye simply wants to know why government agents, the presumed targets of the attack, survived and her children did not. Was there a warning? If so, who got it? Who had prior knowledge? Was there a mistake? There is more CNN video of Edye standing in her boys' bedroom, looking distraught. 'What do you say when people ask you if you have children?' she asks the camera in amazement. 'I *had* children. My children are dead. What do you say?' Then Edye cries uncontrollably and Kathy switches off the video.

The Bureau of Alcohol Tobacco and Firearms, part of the US Treasury department, has a public image of incompetence. It was BATF agents who engineered the spectacularly botched raid on David Koresh's Branch Davidian cult compound at Waco, Texas, in February 1993. The FBI, which has its own growing reputation for incompetence, took over the handling of the Branch Davidian siege and sent in a tank with tear gas to try to end the stand-off. Live on American network television the result, on 19 April 1993, was that the compound caught fire, killing all those inside, including the children of cult members.

Many Americans are in tune with the ideas of Conspiracy Central, believing that the FBI cold-heartedly planned the final conflagration. Those of us who spent a long time in the Texas cow pastures observing the Waco siege, and many hours in the company of US government agents, suspect something quite different. As the government's own inquiry concluded, Waco was almost certainly just another botched job by the FBI which does not live up to the image glamorized by Hollywood.

In the 1990s the FBI and BATF have bounced from one public failure to another. In August 1992, FBI agents shot and killed the wife and son of a white separatist, Randy Weaver, at his isolated cabin in Ruby Ridge, Idaho, in what became a *cause célèbre* for the far Right. Mrs Weaver was killed while holding an infant in her hands. Randy Weaver's crime was to possess a sawn-off shotgun, which is not so unusual in rural areas of the United States. The FBI not only botched the arrest of Mr Weaver, but senior officials then covered up their errors in a scandal which reached to the top of FBI headquarters. And it was not the only one. After the bombing of the Olympic Games in Atlanta in the summer of 1996, the FBI focused their attention on the security guard, Richard Jewell, who discovered the bomb. News leaked. The FBI was eventually forced publicly to clear Mr Jewell of any involvement. But beyond this humiliation, it was revealed that agents tried to trap Mr Jewell into waiving his legal rights by pretending they wanted to make a 'training video' on how he discovered the bomb. This was egregious FBI arrogance and duplicity, producing yet another internal inquiry. At the same time the agency was riven by internal dissent over its famous crime labs.

FBI laboratories are used to provide forensic evidence in the most famous criminal cases in the United States and beyond – the downing of the Pan Am 103 jumbo jet over Lockerbie, Scotland, or the bombing of the World Trade Center in New York. One of the leading FBI forensic scientists publicly alleged that the crime labs were sloppily and incompetently run, and that some of his colleagues twisted scientific evidence to help the prosecution in important cases. Another embarrassing inquiry. In January 1997, after a damning Department of Justice report, the FBI transferred four senior employees, including the heads of the chemistry and explosives units. The investigation concluded that bags of evidence in the Oklahoma City bombing case were among those mishandled, mislabelled and mixed up. Then there was Waco and the deaths of children inside the Branch Davidian compound. Yet another inquiry. There was even the strange case of the FBI agent in the White House who published memoirs betraying his position of trust by retelling old rumours and sleazy stories about President and Mrs Clinton.

Added together, by the late 1990s, FBI agents who were supposed to be defenders of American liberty began to look like the average shady secret policemen from cold war Eastern Europe: over-zealous, over armed, under-intelligent and prepared to do almost anything to cover their own incompetence.

In response to the Wilburns' inquiries and cataloguing of conspiracy theories, the FBI and other US government agencies routinely denied that anyone received prior warning of the Oklahoma bombing. BATF agents were injured by the blast, contrary to Edye Smith's assertions. Secret Service agents, a sister operation to the BATF and also part of the US Treasury department, were killed in the bombing. It is inconceivable, according to the official version of events, that the BATF would be tipped off about an impending attack and not warn other people, including the Secret Service.

The room in the Wilburns' house is silent for a few minutes until I tell Glenn about the official denials of a conspiracy. He shrugs his big shoulders and replies that he believes very little from official sources. Why would anyone think the government was telling the truth? Trust in the US federal government has become one of the most notable casualties of the United States of Anger. I switch tack and ask him how he conducts his own private investigation. He leads me into the kitchen where he sorts through a pile of cassette recordings. The official version, he says, is that two people have been charged with the Oklahoma bombing — two drifters who were once US Army buddies, Tim McVeigh and Terry Nichols. Nichols, even the prosecution accepts, was *not* in Oklahoma City at the time of the bombing.

That means, Glenn says with bitter sarcasm, that McVeigh — whom he describes as an 'idiot' — somehow drove a rented Ryder truck filled with home-made explosives all the way from Kansas to Oklahoma City without blowing himself up. Then he found a parking space right in front of a busy office building during rush hour, detonated the bomb and escaped in his own Ford Mercury Marquis car, all by himself. Glenn is disgusted at the arrogance of the FBI assuming the American public is so stupid it will swallow this story. He points out that the 'master terrorist' McVeigh, who has achieved all these extraordinary things, is nevertheless so stupid as to drive a car without a rear licence plate. Tim McVeigh was arrested not as a result of detective work by the FBI but because an alert Highway Patrol officer pulled him over about the licence plate and then charged him with illegal possession of a firearm. It was ninety minutes after the bombing. McVeigh was ninety miles from Oklahoma City. The speed limit was fifty-five miles an hour, about a mile a minute.

Glenn is shaking with anger at the absurdity of the prosecution case. He takes a deep breath and tells me how he got one witness, Kyle Hunt, to talk. Mr Hunt was — like most of those Glenn confronted — extremely reluctant. 'Wouldn't talk to me at first,' Glenn says, finding the right tape of their telephone conversation and popping it into a player. On the tape Glenn very politely introduces himself to Kyle Hunt as someone whose grandchildren were killed in the bombing. 'And I was given your name.'

Kyle Hunt wants none of this. He has been interviewed by the FBI who have warned witnesses not to talk about the case. 'I really don't want to discuss it over the phone,' Mr Hunt's tape-recorded voice pleads. He would prefer to 'confine my comments to the authorities'.

'The authorities didn't have grandsons in that building,' Glenn politely insists. 'And I *did*. I'm having to run over people to get at the truth.'

The argument is so compelling that within minutes Glenn has cracked open Kyle Hunt like a can of Budweiser. 'I don't want to do anything to jeopardize the investigation,' Mr Hunt protests feebly. 'What I saw is just a minute part . . .'

And then he tells his story.

He was driving in the vicinity of the Alfred P. Murrah federal building half an hour before the bomb went off. He saw a Ryder truck. The prosecution case was that in pursuit of anti-government grudges, specifically the destruction of the Branch Davidian religious compound at Waco on 19 April 1993, McVeigh and Nichols conspired to blow up the Murrah federal building exactly two years later with the bomb in the truck. On the tape, Kyle Hunt is now singing like a canary. He saw someone driving a car behind the truck. There was a total of four people involved, McVeigh and three others. One of them was a 'guy in the back seat . . . with long hair, in total contrast to McVeigh.' McVeigh looked like a clean-cut soldier. The other fellow was a hell's angel biker type or a hippy.

'Caucasians?' Glenn asks.

'They both were,' Kyle Hunt confirms, saying he saw all this at the intersection of Broadway and Main in downtown Oklahoma City, at 8.35 a.m., half an hour before the bomb exploded.

Glenn stops the tape and looks at me, triumphantly. For the first time a smile, a real smile, cracks his white face. He has proved to his own satisfaction that the prosecution case stinks, that there was definitely a wider conspiracy. Terry Nichols was back home in Kansas. McVeigh was in Oklahoma City with – depending on which of Glenn's witnesses you prefer – one, two, three, maybe four other people. Kyle Hunt says on the tape that McVeigh was driving a car, 'an old four-door Ford product' – presumably the Mercury Marquis. Hunt remembers the time because 'I was late for an 8.30 appointment'.

He remembers McVeigh because of his striking skinhead appearance and demeanour. When Hunt looked at him in the traffic 'I got that icy-cold go-to-hell look.'

'Tim's not a very smart man,' Glenn repeats, showing me pictures of McVeigh he obtained from 'a source' in the military facility where McVeigh was originally held. 'He's an idiot, a real idiot . . . He's a sergeant, not an officer.'

'Of all the people that we interviewed,' Kathy continues, 'who saw McVeigh that morning, *no one* saw McVeigh alone. *Everyone* saw him with someone.'

Stephen Jones, McVeigh's lawyer, always planned to use this kind of evidence to muddy the prosecution case. Jones is well respected in Oklahoma. He is courtly, conservative and shrewd, conversing just as easily about the strengths of Margaret Thatcher as the problems facing the Republicans in Congress in Washington. He dresses in dark blue pinstripes and lawyerly red shirts with white collars and sober ties. 'Since 1968,' Jones told me before the trial, 'there has been no major terrorist event in the world that was the result of two men. Terrorism requires an infrastructure.'

Pointing to the history of large home-made bombs in Northern Ireland, Jones said that such explosives are inherently unstable and prone to blowing up the people who are trying to deliver them. 'We are supposed to believe,' he scoffed of the prosecution case, 'that Tim McVeigh and Tim McVeigh *alone* drove a deadly 5,000-pound bomb 300 miles without blowing himself up . . . In the words of one of your [British] experts, I'm not saying your chaps can't do it. I'm just saying that no one has ever done it like that before. And if they were able to do it, would you make them available to every Western security service so we can find out how they did it? Because no one else has been able to do it that way though God knows they have tried.'

One of the curiosities of the proceedings was that, from the earliest stages, McVeigh's defence lawyer and the Wilburns *agreed* about the inadequacies of the government case. Another was how resourceful the Wilburns, the grandparents next door, proved to be in conducting their own investigation.

As de Tocqueville observed, the ordinary citizens of the United States are confident they can achieve – and often do achieve –

remarkable things, while those who are supposed to lead them are far less impressive. The Wilburns passed on to interested journalists the names and telephone numbers of those of their 'witnesses' who were prepared to talk publicly. One, Dave Snyder, agreed to meet at a street corner in Oklahoma City's 'Bricktown' close to where he claims he saw the bombers. Bricktown is a Victorian red-brick warehouse district, now modernized and full of classy bars, restaurants and brew-pubs. Dave is smoking a cigarette and wearing a blue denim jacket with a carelessly buttoned denim bib top. He has a small moustache and there are wrinkles round his eyes as he concentrates on his story. On the morning of the bombing Dave was waiting for two men to deliver a truckload of computer supplies, standing on the street as we are doing now. Dave went to the north side of the building and looked up to the intersection of Oklahoma Avenue and Sheridan Avenue.

'I seen a Ryder truck coming from the east,' he explains, pointing and squinting in the early morning sunshine. 'When the truck turned wide as if it had a heavy load, I said, yessir, they had something in there.' Assuming this was his anticipated load of computers, Snyder stepped out to greet it when 'the passenger gives me this go-to-hell kind of look . . . this is Tim McVeigh. He's in the passenger seat, fifteen feet from me. I am 100 per cent sure.'

Remarkably, Snyder and Kyle Hunt both describe Tim McVeigh in almost the same words. Snyder admits he was in a bad mood that morning and he muttered something to the scowling short-haired passenger. When I asked what he said, he smiled.

'You really want to hear it?'

'Sure.'

'I told him, f*** you, you skinhead looking motherf***er.'

It seemed an adequate description of the man convicted and sentenced to death for the Oklahoma City bombing. But if McVeigh was the passenger, then the riddle continued. Who was the driver? 'He could be Cuban, Latino, he had a pretty good tan,' Snyder asserts. 'This man has olive-coloured skin and a thin pencil moustache shaved close to the lips like in the old gangster movies.'

Snyder told his sister, an amateur artist, and she came up with a sketch of the mystery man which he showed me. 'That man is still walking around. He's not in jail.'

Back in Glenn and Kathy's house another journalist calls Conspiracy Central asking for directions to where they live. He has been out talking to one of the former members of the Grand Jury originally empanelled to assess the evidence against McVeigh and Nichols. The Grand Jury indicted those two together with 'others unknown', but Glenn insists that the FBI is discounting the evidence of other conspirators. He refuses to give government agents the benefit of the doubt for what they have achieved, tracking down the Ryder truck, arresting McVeigh and Nichols.

While Glenn is offering directions to the visiting reporter, I walk back out into the hallway and start looking at the photographs on the walls. There is a personal letter from President Clinton dated 15 May 1995. It reads, 'I will not rest until the perpetrators of this evil are brought to justice.' The letter is beautifully framed alongside the photos of Chase and Colton and Marilyn Monroe in a clinging evening dress. When Glenn gets off the phone I mention the Clinton letter and he scoffs. The president, he says reciting the familiar refrain, is a 'draft-dodging, pot-smoking, womanizer'. I decided this was a topic best avoided and turned again to Glenn's collection of conspiracy theories.

'There was a bomb squad downtown,' he asserts, pursuing the idea that the government had prior knowledge of an attack.

'No,' I contradict him. 'There was no bomb squad downtown according to the local Oklahoma City Police Department, Oklahoma Highway Patrol and all the other agencies involved.'

Glenn refuses to believe their denials. 'I want to know *why* the bomb squad was there.'

Our conversation takes a turn for the worse. An old dismissive phrase about conspiracy theories comes to mind: 'If I had never

believed it, I would not have seen it with my own mind.' Trying
to counter Glenn's earnest beliefs with facts is like trying to
persuade him that the Loch Ness Monster does not exist. He is
trying to show me the suspicious ripples.

'Does that mean that *six* witnesses fabricated their stories?'
he shoots back. Six witnesses have told the Wilburns that there
was some kind of a sting operation the night before the bombing.
It involved, Glenn assures me, fifteen to seventeen ATF agents
brought in from out of town. They expected the Murrah federal
building to be blown up at 3 a.m., when no one was inside. There
was some kind of government informant connected to the bombers
and this person tipped them off. But, I repeat, every single federal
agency or government official denies all of this. It is simply not
true. 'Ah-ha,' Glenn says. 'They would say that, wouldn't they?
The government agencies are lying about what happened because
the truth will embarrass them. The US government lied to its
citizens about Watergate. About the Vietnam war. About the Iran-
Contra affair. Why would it now be telling the truth?'

I take a deep breath. Conspiracy theories are not *logical*
arguments. They are *theological* arguments. They are snake-
handling politics, as always turning upon the triumph of belief
over reason. But I admit to Glenn that he has a compelling basis
to be extremely sceptical of the official view of this case. We
seem to be getting along again. Glenn points out that the FBI
originally released a wanted poster showing Tim McVeigh as
'John Doe Number One', plus a thickset man in a baseball cap,
'John Doe Number Two'. The FBI are no longer publicly
interested in John Doe Number Two. How come?

'There's not just a John Doe Two,' Glenn explains. 'There's a
John Doe Two, Three, Four and possibly Five.'

'I want the truth,' Kathy butts in. 'I don't want this to happen
to anyone else.'

The drive and compulsion of the Wilburns is extraordinary.
And it is not necessary to believe all their theories to recognize
that they represent a uniquely American phenomenon in the
1990s: the outraged, angry citizens who doubt the institutions of

their own country, a politicized version of the woman angry about the alligator on Sanibel Island.

In the 1960s it was the young and the Left who thought the US federal government had betrayed the American Ideal over Vietnam. In the 1990s it is grandparents like the Wilburns, taxpayers not hippies, political conservatives not liberals. And the decency of the Wilburns points to the worst of the American sickness. Solid, patriotic citizens do not trust the institutions of their own government to tell them the truth about a matter of life and death. No democracy can survive such anger and distrust indefinitely. When President Clinton talks of 'building a bridge to the twenty-first century', it is the bridge of trust between the citizens of the United States and their own government which is most in need of construction or repair.

The Governor of Oklahoma, Frank Keating, himself a former FBI agent, is critical of the Wilburns' conspiracy theories. But even he admits that there may well have been a wider conspiracy behind the bombing.

'It *could* be two people,' he told me in the spring of 1996. 'It could be three people. It could be five people. I don't think it's possible to have a very large conspiracy because of the horror of this, everybody would be pointing the finger at everybody else. I think it's probably very small. Could there be other people? Yes . . . But the government has got to go with what it has got. And it's got two defendants now and has got to try them, win or lose.' But, in another curious twist, the anger of Kathy and Glenn towards the US government is not far removed from the anger of Tim McVeigh himself. McVeigh, as everyone who followed the Oklahoma bombing trial knows, is a veteran of the Gulf war. But when the war ended, unlike the veterans of the Second World War or Korea, unlike the immigrant from Belfast, Alex Munro of Levittown who easily found a well-paid job, Tim McVeigh never did. The rules of the old order had collapsed by the time McVeigh left the US Army.

McVeigh returned to his family home in upstate New York and wrote angry, paranoid letters to the local newspaper, the

Lockport Union Sun and Journal, about the decline of his country. The first letter was published on 11 February 1992, a year after victory in the Gulf war, while the economy of the United States was still in recession, and while Governor Bill Clinton was fighting to become the Democratic presidential nominee.

This was the time during which President Bush could still optimistically proclaim the charms of a New World Order, and publicly contrast his 'character' with that of Bill Clinton. Yet voters knew that it was in Mr Bush's 'character' to make the campaign promise: 'Read My Lips – No New Taxes' in 1988, then break it when he was elected.

'Taxes are a joke,' Tim McVeigh wrote in his letter to the newspaper. 'Regardless of what a political candidate "promises" they will increase ... The "American Dream" of the middle class has all but disappeared, substituted with people struggling just to buy next week's groceries ... Politicians are out of control. Their yearly salaries are more than an average person will see in a lifetime.'[2] So far, McVeigh's letter could have been written by the Wilburns or most of the other middle-class government sceptics who have featured in this book. He sounds like the diners in Choo Choo Caron's New Hampshire restaurant, or Choo Choo himself. Claude Morin could have written the letter. Dr Jim in Arkansas. The car workers in Dayton or Cleveland, Ohio. Jerry Dupke and Bill Visnaw in Macomb County, Michigan. But then McVeigh's letter goes much further, to the heart of the United States of Anger.

'Racism on the rise? You had better believe it! America's frustrations venting themselves? Is it a valid frustration? Who is to blame for the mess? At a point when the world has seen Communism falter as an imperfect system to manage people, democracy seems to be headed down the same road.' Tim McVeigh, former model soldier, a man who had served his democratically elected government, pushes towards the angriest of views – that American democracy is a sham, and in any event doomed.

McVeigh's letter rambles about a 'perfect utopian government', echoing the views of European extremists who see fascism as a *'terza posizione'*, a third position, between Communism and failing democracy. McVeigh then strongly asserts the worst of the doom-mongering views: 'America is in serious decline!' he writes.

In the letter's last paragraph he gives an idea how the decline might be reversed. The day the Waco siege ended and the day of the Oklahoma bombing, 19 April, is known on the right-wing fringes of American society as 'Patriots' Day', the anniversary of one of the events in the war against the British colonial masters. McVeigh appears to suggest that the crisis of the United States in the 1990s is as profound as any faced by the Patriots of 1776. He refers to the dumping of tea in Boston harbour as a protest against British taxes. 'We have no proverbial tea to dump,' his letter says. 'Should we instead sink a ship full of Japanese imports? Is a civil war imminent? Do we have to shed blood to reform the current system? I hope it doesn't come to that. *But it might.*' (My italics.)

These are the words of an extremely angry American, a man who was finally convicted for the worst act of domestic terrorism in American history. But what is so startling is how commonplace most of what he wrote seems to be in the 1990s. Even as the US economy swung back from the recession of 1991, the fears of Tim McVeigh remain suffused through the society of the United States – fear of decline from Empire, a corrupt democracy, fraudulent politicians, an unfair economy, foreign enemies and bloodshed. His anger at the US government is, with the most bitter of ironies, shared even by some of the families of the victims of the bombing.

I left the Wilburns' house hoping that Glenn, Kathy and Edye could find out whatever it was they needed to bring them peace, though no amount of understanding can bring true forgiveness of the murderer of children. And real peace is impossible for a country facing a crisis of confidence about everything that makes America *America*. This is the ultimate disconnection of government from people. In a successful democracy, governments do not have to be popular. They merely have to be respected as a legitimate expression of the will of the people.

If government itself seems illegitimate and pernicious to middle-income grandparents like the Wilburns of Oklahoma City, then American democracy is in very great difficulty. This is not healthy scepticism in the American tradition of insisting that no politician is a king and no one above rebuke. It is a national neurosis, the unhealthy belief that the government does not merely make mistakes but actively conspires against its own citizens. Such obsessions have always been on the fringes of American politics – historian Richard Hofstadter's 'paranoid style'. But this is a modern and dangerous variant. A culture of conspiracies has captured the minds of mainstream middle-class families like the Wilburns. It has replaced the red scare fear of Communism with a fed scare fear of the federal government.

In the bedroom of Chase and Colton the music of the carousel is still tinkling. The boys are laughing on videotape. The faces of two little angels look down from the walls. On the big television screen the image of a child's shoe emerges from the rubble. Glenn and Kathy are illuminated, flickering grim and grey, launched on an unending mission for the truth. It is a truth so terrible that their own government dare not speak its name.

Conspiracy Culture from Red Scare to Fed Scare

'The conspiracy theory of society ... comes from abandoning God, and then asking: "Who is in his place?"'

Karl Popper[1]

Washington DC

The most pernicious sign of anger and discontent towards the American political system in the 1990s is that the United States federal government has taken over from Communism as the institution which Americans most often ridicule, distrust, despise and occasionally fear. Two out of three Americans, when asked to describe the biggest threat to the United States in 1994, answered 'Big Government'. Forty years earlier only 16 per cent of Americans named 'Big Government' as a threat. Opinion polls show that three out of four voters do not trust their government to do the right thing when making decisions. Almost four out of five think the government is run mostly by special interests looking out for themselves, while one in five thinks the major institutions of the United States are 'involved in a conspiracy'. Anti-government sentiment and suspicions about conspiracies are particularly strong in small-town America, most notably among middle-income people like the Wilburns rather than the poor.[2]

The result is that, to the angriest Americans, the word 'Washington' is no longer merely a place. It is a state of mind. 'Washington' is angry shorthand for bureaucracy and even repression in the way the word 'Kremlin' was to Americans in the 1950s and

60s. And of all the many reasons why ordinary Americans are convinced their own government is guilty of lying and incompetence, the most important is that *frequently they are proved right.*

The baby boom generation grew up being lied to about the Vietnam war and Watergate, and has subsequently witnessed the endless machinations of the Whitewater affair, or the Iran-Contra conspiracy. Government officials employed by different administrations and from different parties have frequently appeared devious, duplicitous and occasionally been found guilty of serious criminal offences. Statements from politicians are routinely regarded as self-serving lies.

'Read My Lips, No New Taxes,' Vice-President George Bush promised when seeking election to the presidency in 1988. Two years later, when he raised taxes after all, Washington comedians had fun rewriting the slogan. 'Read My Lips,' they joked. 'I Lied.'

Candidate Clinton followed the same pattern. He promised a 'middle-class tax cut' in 1992. He raised taxes in 1993. By the time it was Bob Dole's turn to promise an election year tax cut in 1996, after a career built on fiscally responsible deficit reduction, Americans this time refused to believe him.

Broken political promises are a common failing in all democracies. But what is uniquely American is the way in which prejudices against the institutions of government infuse popular culture. A significant minority of Americans swallow the most outlandish anti-government conspiracy theories in a way which is astonishing and truly alarming. In the absence of a convincing foreign enemy, what was once a 'red scare' during the cold war – fear of Communists subverting the United States and the American way of life – has become a 'fed scare', fear of the US federal government doing the same thing.

The fed scare is yet another manifestation of snake-handling politics, the triumph of belief beyond all reason. Modern conspiracy theories transport Americans into a new realm of public paranoia which makes popular culture on the brink of the twenty-first century seem no more sophisticated than a group of credulous citizens gossiping round the village pump in Salem, Massachusetts, about the satanic conspiracy of the local witches. The gossip stays the same. Only the identity of the witches has changed over the centuries. The supposed witches burned after the infamous seventeenth-century Salem trials were believed to be handmaidens of the Devil. By the 1940s and 50s the witches had traded in their broomsticks for Lenin pins, for John Lennon glasses in the 1960s and 70s, and now in the 1990s they carry White House passes or FBI and CIA identification tags. The 1950s red scare witches and villains of American nightmares were those identified by the US diplomat George Kennan in his famous article in *Foreign Affairs* at the end of the Second World War, which became the intellectual blueprint for the cold war policy of 'containing' Moscow. Kennan's thesis was that Soviet Communism would never rest until it dominated the world. It was indeed a conspiracy theory. But behind it there was a genuine conspiracy.[3]

President Truman and all subsequent administrations recognized the threat and mobilized the entire country to ensure that America survived by first containing, then defeating 'Godless Communism' and the 'Evil Empire'. The witches of the period were not merely foreign Communists but also traitors *within* the United States, spies who sold atomic bomb secrets to Moscow or betrayed Western agents, or complicit 'fellow travellers'. In this cold war atmosphere, enthusiasm for finding real villains degenerated into the red scare. Artists and writers were blacklisted for failing to co-operate with Senator Joe McCarthy's unprincipled investigations. Those not sufficiently enthusiastic about the witch-hunt were regarded as 'soft on Communism' as McCarthy's campaign of half-digested facts and innuendo rolled through government agencies, most notably the State Department and the Pentagon. The bizarre public spectacle of McCarthy's public hearings on Capitol Hill continued until the Senator was finally discredited, the period excoriated as a repeat of the Salem witch trials in Arthur Miller's play *The Crucible*.

These scariest days of the cold war lasted well into the 1960s. In 1964 it was still possible for a presidential candidate, Senator Barry Goldwater, to declare that 'Extremism in the defence of liberty is no vice.' Popular sentiment clearly indicated that however badly the US government occasionally behaved, Moscow was much worse. In a wartime atmosphere, the public was generally willing to give US government officials the benefit of the doubt. But by the 1990s that had changed completely. 'Extremism in the defence of liberty' became the excuse for the creation of armed and dangerous anti-government militias, and even for the bombing of the Oklahoma federal building.

Three current examples of fed scare and conspiracy culture give an idea of the depth of passion and credulity of America's 1990s government haters: the Japanese attack on Pearl Harbor in 1941, the assassination of President John F. Kennedy in 1963 and, finally, the Oklahoma bombing in 1995. Each event was shocking in its wickedness. People say they remember exactly what they were doing when they heard the news. And, in each case, significant sections of the American public believe that the Washington élite is covering up the 'real' story.

The Pearl Harbor conspiracy theory is that President Franklin Roosevelt *knew* that the Japanese were about to launch their 'surprise' attack, but did nothing to prevent it. Roosevelt was so wicked, or so wedded to the idea that the end justifies the means, he calculated that only the shock of 'the day that will live in infamy' could bomb the isolationists in Congress into joining the Second World War. Because the Pearl Harbor garrison was unprepared, 2,397 American lives were lost in the process.

To believe this, you have to be prepared to make one jump beyond the routine debunking of national heroes like FDR in the 1980s and 1990s. Like most American conspiracy theories, you have to believe not only in the wickedness of political leaders, you must also assume that the US government is almost Godlike, omniscient and omnipotent. But it is a fallen god, the Great Satan so hated by the Ayatollah's followers in Iran. In fact, the historical evidence that Roosevelt had an inkling of an attack on Pearl Harbor is extremely shaky, but there is enough to stir the pot of credulity. Besides, like all conspiracy theories, it can never be *disproved*. If the facts do not fit the conspiracy theory then that *must* be because the US federal government has 'covered up' evidence of its own wickedness. In the generation after Watergate, citizens know that cover-ups by the political élite are all too credible.

Conspiracy number two, twenty-two years later, is more familiar – the Kennedy assassination stories. They declare that a lone gunman, Lee Harvey Oswald, could not have killed the president. The Kennedy Conspiracy had to be (take your pick) the CIA, the Russians, the Cubans, the Vietnamese, the Pentagon, the Mafia, Vice-President Lyndon Johnson or an exotic stack of others. In every conspiracy scenario, US government agents were either part of the plot or later found out 'the truth about Kennedy', and will not level with American citizens. Another cover-up. The convenient murder of Oswald by Jack Ruby, seen on television all across the world, lends credence either to the wickedness of US government officials or to their astonishing incompetence. And the subsequent assassinations of Robert Kennedy, Martin Luther King and Malcolm X are (depending on your pick of the conspiracies and cover-ups) all interconnected sub-plots in this Grand Unified Conspiracy Theory, directed by Dark Forces within the United States with the willing complicity of the federal government.

We will return to the third example of a fed scare, the Oklahoma bombing conspiracy, in a moment. But from these first two examples it becomes obvious that the fed scare in the 1990s is not on the wild fringes of popular culture. Like the red scare it has become part of the everyday life of Hollywood movies, network TV, books and journalism. Paranoia about the US government has been accepted as part of the cultural mainstream, with profound implications for American government in the twenty-first century.

Oliver Stone is a leading propagandist of fed scare stories and America's conspiracy culture. He is among the most celebrated Hollywood film directors of his generation and politically on the Left. Stone's movie about the Kennedy assassination, *JFK*, and references in *Nixon* to a cabal of right-wingers who propelled Richard Nixon to power in 1968, are not 'histories'. They are the popularization of political paranoia far beyond any established facts. Such paranoia undoubtedly resonates at a time when so many Americans are angry and unsettled, believing their government actively works against their interests, and when the demonstrable facts about American politics are uninspiring and tainted with corruption. Yet, however bad things are, it is as if Americans have an appetite to go further, desperate to believe the worst about the corruption of their government and society.

Comparing popular treatments of the 1990s fed scare with the 1960s red scare is instructive. In the 1960s, in the aftermath of the Cuban missile crisis and while Vietnam was resulting in countless Americans being brought home in body bags in a proxy war against the red menace, the reality of the superpower struggle was often too brutal for popular television drama. We were, after all, just a few minutes away from nuclear annihilation. A typically escapist TV melodrama of the time was *The Man from U.N.C.L.E.* The heroes were a Russian and an American in an unlikely co-operation of good guys against evil, symbolized by the bad guys of an organization called T.H.R.U.S.H. When Americans wanted to scare themselves with reality, they contemplated mutually assured destruction and the prospect of a new ice age after a nuclear attack, a 'nuclear winter', or they worried about Communists managing to get their man into a position of power in *The Manchurian Candidate*.

By the time Hollywood began to question the legitimacy of the US government's conduct in the cold war it was in cult critiques like the satire *Dr Strangelove*, in which the most lunatic, wicked, crazy characters take over the levers of power in Washington. But by the 1990s, the premiss of *Dr Strangelove* had moved from the edges of cult satire to the centre of popular entertainment.

The heroes of the *X Files*, an equivalent kind of popular escapist TV melodrama to *The Man from U.N.C.L.E.*, spend their time tracking down the new enemies of freedom and the American people. The most dangerous enemies are *within the US government itself*. One of the first things viewers see as the opening credits roll on the *X Files* is a supposed newspaper headline 'Government Denies Knowledge'. We are, from the beginning, deep in conspiracy culture where the big bad government is covering up.

In a typical episode the heroine, Agent Scully, is fighting not Communism but the US Senate Intelligence Committee. The senators are bovine or wicked and she speaks of 'powerful men in this government who flout the law with impunity'. There is, Agent Scully says with all the anger of a Tim McVeigh, a 'culture of lawlessness' in the US government where men pursue 'secret policies' which have led to numerous mysterious crimes. In the same episode it is revealed that Saddam Hussein used a particular kind of germ warfare in the Gulf war, a 'black cancer'.

The US government knew about 'black cancer' but kept it secret amid talk of a 'wide-ranging conspiracy', reinforcing the worst interpretation of the real-life mystery of the Gulf war syndrome. The senators, as Agent Scully observes, are *lawyers*. Lawyers and politicians are the new insult words of the fed scare, the modern equivalent of calling someone a 'Commie'. They are not interested in the truth of her testimony. Instead they want her to betray the whereabouts of her colleague, Agent Mulder. She refuses and when she ends up in jail it is not at the hands of wicked Communists or the evil men of T.H.R.U.S.H. It is because *her own government* imprisons her for contempt of Congress.[4]

The Manichean struggle between good and evil is no longer democracy versus Communist tyranny. In the 1990s it is the American people versus their despotic, corrupt government. Consider this *X Files* script: 'How can we account for our present situation unless we believe that men high in this government are concerting to deliver us to disaster? This must be a project of a great conspiracy, a conspiracy on such a scale so immense as to dwarf any previous such venture in the history of man.'

Actually, that is *not* an *X Files* script, though it could be. It comes from Senator Joe McCarthy defending his anti-Communist witch-hunt in 1951. Same script. Different conspiracy. Different witches.[5]

Or consider the 1996 Hollywood summer blockbuster movie, *Independence Day*, in which aliens try to destroy the earth. The key plot twist again involves the wickedness or stupidity of the US government. It is a hoary fed scare story, that in the 1940s and 50s alien spacecraft crash-landed in the United States, most notably at Roswell, New Mexico. The US government 'covered up' evidence of the UFO sightings. In *Independence Day* the alien spaceship is captured and held in a top-secret government facility in Nevada known as 'Area 51', in the care of a long-haired, idiotic government scientist. The defence secretary, formerly with the CIA, knew about the alien craft and never told the president. The message is that the US government is so wickedly out of control it almost allowed aliens to destroy the world.

Or there is the Sean Connery movie, *The Rock*, in which a group of US soldiers takes over Alcatraz and threatens a chemical gas attack against the city of San Francisco unless the president tells the American people 'the truth' about MIAs – soldiers missing in action in Vietnam and elsewhere.

This is one of the most persistent anti-government conspiracy stories of the past twenty-five years. In real life, the families of US servicemen still unaccounted for in South-East Asia have been told numerous tales of 'Caucasian' prisoners being sighted in remote areas of Laos and Vietnam long after the war ended. The Pentagon is constantly bombarded with inquiries from families and reporters to 'tell the truth' about these supposed living MIAs.

In the movie version of the conspiracy tale, the end comes when the hero takes possession of secret FBI files. In the closing dialogue he asks his wife if she would like to know who really killed President Kennedy. We never hear the answer.

These examples, typical of dozens of others from America's conspiracy culture, demonstrate how the cold war cult satire characters of *Dr Strangelove* – mad government scientists, wicked defence officials, incompetent bureaucrats – are now the commonplace fodder of Hollywood fed scares. In the 1990s, movie scriptwriters do not have to explain *why* the US government is useless or out to get you. It is taken for granted by audiences in the same way that no Second World War movie ever had to explain that the Nazis were the bad guys, and no 1950s movie ever had to point out that the Commies were bent on taking over the world. No longer do we worry about reds under the bed. We worry about feds under the bed. In comedies it is much the same. In Eddie Murphy's *The Honorable Gentleman* the joke is that Murphy is a confidence trickster who ends up in Congress. To no one's surprise he fits right in. They are *all* crooks in Washington, right? As the cartoon character, Pogo, famously put it, we have seen the enemy, and it is *us*.

The anti-government backlash, with hindsight, now looks inevitable. For sixty years since the New Deal the American government expanded to meet the challenge of the Great Depression followed by the totalitarian threats of Japan, Nazism and Communism. The threats have gone. The beast of government remains. There is no peace dividend, no significant shrinkage in the size of government and no public confidence that the government giant is working in the interests of the American people. Conspiracy culture and the 'paranoid style' have always been part of the American tradition. They thrive in the 1990s in a more devastating anti-government fashion than at any time in history because Hollywood directors, TV producers, thriller writers and journalists scent a marketing opportunity in public fear and disillusionment with government for their own fed scare tales.

For example, in 1996, black communities in the United States were roiled by reports that the CIA was behind the crack cocaine epidemic. The story, first reported in the *San Jose Mercury News*, became front page news all over the United States. The story claimed US government officials knew about or sanctioned cocaine shipments as part of the Iran-Contra affair. Like most fed scares this one had been rumoured for years without any compelling proof. The more journalists calmly examined the facts, the more obvious the conclusion: the story was wrong.

Yet the key to understanding why such an appalling, unproven conspiracy is still believed despite the lack of evidence, is simple. The *established* facts about US government actions in the Iran-Contra affair are eccentric enough to make one wonder what else government officials were capable of. The Iran-Contra plot was dreamed up by Marine Colonel Oliver North and his colleagues in the Old Executive office building next to the White House. North called it a 'neat idea'. It was a top-secret real-life conspiracy in which US government agents sold weapons to the Iranians, despite their pariah-regime status as a sponsor of terrorism. Profits from arms sales were then channelled to the Contra guerrillas trying to overthrow the leftist Sandinistas in Nicaragua. It was about as crackpot a covert operation as one could ever conceive, and when it collapsed Ronald Reagan's administration never completely recovered. In the ensuing investigations everyone admitted the guns were shipped to Nicaragua to help overthrow the Sandinistas. But was cocaine regularly shipped back into the United States by the same people, in the same aircraft, as part of a plot to 'destroy' black inner-city communities?

Almost certainly not. Oliver North strongly denies it – though, of course, Colonel North proudly admits he lied to Congress, so his reputation for veracity is not strong. But the unproved and unlikely cocaine conspiracy fulfils a useful function in America's culture of victims because it is easier to turn the CIA into a scapegoat than to say that hundreds of thousands of ordinary Americans are so degenerate or weak that they crave narcotics.

Those Americans credulous enough to believe the incredible, the believers without reason, find it easy to swallow any of the most recent fed scares, where the US federal government is assumed guilty of *something*. Here is a modest sampling of some of the 1990s politics of unreason:

- White House deputy counsel Vincent Foster was found shot dead in a Washington area park in 1993. The culture of conspiracy cranked itself awake with constant speculation that Foster was murdered, even though countless inquiries – including one chaired by highly partisan Republicans – concluded it was suicide.
- William Dannemeyer, a Republican member of Congress from 1979 to 1992, demanded congressional hearings into more than two dozen 'suspicious deaths' among those 'who hold a connection to President Bill Clinton'. He said in a letter to congressional leaders that the total of such deaths 'can only be described as frightening'.
- *Bill Clinton's Circle of Power*, a video narrated by a long-time Clinton-hater from Arkansas, makes the state under Governor Clinton resemble the carnage of a Mafia war in *The Godfather*. The video suggests darkly that people who irritated Governor Clinton in Little Rock were beaten up, with the obvious implication that the Clintons are employing the same methods in Washington. This notorious fed scare video could be purchased by mail order from one of America's well-known televangelists, the Reverend Jerry Falwell of the 'Moral Majority', a man much respected on the Christian Right.
- When US Commerce Secretary and Clinton friend, Ron Brown, died in a plane crash in the former Yugoslavia, on the anti-government militia computer, radio and fax networks it was suddenly 'common knowledge' that Mr Brown had been murdered.
- Supporters of sometime presidential candidate Lyndon LaRouche claim that the Oklahoma conspiracy was really masterminded by British intelligence. The bombing was apparently part of a royalist plot to weaken the United States and take over America as a way towards domination of the world.
- And that brings us back to the most compelling fed scare of the 1990s, the Oklahoma bombing 'government conspiracy'.

This plot by the American government to blow up its own citizens and workers as a pretext for establishing a tyrannical police state was explained to me by James Nichols, the older brother of Terry Nichols and a friend of Tim McVeigh. In April 1995, a few days after the bombing, James Nichols was arrested. Heavily armed FBI agents in bullet-proof vests stormed into his lonely farm in Decker, Michigan. Tim McVeigh had, for a time, lived there.

After questioning, James Nichols was released without charge, and I met him by accident a year later on a flight to Denver, the city where his brother and Tim McVeigh were jailed prior to their trial. James Nichols readily admitted that he despised the US government, denouncing it as a conspiracy against the American people with all the vitriol of Agent Scully in the *X Files*. For a time James Nichols refused to carry a driving licence and gave up his Social Security card since these 'government documents' amounted to 'control' over his life. He was known around Decker for declaring repeatedly that President Clinton was 'unfit to live, let alone be president'. In 1990 he tried to renounce his American citizenship, like his brother Terry, sending a note to the local county clerk declaring himself 'A non-resident alien, non-foreigner, STRANGER!'

James Nichols is balding, in his early forties, talkative, though with a tenuous grasp of syntax, and the earnestness of someone desperate to persuade you he had been abducted by space aliens. He has staring blue eyes and a grey flecked beard. His voice cracks into a strange falsetto under stress. On the day we met he was wearing a checked cotton shirt and blue jeans, looking every inch the farmer on a big day out. He was travelling with his father, a rheumy-eyed man with a thick beard but no moustache, giving him the appearance of a nineteenth-century preacher of solid Amish stock. Also with them was a third man who hovered around in the background, angry-faced and suspicious, refusing to introduce himself or to become involved in the conversation.

When I confronted him with allegations that bomb-making took place on his farm, James Nichols dismissed the idea, saying it was just 'pop bottle bombs' which he described as 'kids' play'.

It was 'mostly Terry and another friend, not Tim' who were making these 'pop bottle bombs'.

I asked James to describe Tim and Terry. They are 'very nice ... polite ... courteous ... trustworthy ... just average people, both of them are'. Terry is 'very conservative, reserved, a homebody'. Did Terry buy vast quantities of fertilizer to make a bomb? A big smile from James. His brother, he confided, does buy a lot of fertilizer in bulk, but then he repackages it in one- or three-pound bags and resells it. 'The profit margin in that is very nice,' James smiled.

Buying huge amounts of fertilizer makes his brother an entrepreneur, not a mad bomber and mass murderer. So what do Terry and Tim think of the government of the United States? James's voice croaked into a falsetto. '*Out of control* ... The federal government of the United States is *out of control.*' And before I could ask the logical question, he answered it. 'If *that* is being government haters, then a lot of Americans are.'

James goes into a favourite rant, listing the fed scare crimes of the American government – the siege at Waco, Ruby Ridge, and so on. 'Tim promoted the truth about Waco,' he says. And the truth, according to James, Tim and Terry, is that agents of the US federal government attacked a group of law-abiding American citizens in David Koresh's Branch Davidian cult compound, tried to take their guns away, then murdered them in their own home by starting a fire which burned women and children alive.

The Branch Davidians were victims of US government tyranny, and James admits that Tim McVeigh cared most deeply about the innocent victims of government 'terrorism' in Waco. That, to James, proves Tim McVeigh could not be guilty of killing innocent victims himself in Oklahoma. 'He's a soldier, not a terrorist.'

'So who did blow up the Oklahoma federal building?' James considered my question for a moment. His answer strayed into the scripts of the *X Files*.

'A lot of people don't want to say the government was involved,' he replied. 'Yet you don't destroy crime scenes before you have independent analysis and investigation of it. That's what they done. They done the same thing at Waco. It's a *cover-up*.'

By 'destroying the crime scene' James Nichols meant that what was left of the Murrah federal building in Oklahoma was demolished by the government and all that is now left is a bare patch of grass. They did the same in Waco, James said, by burning down the Branch Davidian compound. Evidence of government wickedness was destroyed. Everybody in America saw it on TV.

He said all this with an air of finality. I told him I did not understand why the US government would deliberately kill its own people – government workers. James Nichols inhaled deeply. 'The FBI was involved in the first terrorist bombing in this country, in New York,' he shot back, referring to evidence that the FBI had an informer in the group responsible for the World Trade Center bombing and other planned attacks. 'Why wouldn't they be involved in the second?'

That is not the same thing at all, I protested. He still had not explained why the government would deliberately kill its own people. *Why?* At this his voice cracked. His blue eyes rolled in their sockets with the impatience of a true believer confronted by some dupe of the system, a snake-handler surrounded by infidels. 'To promote anti-terrorist legislation,' James replied eventually. 'End *habeas corpus* . . . take American citizens' rights away . . . Show me one government that does not abuse its citizens. They are all guilty of it.'

Abusing citizens is one thing. Deliberately blowing up 168 of them is another. James Nichols is deeply immersed in the pathology of paranoia. He speaks the fed scare language of *The Turner Diaries*, the neo-Nazi novel so beloved of Tim McVeigh, in which the United States government is regarded as an illicit occupying power. His anger is intense, the white heat of a blacksmith's forge. He believes the US government is guilty of institutional cannibalism, eating its own. Oklahoma, as I heard repeatedly on the far Right, was the Reichstag fire of the Clinton administration, the ultimate fed scare, a pretext to prepare America for the future tyranny of a shadowy Washington élite.

Luggage arrived on the conveyor belt at Denver airport and James Nichols said it was time to go. His father, Bill, shook my hand gravely, rubbing his watery eyes and stroking his grizzled beard. In the background the third member of the party appeared again. This time James introduced Bob Popovich as another crusader for truth. Popovich had a rough red beard, a blue T-shirt and a baseball cap.

'Tell him about the book,' Popovich snapped suspiciously at James then walked away, never addressing me directly. James explained that he and Bob were writing a book about this whole affair. They had not yet found a publisher, but were very hopeful. Just what America needs, I decided. Another account of how the government in Washington murders and then lies to its citizens, written by the brother of the man arrested for the Oklahoma bombing. Given the current state of the market for paranoia publishing, it sounded like a sure-fire hit.

Conspiracies, as the philosopher Karl Popper once observed, are a way of explaining a world made complicated and scary without the existence of God. Communism, Jews, Freemasons, black people, the papacy, the CIA and now the US federal government assume the omniscient, omnipotent role, pulling the strings in our darkest nightmares. And this is curiously *comforting*. All conspiracy theories are inevitably optimistic. They assume that *someone* is in charge, however wicked. That means there is a purpose to our suffering in what might otherwise be a purposeless universe. If we could just kill the reds or the feds under the bed, all our worries would be ended. Sadly, human experience suggests otherwise.

James Nichols and I said goodbye. I travelled on to Oklahoma City, arriving just before dark. There was time to look at what remained of the Alfred P. Murrah federal building before nightfall. The rubble was cleared just as Nichols had said ('evidence destroyed' in conspiracy-speak). All around the wire fence pilgrims had attached tokens, scribbled notes, crosses made out of wood, teddy bears, Easter bunnies, wreaths. A US flag flew at half mast. There was a small memorial featuring a granite slab from the Murrah building and a 'Heartland Chapel' where visitors could say a few prayers, sit on wooden benches or read about the gifts from the Jewish and Islamic communities. A man was watering flowers, newly planted in big bowls. Women volunteers in T-shirts were collecting litter to keep the area clear.

A tall white man, six feet eight inches or more, was grasping the fence, his head bowed in prayer. When he finished we struck up a conversation. His name was Gary Jenkins. He said that a minute or two before the bomb exploded he dropped off his best friend, Pete DeMaster, an investigator for the Department of Defense, at the spot where we were standing. 'Ground zero,' Gary said, pointing at the earth under our feet.

This was exactly where the Ryder truck full of explosives was parked. On the day of the bombing, Gary had driven a few blocks when the force of the explosion sent a shock wave through the city. The blast was so great it blew in all the windows of his car. He returned and began searching in the rubble for Pete, but Pete was already dead. Gary breathed deeply. He said that Pete's family had just visited and took me along the fence to show off the wreath they had left – red, white and blue – Pete's patriotic 'favourite colours'. On the wreath was written 'Gone but not Forgotten'. Gary said that he makes the pilgrimage to the site every day to think and pray. The day we met he had visited 355 times in a row. 'Justice is coming soon,' he murmured to Pete, or Pete's spirit. 'Justice is coming.'

I asked him what he thought should happen to Terry Nichols and Tim McVeigh when it came time for their trial. 'I'm a pretty open-minded person,' Gary responded. 'They should have a fair chance.' We talked about the conspiracy theories of the Wilburns and James Nichols. Gary did not believe them, but would like the trial to explore every angle, however weird, every defence. Then, if the accused were found guilty, there should be 'a public execution right here on the site of the building. For them to burn in hell for eternity wouldn't be good enough.'

Everyone will understand the anger of Gary Jenkins – straightforward, human and, above all, normal. But the anger of James Nichols and America's culture of conspiracy is unfathomable, abnormal, based on a perverted sense of victimhood, dangerous, and difficult to defuse. This anger is in the dubious American tradition of unreasoned belief which encouraged men to burn witches in Salem, Communist witches in the McCarthy hearings, and now seeks federal government witches to drag to the stake for their sins. What is most worrying is that the balanced common sense of the majority, those like Gary Jenkins, is being increasingly drowned out by the noisy blasts of paranoia from the angriest minority, those like James Nichols.

Anti-government rage is America's fashion of the 1990s, exceeding anything since the Civil War. Government-hating obsessions are trumpeted daily on the 'new media', talk radio, fax networks and the Internet, in a destabilizing Babel of conspiracies available in every home. If the Babel sounds bad now, it will become intolerable as the new millennium excites the most credulous, angry and dangerous fringes.

To believe that the US government blew up its own people in Oklahoma is worse than asserting that Franklin Roosevelt covered up an early warning of the Japanese attack. It is the equivalent of believing Roosevelt actually *bombed* Pearl Harbor, or that John F. Kennedy was a conspirator in his own assassination. And it illuminates the core problem of the information age, obvious in America but undoubtedly imminent in Britain and Europe: so much of the available information is *bad*.

The earnest belief in nonsense has become a crippling American condition.

Bad News: Garbage In, Garbage Out

'People are not, in general, stupid, but they are often ignorant. In their ignorance they often tolerate ignorant news reporters who, in turn, tolerate ignorant politicians. The result is an ignorant politician making an ignorant speech to be covered by an ignorant reporter and shown in a forty-second clip on television to an ignorant audience.'

Newt Gingrich, Window of Opportunity, *1984*

Columbia, South Carolina

General Sherman was characteristically unkind to Columbia, the state capital of South Carolina. During the civil war he razed the town, sparing little more than the grand Capitol building which today stands among the palmetto and magnolia trees, surrounded by testimonies to the state's military traditions. On the outskirts of Columbia there is a large army base, Fort Jackson. Through the middle of the town there is the Blue Star Memorial Highway dedicated as 'a tribute to the armed forces that have defended the United States of America'. There is a monument to the 'South Carolina dead of the Confederate army', which speaks of those 'who have glorified a fallen cause'. Streets around the Capitol are named after officers who fought in the war of independence. And there is a palmetto tree monument from the people of South Carolina 'to her sons of the Palmetto Regiment who fell in the war with Mexico, 1847'.

Proudly patriotic, not especially rich or poor, in many ways Columbia is an average sort of town. Dr Frank Luntz, a Republican strategist and pollster who helped design Newt Gingrich's

'Contract with America', uses it occasionally as a site for 'focus groups', the marketing ploy of American and British politics. Focus groups were invented to test new products, and in an age where politicians are marketed like cornflakes they are used to gauge the impact of the political 'product' on the 'consumer'. A dozen statistically 'typical' consumers are selected, usually by telephone surveys. The chosen group is invited to a room fitted out with microphones and a large one-way mirror reflecting into the room.

On the other side of the mirror are those interested in the market research, who take notes or record the proceedings on videotape as the focus group consumers are told to consume. They guzzle chocolate bars, breakfast cereals, ice-creams, taco chips or new policy ideas that a political party is trying to test. Then the consumers, or voters, are quizzed on their likes and dislikes.

Dr Luntz had been hired by the Coalition to Defend America, a group of Republicans hawkish on defence, who were concerned that Ronald Reagan's Strategic Defence Initiative, nicknamed 'Star Wars', had been cancelled by the Clinton administration. Columbia, with its military tradition, was thought to be an ideal location to sample the opinions of Americans broadly familiar with defence issues. There were other good reasons. The local congressman was Floyd Spence, chairman of the House of Representatives National Security Committee, one of the most important men in Congress. South Carolina was also home to the veteran senator, Strom Thurmond, who chaired the Senate Armed Services Committee. These two men would be pivotal in deciding how US defence money was to be spent. Congressman Spence and one of Senator Thurmond's aides were invited to watch the focus group in action, to learn what voters thought of the Star Wars idea.

What happened during the next two hours was utterly shocking. It was a revelation of ignorance and misinformation in which not a single one of the participants – average voters – knew the most basic and significant facts about America's defence.

And it was a bizarre case of politicians trying to learn from voters who knew nothing, emphasizing the shortage of reliable information in the supposed information age.

The dozen or so participants were ushered in to a large room to face Frank Luntz. These voters all came from middle-income households with earnings between $25,000 and $50,000 a year. There was one black man, a hospital worker called Clyde, and one black woman with a son in the US military. The rest, split half and half between men and women, were white. They included a prison worker, a certified accountant, a retired man and various self-employed people.

Frank Luntz explained they had been selected as a typical spread of middle- or lower-middle-class Americans. Politically they were Republicans, Independents and Democrats. 'Economically and politically dead on,' Luntz nodded to me as he went into the room to greet the participants. 'This will be middle America responding to defence issues.' Luntz has considerable expertise. He had conducted six focus groups in the previous month for the Republican party.

Virtually every policy emanating from the Republican majority in Congress or the Clinton White House had been tested not only in opinion polls but also in these more intimate settings. Dr Luntz argues that opinion polls give a broad sweep of public opinion, but focus groups enable pollsters and politicians to dissect the national mood to discover in detail the reasons why voters like or dislike certain policies. The presentation of policies, the words used to sell them to voters, can be retuned to have most impact.

The Star Wars group was supposed, therefore, to be middle America speaking its mind. The conversation was decidedly short. Luntz started with a few warm-up questions about America's role in the world. Was the Pentagon downsizing the military budget too fast? Who were America's enemies now? Iraq, Iran, North Korea, Libya, China, the "Middle East", Russia and Japan were all mentioned. Everyone had an opinion, and everyone agreed the United States needed a strong military after the cold war.

With one exception, all the participants in the focus group could be described as articulate. They had differing views but – with that one exception – everyone in the room could explain and argue intelligently and lucidly. This was not a group of stupid people. It was a group of decidedly ignorant people.

The key question from Luntz came quickly. He wanted the dozen participants to imagine what would happen if Russia fired a nuclear missile at Columbia, South Carolina. Everyone said it would be shot down by American defences, though they varied on the details. Every single person was misinformed.

One participant, Ron, thought American fighter planes would knock out the Russian attack with 'anti-missile missiles'. 'Take the missile out from a plane,' he said.

'*Something* intercepts,' said John, but he was not sure which part of Star Wars technology would actually be used.

'Billions' had been spent on advanced high-tech systems, Sylvia commented, to blast enemy missiles out of the sky. The US military would knock the Russian ICBM down.

Luntz went round the room carefully until every participant had committed themselves to stating that, one way or another, the United States had a Star Wars system in operation to save Columbia, South Carolina. Then Luntz told them, politely, they were all talking nonsense. 'In fact the United States has no effective defence . . . we could do nothing about it,' he said.

'I'm *shocked*,' said Jo, a highly articulate widow with two grown-up sons. Just minutes before she had confidently described the non-existent Strategic Defense Initiative 'peace shield' as 'our shield of protection – impenetrable – it will protect us'.

'You mean we have nothing beyond the patriot missile?' asked John, clearly agitated. Patriot missiles were used – with great political success but limited military achievement – as a US countermeasure to Saddam Hussein's SCUD missiles during the Gulf war.

'It is so hard to believe that we don't have anything that could stop it,' Joanne admitted. 'That just boggles the mind.'

After the focus group ended, I chatted to Congressman Spence.

What boggled *his* mind was how little the voters, even in this military town which he represented in Congress, understood about one of the most commonly reported news stories of the past decade. He said he was 'just amazed' by the ignorance of the ordinary voters. Frank Luntz was not amazed.

His polling studies had revealed that on many issues, not merely defence, the American public knew very little, and what they *did* know was often plain wrong. As we saw in Part One, many Americans thought unemployment in the mid-1990s was at 25 per cent – Great Depression levels – when the real figure was around 6 per cent. They also wrongly believed the budget deficit was rising, instead of falling, and that inflation was much worse than it really was.

Typically, Americans thought aid to foreign countries was an enormous slice of the US budget, more than was spent on health care for the elderly. In fact, foreign aid is a tiny percentage of GDP compared to many European countries, and a much smaller part of the US budget than Medicare. 'The truth is that the American people are very badly informed of things that are happening around them,' Dr Luntz admitted. 'Obviously, from the results of this focus group, when they *are* informed about the threat they face they are going to get pretty agitated and pretty angry.' That, presumably, depends upon who is doing the informing and how they go about it. 'In a sense,' Luntz explained, 'what we did was evil because those twelve people will not sleep as well tonight as they did last night and it will be some time before they feel as secure as they did when they walked in here. Because right now they feel very insecure and, unless the US government changes its policy on missile defence, those people will not sleep well for some time to come.'

Politicians manipulating anger and insecurity based on the ignorance of the electorate is nothing new. But if the American electorate was really as badly informed as Dr Luntz, the focus group and the other studies suggested, there were extraordinary opportunities for the angriest voices in America, those preaching racial hatred or anti-government propaganda, to reach and misinform a section of the under-informed public. The puzzle was how the *entire* focus group failed to understand one of the biggest stories in the United States in recent years. Where, I asked Dr Luntz, did they get – or fail to get – their information? Luntz smiled. He recited the self-promoting slogan heard every night on one of the TV networks, his voice heavy with irony. 'More Americans get their news from ABC than any other source.'

ABC television news has a distinguished journalistic history. But Dr Luntz's point was that millions of Americans *fail* to get much news and information from reliable sources like ABC. The American news market is fragmented to an extent unknown in any other industrialized country. Unlike Britain, most of Europe, or even Russia, there is no vigorous national press. The only national newspaper is *USA Today*, which can be purchased in most cities but is often given away free in hotels. Despite its lively reporting it has not yet become a major journalistic force in the United States. A few outstanding regional newspapers like *The New York Times*, *The LA Times* and the *Washington Post* have international reputations and are read outside their natural catchment areas by small numbers of well-informed subscribers, but these are exceptions. The total readership of these three papers is, by British standards, tiny. For most Americans, news is not only local but – compared to Europe – downright parochial. The American élite, tuned into CNN, National Public Radio and even the BBC World Service, will buy *The New York Times*, *The LA Times* or the *Washington Post* and will almost certainly subscribe to quality news magazines like *Newsweek*, *Time*, *US News and World Report* and the *Economist*. But tens of millions of Americans watch very little news except what is broadcast on local TV, do not subscribe to any of the best newspapers and magazines, and appear to have little knowledge of the world beyond their town, or their state.

To put it brutally, America suffers from a deep information gap between the highly informed minority and the vastly uninformed ignorant majority. This gap is as wide as that between rich and poor. The best and brightest Americans of the political élite in Washington, New York and a few other big cities are probably better informed than in other countries. But the vast majority of Americans are information Have-Nots. Like the Columbia focus group, they may be intelligent and articulate people, but they are also astoundingly ignorant of the most basic facts concerning American society and political life.

In a democracy, they have the right to be ignorant. But two trends suggest this information gap will widen. The first is that the 'mainstream' American media are diminishing in importance and are often regarded with suspicion by viewers and readers. The second trend is the rise of 'new media' – talk radio and the Internet – which are increasingly popular sources of information, but with one catch: much of their information is unreliable electronic gossip. Both trends are easy to document.

The biggest story in the American newspaper industry of the 1990s is about cuts, ageing readership and fears of a collapse of the entire industry. Newspapers are closing. *Time* magazine reported that the percentage of American adults reading a daily newspaper had dropped from 78 per cent in 1970 to 64 per cent in 1995.

Typical of most countries, the most sought-after readers, young people, are the least interested. In the 16–24 age group only 52 per cent read a paper daily. The number of daily newspapers had fallen from 1,570 in 1992 to 1,532 in 1995. Network news on television demonstrates an even more precipitous decline. While newcomers like CNN, MSNBC and FOX competed to offer a twenty-four-hour cable service to the interested minority of Americans who want to keep up with the news, the main network broadcasts are dinosaurs, still powerful but ripe for extinction.

In 1981 the 'big three' network news shows – ABC, CBS and NBC – could boast that 41 per cent of all homes tuned in to their broadcasts every night. By 1995 that share had dropped to 26 per cent.[1] Typically, a network news show is a thirty-minute slot. Roughly eight minutes can be subtracted for advertisements and promotional material of various types. A glance at the advertisements is a good indication of who the viewers are. In the case of American network news it is obviously older people. An average selection of ads on network news will include commercials for incontinence pads, laxatives, haemorrhoid treatments, antacids, headache pills and other pain relievers. Switch away from network news to one of the youth-orientated channels like MTV, and you see an utterly different America – Coca-Cola ads and commercials for condoms and tampons.

Judging by the advertisements they show, American network TV news programmes have a special appeal for those who are post-menopausal, incontinent, constipated and sick. In the twenty-two minutes of airtime available for news stories, the editors try to squeeze in whatever their 'agenda' will bear. Again, typically, there will be three or four 'hard' news stories at the start, most often from Washington – a debate in Congress, a White House scandal. But very quickly, as the pace of the commercials increases, the agenda turns to 'soft' news, heart-warming stories of teachers who have triumphed in tough schools or blacks and whites coming together to combat racism. There are frequent medical news stories, hopeful cures for diseases or worrying new ways to die, but foreign news, unless US troops are involved, rarely gets a mention. ABC's *World News Tonight* is rarely about the 'world' beyond the shores of the United States.

Within the tight box left for their reports, network news shows compress stories into bite-sized morsels of a minute and a half or two minutes – with the exception of the heart-warming features and occasional investigations. This 'mainstream' of journalism is increasingly becoming a side-channel, proving far less important to most Americans than in the past. Instead, there has been an explosion in soft-news magazine shows and 'tabloid TV' programmes which resemble real news programmes in the same way alcohol-free beer is like real beer. The idea is the same, but the flavour is very different.

Beyond dropping circulation and audience figures, mainstream journalism has sunk in public estimation. The author and journalist James Fallows demonstrates in his indictment of the news business, *Breaking the News*, that journalists were often in the past regarded as lower-middle-class campaigners for the truth, decent ordinary people in touch with the concerns of average Americans. The journalists Bob Woodward and Carl Bernstein even became heroes for their exposure of the lies of the Nixon administration over Watergate. But in the 1990s, Hollywood movies and popular novels frequently portray journalists as far less sympathetic, arrogant, self-obsessed, with show-business egos and salaries to match, out of touch with average America.

Mr Fallows's criticism is shared by many Americans, to judge from a few recent examples. After a bomb exploded at the Olympic Games in Atlanta in the summer of 1996, CNN, NBC and the *Atlanta Constitution* newspaper immediately leaped to the conclusion that the security guard who discovered the bomb, Richard Jewell, was probably guilty. When he was eventually cleared by the FBI, in January 1997, CNN and NBC made payments to Mr Jewell under threat of a lawsuit. He had been found 'guilty' in the media without a trial and without being charged with any offence.

That same month a North Carolina jury found ABC News liable for $5.5 million in punitive damages after the network used researchers to deceive a supermarket chain. The researchers obtained jobs under false pretences by submitting fabricated work experience details. Then they used hidden cameras to catch supermarket workers selling tainted meat – a story which they had already established from interviews.

The reason for the deception had less to do with journalism than with the show-business demands of television entertainment: get the pictures at all costs. The jury was in no doubt that the TV network had gone too far, whatever their protestations about 'press freedom'. In that same month, TV networks and newspapers competed to retell lurid stories about footballers with the Dallas Cowboys accused of rape. But Dallas police concluded that the woman involved had made up the accusations, and that her complaint had no merit. The footballers were pilloried publicly and repeatedly on the basis of no evidence, and no charges, in a kind of journalistic lynch law.

In each case, mainstream American journalists proudly claimed the right of a free press guaranteed by the First Amendment to the Constitution. But there was little evidence that this 'right' was used responsibly. Every journalist makes mistakes. Every journalist takes risks in what can be a dangerous profession. But these cases demonstrate a degree of unthinking hypocrisy by journalists that they would like to 'expose' in other professions. If it is right for journalists to deceive a supermarket chain in pursuit of allegedly tainted chicken, is it also right for CIA or FBI agents to pretend to be journalists to obtain information relevant to national security and expose much more serious spies or criminals? Is the right to a free press more important than the right to a free trial, and the right to be considered innocent until proven guilty?

Robust reporting, even muckraking, can be a powerful disinfectant, a means of defusing the anger within American society. Instead, journalism has become a target for that anger, just another institution to be distrusted and occasionally loathed or feared. In *Breaking the News*, James Fallows noted that Washington political journalism has bent itself away from explaining how policies affect ordinary Americans. Political reporters, with limited airtime, prefer to avoid the complications of how policies might actually work. Instead they focus on the insider game, how policies boost or reduce the politician's standing in the polls. Like Oscar Wilde's definition of the cynic, journalists risk knowing the price of every political commodity but the value of nothing. Fallows claims that reporting on the Clinton health care proposals of 1993–4 was typical, as he puts it in the book's subtitle, of the way in which 'the media undermine American democracy'.[2]

The Clinton health proposals were frequently reported as signifying an up or a down for the president in the opinion polls. The true nature of the plan was not fully explored by much of the American media and therefore could not be understood by the public. That meant the health care 'debate' was not about how proposal X would help Mrs Smith in Wisconsin get her illness treated. It tended to focus instead on how a successful TV advertising campaign by health care lobbyists killed the Clinton plan, with serious political implications for the presidency. It was often not about health at all, but about the insider's game of Washington politics as usual.

Anyone who watched the 1992 or 1996 presidential election debates will recognize how disconnected 'mainstream' journalism has become from viewers and readers. Typical of the American information gap, when given the opportunity to ask presidential candidates a question, reporters and ordinary people proved to be interested in utterly different subjects. Ordinary voters who were allowed to grill Senator Dole and President Clinton in San Diego in 1996 wanted straight answers to plain questions: 'How can you cut taxes without ballooning the deficit?' 'How can education/race relations/health care be improved?' 'What will you do about boosting pay for serving military personnel?' In other words, when offered the chance, voters are single-minded and direct. They want answers about what Government can *do* for them.

'Informed' questions from reporters in the average White House news conference, however, are remarkably different. Generally they are not about how government policies might help citizens, but are, instead, a kind of journalistic 'gotcha' game, dripping with a sense of wickedness and corruption: 'Will you pardon those convicted of offences in the Whitewater affair?' 'What influence was bought by Indonesian bankers for funds paid to the Democratic party?' 'Who had access to FBI files in the White House?'

This points to a simple fact. All journalists are biased. And they are all biased in the same way – not for the Left or Right, but in favour of the Big Story. Among informed political and journalistic élites on both sides of the Atlantic, 'gotcha' questions are extremely important. They lead to the next scandal, the next revelation of a cover-up, the next lead story.

But, at the other end of America's information gap, these matters were not important at all to the ordinary voters who questioned the candidates during the election. They wanted facts about policies that might affect them. This disconnection between journalists and their readers or audience does not directly mean the reporters are wrong. White House scandals *are* significant. But journalists since Watergate have become obsessed with the idea of government as a conspiracy against the people, a sham of spin doctors in which the core assumption is that the politicians are always lying. Politicians, obligingly, often prove that this assumption is correct.

The purpose of journalism in this climate tends, therefore, towards exposing wrongdoing rather than informing the public. Both are important, but in the tight little packages squeezing in between the ads on television, the TV networks err heavily against information or exposition and in favour of confrontation and exposés. Journalists, typically, do not win awards for clear expositions of boring but worthy subjects. They do win awards for uncovering wrongdoing in high places and naming the guilty men.

The result is that information age journalists often fail to address the real hunger for bread-and-butter facts, especially about what government can do and how it might do it better. Americans are swamped by information, but much of it is not what they want, or need. Or it is unreliable. And far from their traditional role as the voice of the people, Washington journalists risk being regarded as a kind of commentariat, a permanent Greek chorus burbling about the action of the politicians but deaf to the real world off the political stage. In consequence, the people of the United States have lost or are rapidly losing faith not merely in the politicians but also in reporters who appear to be part of the same inside-the-Beltway political tribe.

Journalists can survive if they are not loved. They can survive factual errors made in good faith. They can even survive errors of judgement – like the coverage of Richard Jewell in the Atlanta bombing story — if the public believes that a free press is worth protecting, despite occasionally serious lapses. But mainstream journalism cannot survive if readers and viewers do not trust its reports.

One result of this mistrust is that Americans are looking elsewhere for their news. In yet another American paradox, mainstream journalism comes under increasing suspicion, despite its attempts to be fair, accurate and not committed to any political viewpoint. But the pseudo-journalism of the 'new media' is regarded by enthusiasts as having the accuracy of Holy Writ, despite — or perhaps as a result of — its proud political bias. And in that context, the most exciting new phenomenon of 1990s mass communication in the United States is the rise of talk radio.

'I *am* equal time,' the popular radio talk show host, Rush Limbaugh, bellows repeatedly when challenged that only con-servative views are given a fair hearing on his show. 'I *am* equal time.' Mr Limbaugh, who claims to be the number-one radio talk show host with 20 million listeners, says he is a counterweight to the despised 'liberal' mainstream media. He and his imitators have created a dynamic new radio culture in what was assumed to be the 'television age'.

Bill Adams, a professor of Public Administration at George Washington University, indicates the success and importance of talk radio by producing a digest of what appears on the shows in a newssheet called 'Talk Daily'. His subscribers come from within America's well-informed political élite. They recognize the significance of the new medium, even if many of them cannot bear to listen to it. Among those who buy 'Talk Daily' as a means of taking the blood pressure of the American people are the White House, the Senate, the House of Representatives, universities and numerous mainstream TV programmes and newspapers.

Their interest is recognition that talk radio has become the most popular radio format in the United States, surpassing rock and roll or country and western, and subverting the 'mainstream' media. Professor Adams estimates some 1,200 of the 8,000–9,000 radio stations in the country are now, as the slogan says, 'All Talk, All the Time'.

'Talk radio reaches tens of millions of Americans every day,' Professor Adams says. 'Roughly one out of every five or six Americans listens to talk radio every twenty-four hours. It has a big audience. More people listen to Rush Limbaugh than read the *Washington Post, The New York Times, The LA Times* and the *Chicago Tribune* put together *and doubled.*' That is because, according to Professor Adams, talk radio is regarded by listeners as 'an alternative to the traditional mainstream media that many of them do not trust.' Newly successful radio hosts include former Iran-Contra conspirator Colonel Oliver North and G. Gordon Liddy, 'the G-Man', who was one of the Watergate conspirators.

The Watergate 'plumbers' burgled the Democratic National Committee headquarters during the 1972 election campaign on behalf of Richard Nixon. Legend has it that Liddy proved his tough-guy machismo by holding his hand over a cigarette lighter flame until the skin sizzled. Today he claims the second highest talk radio ratings after Limbaugh, pulling in 8–10 million listeners on 270 radio stations from Alaska and Hawaii to Virginia and Florida. Mr Liddy broadcasts every day from 11 a.m. to 3 p.m. from a tiny cupboard of a studio in Fairfax, Virginia, a Washington suburb. He has a shaved bald head and a droopy brown moustache which makes him look as if he is permanently scowling. The 'G-Man' or 'the Darth Vader of the Nixon adminis-tration', as he calls himself, was dressed impeccably in a smart hound's-tooth check suit as he sat delivering for the entertain-ment of his audience the kind of trenchant conservative views which are loathed by the Clinton administration and unheard of from the supposedly impartial news presenters or anchors on the mainstream media.

Liddy on sex education in schools: 'Children are spending too much time learning how to put condoms on bananas and not enough time on the core curriculum.' On the law banning certain classes of assault weapons: 'It's as phoney as Bill Clinton's wedding vows.' And on the White House: 'More illegal activities by Hillary Clinton ... More wrongdoing ... it's just like a fountain of illegality, a fountain of felonious activity from Hillary on down.'

But Liddy goes well beyond even this robust political commentary. In the aftermath of the raid on David Koresh's cult headquarters in Waco, he advised listeners how to shoot US government agents: 'Head shots! Head shots!' G. Gordon Liddy said. 'Kill the sons of bitches.'

In Britain and most of Europe such comments would destroy Mr Liddy's career. European audiences would never stand for a radio broadcast advocating the best way to kill police or government agents. But in the United States Mr Liddy's radio show has prospered as a result of the furore it has caused, even though, in the aftermath of the Oklahoma bombing, many Americans began to wonder if talk radio was going too far.

Had it contributed to an angry anti-government atmosphere? President Clinton certainly seemed to think so. He criticized the 'purveyors of hatred and division', the 'promoters of paranoia', and the 'loud and angry voices' in American political life. Everybody knew he was talking about talk radio, and Liddy was an obvious target. Five days after the bombing the president was most indignant. 'We must stand up and speak against reckless speech that can push fragile people over the edge beyond the bounds of civilized conduct and take this country into a dark place.'

In the dark place of his Fairfax studio the G-Man was warming up. 'It is I, G. Gordon, here on Radio *Free* DC,' Liddy began the next segment of his show and we began to talk. The talk radio format, Liddy explained, was notorious and popular for the same reason: because it is so conservative. The mainstream media, the TV networks and the big newspapers are seen to be élitist, 'perceived by the public to be quite to the Left, and we benefit by default'.

Liddy's programme is 'interactive'. People talk *back* to talk radio hosts in a way in which they cannot to the omniscient demigods who anchor the main network television shows.

American TV news anchors are at the peak of the mainstream media commentariat. The best paid earn film-star wages, millions of dollars a year, to read what amounts to about five minutes of words in a twenty-two-minute news bulletin once a night. In Liddy's view, most Americans are disconnected from the broadcasts of the élite, compared to the down-home intimacy of talk radio which, as he described it, sounded like the perfect medium for the United States of Anger.

'The vast majority of American citizens these days are extremely sceptical about politics and politicians on both sides of the fence,' Gordon Liddy said. 'Both Democrat and Republican.' The reasons are obvious. 'George Bush was turned out of office essentially because he violated a promise. He said to the American people read my lips, I will not raise your taxes. Then he raised taxes. The great revolt of 1994 was because Bill Clinton said if you elect me your president I will propose a middle-class tax cut. He then strapped to the backs of the American people the largest tax increase in the history of this nation, indeed in the history of the world. So both sides are viewed sceptically by the electorate.'

Unlike the mainstream media, which broadcasts the perpetually good economic news of America in the aggregate, Liddy is tapped in to the discontent of America the anecdotal. 'In spite of the economic news,' he said, 'there has been a decrease in real income, disposable income after taxes. And so [listeners] sit there and they read that economic news is good in the newspapers, and they say, if that's true, how come I cannot afford [what I used to be able to afford]? Why are things so tough? It's because their real income is down, and for that reason they are not happy.'

But, I wondered, doesn't talk radio contribute to America's sense of pessimism, full of the 'angry voices' that so worried President Clinton? 'Well, he named *me*,' Liddy responded. 'I was the only one that he named. For which I am very grateful. I ended up getting the Freedom of Speech Award from my peers as a result. He is notorious for his temper. He is like a two-year-old.

If you say "no" to a two-year-old you get a temper tantrum, and that's what you get with Bill Clinton.'

Talk radio's popularity is, therefore, easy to understand in an angry and discontented time. Americans, disconnected from each other by so many of the stresses within their society, can connect in the electronic town meeting. Talk radio is popular because it is also *populist*. Liddy views the world not as one of the Washington élite, quoting Labor Department employment statistics. Instead he speaks like his audience, like many of the people in this book: sceptical about politicians, angry about the system, critical of the growth of government and recognizing that all the 'good' economic statistics quoted by the inside-the-Beltway élite are quite alien in the lives most people lead. If listeners find anger in Liddy's words, it is the anger of Caliban seeing his reflection in the mirror. But Liddy, whatever the White House may argue, is no demon. He allows, indeed encourages, Democrats as guests or as telephone callers. And on the day of our conversation he corrected callers who believed some of the fantastic conspiracy theories that swirled around America, conspiracies he described as 'nuts'.

It is vital to recognize, whether you care for his politics or not, that on the scale of the 'new media', G. Gordon Liddy is positively a voice of sanity and reason compared to many of the others.

Retune your radio elsewhere on the dial, log on to the Internet or hook in to the new 'patriot' fax networks, and you discover far angrier voices. The Anti-Defamation League has studied some of them. The ADL report 'Poisoning the Airwaves: the Extremist Message of Hate on Shortwave Radio' is an examination of the worst of the on-air fed scare, and a revelation of the worst of the bad news and perverted 'information' now available in America's information explosion.

Some broadcasters routinely blame the Oklahoma City bombing on the US government, on the Clintons, the Attorney-General Janet Reno, or the Israeli spy service Mossad. The ADL report says one radio talk show host allegedly broadcast instructions on how to build a bomb with easily obtainable parts. Another spoke of 'how the Clintons' agenda very closely resembles what happened in Nazi Germany in the 1930s'. A third spoke of the Oklahoma bombing, in the language of James Nichols, as 'the New World Order's Reichstag fire'.

'Step back three paces and look up 15 degrees to see who is pulling the strings,' Michigan Militia at Large member Mark Koernke said on his talk radio show, in a typical offering of the on-air conspiracy broadcasters.

Pastor Pete Peters, another talk show host of the far Right, in a broadcast on 18 March 1995 forecast that a 'world court' would one day drag Americans before a United Nations tribunal to punish them for failing to submit to a one world government, run, presumably, by Boutros Boutros Ghali. 'We are Christians and we do not unite with a bunch of people-starving cockroach-protecting Hindus or a spear-chucking big sun-worshipping heathen,' the ADL report quotes Pastor Peters as saying. 'We're not giving up our guns! We might give up our ammo . . . yeah, one bullet at a time.'

Pastor Peters was broadcasting on *NewsLight*, a programme aired not only on shortwave, which picks up a tiny minority of listeners, but also by commercial radio stations including televangelist Jimmy Swaggart's Evangelistic Association on WJYM from Bowling Green, Ohio, plus stations in Arizona and California.

Other fringe talk 'celebrities' call black people 'mud people' and Jews the 'children of Satan'. The ADL also reports that associated publications of the radio extremists include a September 1994 supplement to a far-Right magazine which wondered: 'Is America on the verge of war? Is a national emergency about to be declared and America placed under martial law? Is America on the brink of occupation by military troops under United Nations control?'

The paranoia of the far Right extends to other 'new media' off the radio dial. The American Patriot Fax Network acts as one of the most bizarre clearing houses for far-Right and libertarian information. It works rather like the computer links between militia groups. To receive 'information' you dial an eleven-digit number on a fax machine and listen for recorded instructions. A stream of documents, usually outlining horrendous conspiracies by the US government against its citizens, will follow. One, from APFN founder Kenneth Vardon, shows the United States flag flying upside down, a universally recognized symbol of acute distress.

'Friends Faxing Friends', it says on the masthead, and then speaks of the group as 'the spiritual heir of Sam Adams and other patriots'. The fax, with typically mangled syntax, then outlines the purpose of the network. 'The resulting communications from all across America,' the fax says, 'showing a united liberty force of such great numbers would be difficult for the polititions [*sic*] to ignore.' Another fax says 'Anyone can be an APFN friend,' which is more or less true. All you need is a fax machine or fax modem on your computer, plus the telephone number to call.

An even more important channel used by angry Americans to talk to one another is the Internet. Try looking up computerized newsgroups like alt.conspiracy or talk.politics.guns. Or you can find bulletin boards with names like Paul Revere Net, Liberty Net and Patriot Net. Dial in, switch on, link up, and you find this kind of endlessly recycled 'information' from a group identifying themselves as the National Vietnam POW Strike Force. 'Jack-booted government thugs,' their faxed communication says, 'are too nice words to describe the BATF and FBI.'

Referring to the assault on David Koresh's Branch Davidian compound, the fax calls the FBI 'Federal Baby Incinerators' and the BATF 'Baby Assassinators Traitors and Faggots'. In a way typical of the identification of the media élite with government conspiracies, a well-known network television reporter who is the specific target of hatred is described as a 'totally sold out Liberal Establishment Faggot (LEMF) on the payroll of the CIA'.

And then comes the punchline. It is, yet again, about the bombing of the Alfred P. Murrah federal building in Oklahoma

City. 'Clinton's ordering the bombing of the Murrah building is exactly parallel to Adolf Hitler's secretly ordered burning of the Reichstag in 1933 to foment hysteria and institute draconian martial law to stop terrorism.' The fax goes on to claim that the alleged Oklahoma bombers (Tim McVeigh and Terry Nichols) are 'patsies' set up by the US government, and that a witness who can refute the government's case 'mysteriously' died. Other faxes rail against 'Big Brother Bill [Clinton] and his ally the controlled press'. The author notes 'you can personally judge how close you are to total slavery by how much you believe the free press'. There are hundreds, probably thousands, of other examples.[3]

In this way the fed scare and conspiracy stories go round and round in an electric echo chamber of belief beyond reason on the new media. Kenneth S. Stern, in his revealing book on the angry militia movement, *A Force Upon the Plain*, notes that there were instructions posted on the Internet under newsgroup rec.pyrotechnics for the recipe for Sarin, the nerve gas used in the Tokyo subway. Three weeks before the Oklahoma City bombing there were instructions available on the Internet for building the kind of bomb which was used in Oklahoma, a device constructed from the fertilizer ammonium nitrate. There was even the promise to share the formula for C-4 military plastic explosives.

A much respected journalist, Pierre Salinger, formerly of ABC News, was even hooked by one of the crazy stories that had appeared on the Internet. After TWA flight 800 mysteriously crashed off Long Island, New York in the summer of 1996, Salinger was given a document by someone he described as a top French intelligence official. The document read like every journalist's idea of an astounding scoop. It said that TWA 800 was shot down by a US Navy Aegis missile. There was a cover-up of Watergate proportions. Innocent passengers blown to pieces by the American navy! Hold the front page! But there was one catch. Mr Salinger did not know it at the time, but the Internet had become a kind of electronic lavatory wall, full of pages of speculative and unproven material, a manifestation of a phenom-enon known to computer programmers as GIGO – Garbage In, Garbage Out. If a system is programmed with unreliable information, it multiplies and comes out in unexpected places. The new media have become the loudest and most obvious example of GIGO in history. The Salinger 'scoop' had been on the Internet for a long time with no evidence to support it.

Journalists who had tried to check its veracity concluded there was no proof that would lead to a credible report, and so ignored this example of an Internet conspiracy theory, but Mr Salinger was less familiar with the Net and its capacity to ensnare. In an attempt to clear up the mess and clean up the Internet's GIGO culture, *Slate*, the Microsoft on-line magazine introduced 'The Tangled Web', a welcome attempt to correct the more ludicrous on-line fictions by exposing the lack of evidence behind them, the faulty reasoning or factual inaccuracies. Yet for every correction there always seem to be a hundred more conspiracies.

'Listen, Globalists,' officer Jack McLamb, a former Phoenix, Arizona police officer and sometime talk show host warned in one fax obtained through the APFN. 'It is only when a government begins to enslave the people that the "leaders" rightly fear guns in the hands of the citizens. Seventy-million plus good Americans [militia] own guns. Most, including many of us in uniform, will not die keeping them, but alas will see that those who would try to take them die in trying.'

What are we to make of all this? These most angry voices represent a trickle off the mainstream of American society, but they cannot be ignored. The words of respected figures like Pat Robertson validate some of the crazier theories of the dangerous fringes. And since the mainstream media and political leaders are objects of suspicion, there appears to be little to stop the drift towards a dangerous paranoia for the angriest Americans.

In the worst case, America risks exactly the opposite of the excesses of the French Revolution. There are no American zealots worshipping at the temple of the Goddess of Reason. But there are plenty of American zealots crowding around the Goddess of

Unreason, listening to the recycling of dangerous nonsense, of which there is an abundance in the 'new media' of the 1990s. The fragmentation and decline of the mainstream media has left not merely an information gap between the well informed and the ignorant, it has increased choice to the point at which we can select the *kind* of news we wish to hear. We can read newspapers of record, *The New York Times* and the rest, or we can choose the softer news and heart-warming stories of the feature shows and magazine programmes. But we can also decide to take the angrier options, either on popular talk radio or its far more extreme variants. For those angriest Americans it is unlikely that any of the information options they choose will upset their paranoid view of the world or their worship of unreason. That suggests an extremely grim conclusion.

News tends to be subversive. The truth is as strong a disinfectant as bright sunlight and fresh air. It overcomes prejudices and paints a complex picture of the way in which human societies function. But the proliferating choice of different types of biased information suggests that the most committed and irrational people will choose only that 'news' which reinforces their own prejudices about race relations, government conspiracies, abortion, gun control and the rest. Obviously this is not unique to the United States. On the political Right and Left, British readers of the *Daily Telegraph* or the *Guardian* know what they are buying, and generally share the underlying political assumptions of these newspapers. To do otherwise would be irrational. Who wants to wake up to a newspaper whose views consistently make them angry?

On both sides of the Atlantic there is an honourable tradition of quality newspapers like these separating more objective news coverage from comment and editorial. But the big difference comes in the electronic media. In Britain, radio and television news strives to be impartial and, indeed, broadcasters have a legal obligation not to adopt a party political propagandist tone. In the United States, network TV news follows different rules but broadly works within a similarly impartial framework. But the widening of the choice of news has resulted in some of it not being 'news' at all.

At its worst, America's junk news is little more than propaganda for extremist or bizarre causes. Instead of exposing wide audiences to contradictory views, the impact of the new media may well be simply to reinforce the anger of the angriest Americans, turning out reasonable counter-arguments and reducing news to the battle between 'us' and 'them'.

For a glimpse of where this may lead, there are clues in some of the most bizarre hearings ever conducted on Capitol Hill, those of 15 June 1995. The date was two months after the explosion of the Oklahoma City bomb. Congress was shaken by the bombing and the revelations that armed anti-government militias had proliferated across the country, a reservoir of anger that had been seriously under-reported by the mainstream media until the bombing forced America's dangerous culture of conspiracies on to the nightly news agenda.

In a senate hearing room, a group of anti-government militia leaders assembled behind a long wooden table. The hearing chairman, Pennsylvania Senator Arlen Specter, had invited the leaders to explain their 'philosophy' and their sense of hatred of the US federal government. It was the venting of steam from an especially angry volcano, and the mirror image of the McCarthy hearings of the 1940s and 50s. In the cold war, senators and members of the House of Un-American Activities Committee were searching for the red menace by publicly interrogating and sometimes humiliating American citizens. In the 1990s version, just as in the *X Files*, it was the committee and the *government itself* which was held in contempt by the ordinary citizens before it. John Trochmann of the Militia of Montana, looking every inch like an Old Testament prophet with his long beard and fierce demeanour, lectured the senators on how the 'office of the presidency has been turned into a position of dictatorial oppression'.

He claimed that the US government 'defines human beings as a biological resource under [the] United Nations Ecosystem

Management Programme'. The US government 'allows our military to be ordered and controlled by foreigners'. Then, in a typical attack, he denounced the mainstream US media as being 'twisted, slanted, biased . . . [they] take their signals from a few private, covert special-interest groups bent on destroying what's left of the American way'.

'Thank you very much, Mr Trochmann,' Senator Specter said solemnly. Trochmann's lecture set the tone of what was to follow, a clash of two utterly disconnected cultures. Conducting the hearing and listening from the press galleries were some of the best informed politicians, staff and journalists anywhere in the world. In front of them, from Montana, Michigan, Ohio and elsewhere, were men who seemed to inhabit a different country, an America full of strange fears, terrors and suspicions. There were those who thought that the United Nations was flying black helicopters in American airspace as a prelude to seizing power in the United States. There are secret directions written on the back of highway traffic signs at road junctions, showing the UN troops how to take over the country. American citizens have been brainwashed, computer chips inserted in their buttocks. Russian troops are poised to take over America, and are already in position on US soil, hidden in top-secret bases ready to spring out and lock up genuine 'patriots'. Los Angeles street gangs, the Bloods and Crips, are going to be the shock troops of the New World Order.

Robert Fletcher, John Trochmann's colleague in the Militia of Montana, spoke next. He is something of a superstar on the far Right, a man whose capacity for argument led to his colleagues speaking of him as 'Fletcherizing' people who disagree with him. Mr Fletcher began by alleging that there was not one but two explosions in the Oklahoma federal building on 19 April 1995. Or perhaps three. The government's version of the bombing, Mr Fletcher said, is 'absolute baloney'.

James Johnson of the Ohio Unorganized Militia gave the senators a taste of the problem facing them. 'We're the *calm* ones,' he said of himself and the other militia leaders, compared to their more extreme followers. 'We're the ones who calm people down . . . The only thing standing between some of the current legislation being contemplated [on gun control and other matters] and armed conflict, is *time* . . . And I have heard more and more people say, "if one of these black-suited armour-wearing state-sponsored terrorists comes kicking down my door, I'm going to blow somebody away".'

The people with this attitude to the FBI and BATF, Mr Johnson said, are not extremists. They 'call themselves American citizens who are getting tired of confiscatory tax rates [and] increasingly heavy regulations'.

Norman Olson of the Michigan Militia spoke of his understanding of the motives of the Oklahoma bombers and the 'dynamic of retribution' for the 'attack' by government agents on Waco. 'Revenge and retribution,' he said, citing the Old Testament, 'are a natural dynamic which occurs when justice is taken out of the equation.'

Most extraordinary of all was the belief that the US government has weather tampering technology, calling up storms and droughts to bring starvation to the American people. Democratic Senator Herb Kohl of Wisconsin began to question Robert Fletcher on his assertion that 'the American government has created weather tampering techniques so that a New World Order will be able to starve millions of Americans and to control the rest'.

The committee room, in hushed amazement, turned to hear the words of Mr Fletcher. 'Well,' Mr Fletcher prevaricated, 'what I was trying to say is exactly what I said. There is [*sic*] weather control techniques.' Mr Fletcher has alleged that earthquakes, including Japan's Kobe earthquake, the flooding of the Mississippi River and droughts in Ethiopia are part of a New World Order conspiracy to kill billions of people.

Senator Kohl responded as if he could not quite comprehend. 'You're saying the government has created weather tampering techniques so that the New World Order will be able to starve millions of Americans . . .'

'*Worldwide,*' Mr Fletcher interrupted.

'. . . millions of Americans and to control the rest,' Senator Kohl completed his sentence, still not quite comprehending that the conspiracy he had uncovered stretched far beyond the boundaries of the United States.

'Yes, sir,' Mr Fletcher answered. 'And that's my belief.' Robert Fletcher had 'proof' and spoke of 'weather wars'. It was already happening in the mid-West. 'If you think that eighty-five tornadoes takes place [sic] in the middle of our growing area by simultaneous accident, I'm sorry.'

These hearings and the pathology of paranoia they reveal are the logical extension of the decline of the mainstream media in the United States and the proliferation of unreliable information at the extremes. There is no corrective viewpoint available to Mr Fletcher on CBS television or in *The Los Angeles Times* because typically he would dismiss these news sources as examples of the journalism of an out-of-touch liberal media élite. Instead he can tune in or switch on to any number of new media outlets which reflect, validate and extend his views.

Senator Specter said that there were 224 armed militia groups in the United States around the time of the Oklahoma bombing. Their membership has been variously estimated at between 10,000 and 40,000 people. These numbers are, of course, tiny. Few Americans will give up weekends to prance around in the backwoods in combat fatigues to defend the United States from phantom UN black helicopters and hidden Russian troops. But as arrests of militia members in Arizona, Washington State and Georgia have proved, armed and dangerous anti-government bands are now a chronic problem for the United States, despite their relatively small numbers. They engage in bank robberies, anti-Semitic and racist attacks, bombings of federal property, attacks on federal agents and other serious crimes. As Europeans know well from terrorist groups in Ireland, Spain and elsewhere, small numbers of determined or deluded people who put their beliefs beyond all reason can murder and cause mayhem for years. Besides, if these small right-wing groups can be this troublesome in the good times of 1990s America, how might things be when the economy, inevitably, turns sour? Or when the more 'reputable' fed scare proponents crank themselves into an even higher gear of righteous excitement at the thought of the approaching new millennium?

The United States suffers a worrying link between ignorance and credulity. As the South Carolina focus group showed, many intelligent American citizens are ignorant of the major political issues of the day, yet angry or disappointed that the government has not 'solved' these issues. This ignorance makes it relatively easy for a small minority, led by the unscrupulous or the fanatical, to drift towards belief in the most bizarre conspiracies, fomented by the worst examples of the 'new media', in which ignorance is not corrected. It is elevated to the level of a sacrament.

Suspicion of the mainstream media is hardly unique to the United States, but the level of suspicion is a phenomenon which appears to be uniquely American. Ignorance in a democracy is dangerous, especially when political leaders increasingly look to opinion polls and focus groups for guidance, and where the media's ability to correct conspiracy stories is limited by suspicion of the media itself. Speaker Newt Gingrich spotted the obvious result: 'People are not, in general, stupid, but they are often ignorant. In their ignorance they often tolerate ignorant news reporters who, in turn, tolerate ignorant politicians. The result is an ignorant politician making an ignorant speech to be covered by an ignorant reporter and shown in a forty-second clip on television to an ignorant audience.'

Mr Gingrich's words may amount to an important criticism of all the mainstream media, but the extremes of the alternative media can be far more damaging. At the end of the American century, President John F. Kennedy's words have an eerie ring. In the speech he was scheduled to deliver in Dallas on the day he was assassinated in November 1963, he referred to the worst of America's conspiracy culture. President Kennedy could have been forecasting the least rational of the information available on the Internet, talk radio or the American Patriot Fax Network, the electronic churches of the Goddess of Unreason.

'There will always be dissident voices . . . perceiving gloom on every side and seeking influence without responsibility. But today other voices are heard in the land – voices preaching doctrines wholly unrelated to reality . . . They fear [the] supposed hordes of civil servants far more than the actual hordes of opposing armies. We cannot expect that everyone . . . will talk sense to the American people. But we can hope that fewer people will listen to nonsense.'[4]

Yes, indeed. We can hope.

Why Americans Hate Washington

Jamestown, Virginia

This journey around a disconnected America ends where the United States began. It is a tale of two rivers, the James River in Virginia and the Potomac a hundred or so miles to the north, on which America built its capital city. It is a tale of two worlds, the real America and Washington DC. And, above all, it is a tale of two views of America, the optimism that most Europeans see as a traditional American characteristic, and a new sense of pessimism among Americans who feel the country has lost its way – politically, culturally, morally and even spiritually. By understanding the gulf between the government and the governed, the gap between those who live on the Potomac and the rest of America, we may begin to see clues as to how the United States might overcome anger and apathy and reverse the damaging trends of the past thirty years.

Walking along the banks of the James River at the site of the unhappy colony of Jamestown, you cannot help but think they must have been world-class optimists, those first Europeans who sailed here in the seventeenth century. It was a mosquito-ridden forest then. It is not much better now. Three small wooden ships, full-sized reconstructions of those used by the colonists to cross the Atlantic, are bobbing like toys in the water, their ropes and rigging creaking in the breeze. You would not trust ships like these to take you across the river, never mind across the Atlantic Ocean, and it is difficult to imagine what persuaded the first Europeans they could survive and prosper in Virginia.

They landed here, full of hope, in the spring of 1607. A total of 144 settlers from the Virginia Company had left England but thirty-nine died on the Atlantic crossing. The remaining 105 came ashore and tried to carve a new life in the New World. Only thirty-two made it through the first winter alive. They called their rough settlement 'James Fort' and, later, Jamestown after King James I. In the forests Pocahontas, daughter of the great Indian chief Powhatan, befriended the British settlers and, according to legend, saved Captain John Smith from certain death. In September 1996 archaeologists announced they had uncovered outlines of the original fort, the remains of the first permanent English settlement in the New World.

A grave revealed the skeleton of a white male in his early twenties who probably died of gunshot wounds, suggesting mutiny or murder and the unhappiness of the earliest days of the English conquest. 'We have discovered America's birthplace,' Virginia Governor George Allen declared of the Jamestown excavations, with forgivable pride.

The James River colonists eventually succeeded – despite enduring every possible calamity. They had settled in a swamp in the middle of a powerful Indian confederacy which launched its first attack two weeks after the British arrived. The settlers were unable to grow the crops they had planned. They succumbed to heat, disease, bitter winters, malnutrition and Powhatan's warriors. 'So lamentable is our scarcity,' one colonist wrote, 'that we were constrained to eat dogs, cats, rats, snakes, toadstools, horsehides and whatnot.'

One man was executed for cannibalism after eating part of his dead wife. Then a miracle arrived in the unlikely shape of the Virginia tobacco leaf. A hybrid tobacco was developed by John Rolfe, who married Pocahontas, and the practical settlers made so much money selling their addictive cash crop in the Old World that eventually the great Virginia plantations became economically secure enough to enable Thomas Jefferson, George Washington and others to enshrine the New World's optimism in the breath-taking promise of the Declaration of Independence.

'We hold these truths to be self-evident,' it declares, 'that all men are created equal, that they are endowed by their creator with certain unalienable rights and among these are the rights to life, liberty and the pursuit of happiness, that to secure these rights governments are instituted among men.' For slave-owning farmers like Jefferson the 'all men' who were created equal did not include those of African origin. But for whites the promise was of abundant land coupled with the belief that hard work and the grace of God would mean every generation of Americans would do better than their parents.

All presidential elections, and all politics, are about that one sentence in the Declaration of Independence. Specifically, every American seeking political office has to explain to voters how government can best secure these 'rights' which helped Americans prosper and conquer a continent stretching from the James River to the Pacific Ocean. If the central issue of modern American politics has been around for more than 200 years, the criticism that elections are sleazy affairs is not new either. In fact, distaste for American politicians is as old as America.

In 1800, candidate John Adams was described as a 'fool, hypocrite, criminal tyrant'. In the same year, Thomas Jefferson's opponents argued that electing the Virginian would ensure that 'murder, robbery, rape, adultery and incest will be openly taught and practiced'. In 1844, candidate Henry Clay was described as spending 'his days at the gambling table and his nights in a brothel'. H. L. Mencken described Franklin Roosevelt as such a political opportunist that if he became convinced cannibalism would secure him votes, FDR would fatten a missionary at the White House immediately. All this makes Republican rhetoric about Bill Clinton being a 'womanizing, pot smoking, draft dodger' sound feeble by comparison.

But if there has always been a robust and healthy suspicion of the governing class, there has also always been a consensus in American history that the political system works to represent its citizens. Whatever the perils of the moment, Americans have usually been optimistic that their country would emerge from repeated crises better and stronger. Despite 1990s peace and prosperity, much of this consensus has gone. As *The State of Disunion* survey from the University of Virginia put it, 'what stands out is the American people's pervasive pessimism about the actual state of our nation's institutions and the state of America as a whole. A mere 10 per cent . . . felt that the United States is improving overall, and only one out of ten would go so far as to say that this improvement is strong. A full 50 per cent . . . admitted to the view that the US is actually in decline.'[1]

To understand the task President Clinton and other political leaders face in reconnecting an angry, anxious and pessimistic America, consider an average day in the capital on the Potomac River and think how it is viewed by ordinary citizens here on the James River in Virginia, the successors of the first colonists.

It is 6 June 1996. You are a hard-working patriot living near Jamestown. You finish ten hours at work because you need the overtime. You have a second job at the weekends to pay for extras. Your spouse is on a different shift and not home yet. You both work so hard you rarely see each other. So you fix a meal for the kids, pop a can of beer and settle down to watch the TV news, exhausted as you stretch out on your La-Z-Boy recliner. The news is all about the farce on the other river, the Potomac. The newsreader says the chairman of the Senate Banking Committee, Alphonse D'Amato, made a one-day profit of $37,000 in stock market trading through a securities company. The company is being investigated for possible wrongdoing in thirty states, but the senator says that he 'received no special treatment'. Yet somehow he pulled in $37,000 in one *day* which is more than you make in a *year*. It turns out the brokerage firm assigned him a large number of shares in a hot issue of new stock which then soared. Would they do the same for you? Jeez.

Down here on the James River you don't pay much attention to what happens on the Potomac, three hours' drive away, but you do know that Senator D'Amato's banking committee is supposed to be the *watchdog* on securities matters, which sounds like a bad joke. Who watches the watchdog? You consider putting your foot through the television, when the reporter says that the senator is also leading the congressional investigation on the ethics of President Clinton in the Whitewater scandal. You start laughing uncontrollably. Al D'Amato investigating political ethics is like a fox looking into henhouse security.

You are about to switch channels when the next news story brings you up short. More Potomac palaver. You notice that the reporters in Washington sound, and even look, suspiciously like the politicians. They talk the same weird jargon so that sometimes it is difficult to tell them apart. This reporter says the Senate Majority leader, Bob Dole, is orchestrating the last vote of his thirty-five years in Congress on an issue he claims is of vital importance to every American. It is an amendment to the Constitution of the United States to balance the budget. Wow! *Changing the Constitution!* Now that *is* something.[2]

So you listen carefully until you realize Senator Dole is not Thomas Jefferson. He is not actually balancing the budget. No, sir. That would involve boring stuff about cutting spending or raising taxes. Instead, the crowning achievement of Senator Dole's career is a vote which instructs *future* generations of politicians that *they* have to balance the budget. Or else. These guys in Washington, you think. Must have caught some kind of Potomac fever. Imagine telling your wife when she gets home that you did not mow the lawn but put in operation a plan to instruct future generations of your family to do so. The Jamestown Lawn Mowing Amendment. Here you are working at a real job to earn real money to pay real bills on the James River, while up there on the Potomac they are living in a kind of *Alice-in-Wonderland* world of virtue tomorrow and virtue yesterday but never demonstrating virtue today. When Senator Dole tells you he's 'a doer not a talker', alarm bells ring in your head. You know that is the language they speak up in Washington. It means precisely the opposite of what it means in the real America.

You try to imagine that the year is 1607 and the Jamestown Colony just down the road is filled with members of Congress. You and the other working stiffs are (naturally) in the fields sweating to plant corn and fortify the wooden stockade in case the Indians attack again. But the congressmen are not working. They are the lilies of the field. They toil not. Neither do they spin. Instead they are arguing under a shade tree about constitutional amendments to outlaw starvation, while simultaneously resisting the temptation to pick up a shovel or build up the fort walls. *Now* you know why, in the real America, people joke that Washington DC stands for Dysfunctional City.

You finish your beer and throw the can in the recycling bin. This country was born in a rebellion against British taxation at the Boston tea party when patriots tipped tea into the harbour. That rebellion finally succeeded here in southern Virginia a few miles down the road at Yorktown. Bottled up by the French fleet offshore, the arrogant, out-of-touch British surrendered the colonies to George Washington's ragtag American patriots, while their band played 'The World Turned Upside Down'. The British could not believe they had lost. The trouble is that now Washington DC is as disconnected from your life and the lives of ordinary Americans as the London court of King George III ever was from the distant colonists in Virginia. They even speak a different language – fluent Potomac – infectious but ultimately sterile.

At the start of the 1996 election season the *Washington Post* carried an article on the state of American politics. Steve Moore of the Cato Institute, a right-wing think-tank, fretted about the Republican political message. 'I and others,' Moore told the *Post*, in the Potomac language, 'have been saying for the last year that "shrink the government" is not enough. It has to be "shrink the government, grow the economy". My complaint, even in 1994, was that growth message was lacking. If you look at the Contract with America, its deficiency was, where's the growth message?'

Down here on the James River, real Americans do not talk like this. Outside the Potomac-speakers in Washington DC *no one* talks like this. George Bush's infamous slogan, 'Read My Lips, No New Taxes', was a promise in the Potomac tongue, signifying precisely the opposite of what the words mean in the real America. Bill Clinton's Potomac-speak was 'a middle-class tax cut', which translates into real American as 'a middle-class tax *increase*'. He also promised to run the 'most ethical' administration in history. That translates from the Potomac language as: 'Whitewater-filegate-travelgate-questionable-political-contributions' investigations and sleaze.

'Yes, like everyone else, we're not perfect,' Clinton adviser George Stephanopoulos admitted after the 1996 election campaign. 'But it wouldn't hurt to give elected officials a little bit more of the benefit of the doubt.'[3] Not a chance in the 1990s. Mr Stephanopoulos had clearly forgotten the old Arkansas wisdom often quoted by his boss, President Clinton.

'Fool me once,' Mr Clinton forever repeats in his best Southern drawl, 'shame on *you*. Fool me twice, shame on *me*.' Having been fooled so often, even if the fictitious Jamestown citizen does not swallow the nuttiest anti-government conspiracy theories he sees on TV and hears on the radio, why would he offer government 'the benefit of the doubt'? Why would any American? Just think of the news from the Potomac that has filtered down to the rest of America in the past thirty years.

That most famous of Vietnam war hawks, Lyndon Johnson's Defense Secretary, Robert McNamara, admitted that he knew in the 1960s that the Vietnam war was probably hopeless, and yet he publicly argued that the war was winnable. The United States government ploughed on in a futile effort which eventually cost 58,000 American lives. The Nixon administration also lied about the war, extending it to Cambodia and prolonging the conflict for political reasons when they could have achieved peace earlier. President Nixon and his officials lied about Watergate. Reagan administration officials lied about the Iran-Contra affair. The alleged lies of some Clinton administration officials led to criminal indictments and so many investigations that down here in Jamestown it is difficult to keep them all straight in your head.

In this decade, where Mr Stephanopoulos seeks 'the benefit of the doubt' for government, the governing bureaucracy seems to get bigger while delivering less. As we have seen, for the first time in history there were more Americans working for various parts of the government than in manufacturing industry. According to Martin Gross's compendium of waste and abuse, *The Political Racket*, there are 19.5 million government workers in the United States, including local, state and federal government, in the 1990s. Since 1975 the number of government workers has increased by 5 million, while the number of manufacturing jobs has remained static. In the Second World War, Gross says, the United States had one civilian defence worker for every five men in uniform. By the 1970s that was one for three. In the 1990s it is one for two. It is hardly surprising that there is a fed scare in the 1990s. Behind the red scare there was a real red menace. Behind the fed scare Americans see the real fed menace.

One small example: the House of Representatives and the Senate both employ chaplains on the public payroll, both earning six-figure salaries to minister to the spiritual needs of members of Congress. Undoubtedly politicians need moral counsel, but why does it have to be at taxpayers' expense? Why not volunteer clergy from Washington parishes?

And one big example: the US Department of Agriculture has grown for decades while the number of farmers in America has shrunk. Gross says that in 1935 there were 6.3 million farmers and 20,000 USDA employees. By 1992 the number of farmers had dropped by a third, while the number of USDA bureaucrats had tripled. At the same time, members of Congress have expanded their personal bureaucracies. There are 435 members of the House of Representatives and 100 senators. These 535 politicians employ at the very least 20,000 staff. One study by Professor Anthony King of Essex University says that the total is more like 32,000. No one doubts that Congress is the most heavily staffed legislature in the world. About 3,700 staff are assigned to various committees. But the 'personal' staff of members of Congress had grown from 3,556 in 1957 to 11,572 in 1991. An administrative assistant to a member of Congress earns more than $100,000 a year, bringing the total cost to taxpayers (including office space and medical benefits) to $1.5 billion a year. Each member of Congress can also obtain taxpayer financing for up to three offices in his or her home district.[4]

President Clinton has had some modest success in trimming the bureaucracy. New ethics rules have attempted to stop the most obvious abuses – junkets, golf trips to Florida and Hawaii paid for by lobbyists, expensive dinners and fat fees called 'honoraria' given to members of Congress for speaking engagements. American journalists have repeatedly documented abuses.

Every Monday night, ABC TV *World News Tonight* runs a segment called 'Your Money' which focuses on the government's waste of taxpayers' money as a result of incompetence or wickedness. The reporting is strong and well researched. But the overall implication is that government spending is *always* stupid or wicked, and government functionaries are *always* fools or knaves. All democratic governments deserve to be held accountable for waste, greed and corruption, and the US federal government has shown plenty of talent for all three. But surely it must do *something* right? Clean up the water supplies? Air pollution? Immunize children? Medical research? The Centers for Disease Control? Weather forecasting? Coastguard rescues? And as any foreign reporter knows, the bureaucrats in Washington are far more helpful than their counterparts in London, Paris or Bonn. They genuinely welcome media scrutiny and are prepared to offer access even to 'secret' facilities in the hope of keeping the public informed.

But – just as with anti-government stories in Hollywood movies, TV shows and thrillers – journalists find there is a strong appetite from viewers for tales of government misdeeds. A member of Congress told me she was investigated and then 'ambushed' in her office by journalists from a TV programme. The journalists were probing – legitimately – the ridiculous perks members of Congress award themselves. In her case it was a congressionally sanctioned retirement pension of $75,000 a year. Because of her life expectancy, under normal actuarial conditions her retirement could cost the taxpayers $4 million.

This was a legitimate journalistic exposé of a Congress as

disconnected from the financial pressures of the rest of America as the Soviet Politburo was from Russia's peasants. But the story also reveals how the fed scare plays to the American TV news audience of the 1990s. The congresswoman knew the reporter well. Washington, as the suspicious citizen on the James River is right to suspect, is indeed a cosy kind of political village where journalists, politicians and bureaucrats inevitably find themselves friends and neighbours, speaking easily in their shared Potomac tongue. After the 'ambush' the reporter confided to the congresswoman that his TV network had originally planned to cancel his show. Then, in one edition they ran an investigative report on vacations taken by members of Congress, paid for by rich lobbyists. The anti-government report was such a success with viewers (and consequently advertisers) that the programme was not cancelled after all.

The moral: journalistic careers can be saved by bashing the US government. Nobody has ever made a successful career out of exposing what government does well, because that is not journalism. It is public relations. Government-bashing has therefore become a thriving industry, from Hollywood movie conspiracies right down to the evening news and pressure groups of 'concerned citizens'.

There is even an annual publication called the *Pig Book*, produced by 'Citizens Against Government Waste'. For a copy you call 1 800 BE ANGRY and they will send you a slim volume with a bloated pig on the cover, detailing dozens of reasons why you *should* be angry about government waste, mismanagement and inefficiency.

In the 1995 *Pig Book* the authors detail eighty-eight projects of allegedly wasted money costing taxpayers a billion dollars. They claim this is only a fraction of the total of $10 billion in government waste for that year. For example, $15 million was earmarked for a bridge to Ellis Island, despite the fact that the National Park Service, which runs the monument, says it does not want a bridge because it would negate the entire history of what is, after all, an *island*. Whether these expenditures are good or bad is beside the point. The important fact is that the *Pig Book* clearly strikes the angry public mood which assumes members of Congress are among the biggest swine who misuse taxpayer funds in Washington DC.

The sense of hatred of official Washington goes beyond the White House and Congress. The Pike and Church Congressional hearings into CIA abuses in the 1970s revealed that taxpayers' money was being used to spy illegally on American citizens in the anti-war movement and to finance often risible assassination attempts on enemies abroad. The CIA soberly considered whether making Fidel Castro's beard fall out would destroy his revolution. *X Files* scriptwriters would reject that idea as absurd. Unhappiness over CIA incompetence led the agency to change directors on average once a year for the five years after the cold war ended. The CIA even failed in its most important mission of fifty years. It did *not* predict the collapse of the Soviet Union. More than the Aldrich Ames spy scandal, this was the real public relations scandal of American intelligence. It never looked especially intelligent.

Add in revelations that the US government conducted what are known as the Tuskegee medical experiments, in which black men were deliberately not treated for syphilis to study how the disease progressed. Throw in the unveiling of years of deception by the Energy Department over the nuclear weapons programme, most especially human radiation experiments. Stir on top Waco, Ruby Ridge, Oklahoma and the Atlanta bombing, and why would any American extend the 'benefit of the doubt', as George Stephanopoulos suggested, to government officials even when evidence of wrongdoing is slim? In this atmosphere, by the late 1990s Washington's inside-the-Beltway crowd of politicians and top journalists were regarded by many Americans with a mixture of envy, distaste and scepticism similar to the way in which ordinary Russians regarded the privileged communist élite known as the *nomenklatura*.

Republican Senator Conrad Burns of Wyoming — a state typical of the West, where many voters feel especially disconnected from

Washington – told me in 1989 that his constituents had a very limited idea of what they wanted from the federal government. He summed it up in three sentences: 'Defend our shores. Deliver our mail. And we'll call you when we need you.'

By the 1990s, Senator Burns's constituents and millions of other Americans were left wondering who would defend them from the rapacity of the federal government itself. It was as if the distant, arrogant monarchy of George III had been replaced by a geographically close but profoundly distant political culture in Washington. Even if the conspiracy-believers and the most angry government-bashers are discounted, the practical, can-do spirit of America finds little voice in the can't-do American capital. In the most pessimistic view, Washington is not so much a conspiracy as potentially a twenty-first-century equivalent of the eighteenth-century English court – voluptuous, corrupt, immoral, decadent, out of touch and ultimately irrelevant to the lives of most citizens. Thomas Jefferson suggested that a little rebellion now and then was a good thing. It is hardly surprising that many Americans – not merely the angriest fringes – take him at his word and offer strong medicine for the American sickness.

Some want shock therapy, limiting the terms of members of Congress so they can only serve a maximum of twelve years. Then they will be barred from re-election. Others want to bleed the body politic of money, offering constitutional amendments to balance the budget and force the politicians to act responsibly. Still others want the balance of power to shift strongly away from Washington for the first time in sixty years, back to the states, scrapping a whole string of federal government agencies including the Education and Commerce departments. In welfare reform and other social policies this movement is picking up steam.

And many talk of faith healing – a moral, spiritual and political revival to prepare America for the new century by rebuilding a civil society, encouraging the warm tradition of volunteerism in American life, and ensuring that if politicians will never be angels, at least they will cease to behave like pigs with their snouts in the public trough.

Concerned Americans, the successors of the hardy pioneers who built Jamestown and eventually created the United States, see evidence all around them of the crisis of confidence in America's political system, apathy towards politics, ignorance of the issues, angry social and cultural trends, and an increasing gap between rich and poor. There really is an alligator in the pond, and it will not do to say that nothing can be done. But the person who, above all, has to come up with solutions to defuse the United States of Anger is, by a cruel irony of fate, also the target for the worst fury of the angriest of his fellow citizens — those who hate Washington with the greatest passion. His name is William Jefferson Clinton.

PART FOUR
AFTER ANGER

'Government is not the problem; government is not the solution. We, the American people, we are the solution . . . And we need a new sense of responsibility for a new century. There is work to do, work the government alone cannot do . . . Each and every one of us, in our own way, must assume personal responsibility . . . With a new vision of government, a new sense of responsibility, a new spirit of community, we will sustain America's journey. The promise we sought in a new land, we will find again in a land of New Promise . . . Our streets will echo with the laughter of children, because our neighbourhoods are safe again. Everyone who can work, will work, with today's permanent underclass a part of tomorrow's growing middle class.'

President Bill Clinton, second Inaugural Address, January 1997

'We are the final generation of an old civilization and the first generation of a new one . . . Much of our personal confusion, anguish and disorientation can be traced directly to the conflict within us and within our political institutions . . .'

Alvin and Heidi Toffler, Creating a New Civilization

Governor Zipper Problem and the United States of Anger

Bill Clinton's reputation preceded him. It usually does. One hot night in the summer of 1991, a group of journalists and party workers who had attached themselves to the Democratic campaign to unseat George Bush, gathered in a bar in Iowa to discuss over ice-cold beer the forthcoming presidential election campaign.

'Tsongas can't do it,' one of the political reporters said of the candidate we were at that time following, Senator Paul Tsongas. 'But Clinton might.'

'Clinton?' one of the Democratic party workers grinned. 'You mean Governor Zipper Problem.'

The bar erupted with laughter as the cosy gathering of reporters and political operatives shared rumours and stories of the dangerous liaisons behind the joke. It was to be another seven months before most Americans, at the other end of the information gap, would understand the reasons for such hilarity. By mid-1991 Bill Clinton remained largely unknown outside his native Arkansas, yet six months later the sexual scandals, questions about his avoidance of the Vietnam war draft, and about his use of marijuana, ensured he was soon to be a household name across the United States. A few months later he was elected to the most powerful political office in the world. This talented, energetic, inspiring yet clearly flawed man inherited the problems of the United States of Anger, most especially the responsibility – in his own words – to ensure that America 'comes together' rather than 'comes apart'.

Can Clinton do it? Can anyone reconnect Americans with their system of government and with each other in the new millennium?

The task of political leadership would appear to tax the powers of a Lincoln or a Roosevelt. It requires political and social reforms plus a kind of moral rebirth of responsibility from the federal government, and also from the American people at what Mr Clinton called the dawn of another century and 'another time to choose'.

Before speculating on what Americans may indeed choose for their future, with profound resonance for American allies, for Britain, Europe and much of the rest of the world, it is important to recognize the limitations of the Clinton presidency. To say that Bill Clinton is the 'most powerful man in the world' may be true, but it misses the point. The greatest blessing of the American system of divided government is that 'the most powerful man in the world' has severe limitations on his power, and in peacetime an American president is, in many ways, not extraordinarily powerful after all. In Bill Clinton's case, that power has been further diluted by a simple yet disturbing fact: Mr Clinton and his wife have become the lightning conductors for the United States of Anger.

The Clintons are despised by a vocal minority of the angriest Americans well beyond any failures of specific policies, and despite a successful economic programme which cut the budget deficit, created a record 11 million new jobs in four years and promised a balanced budget by 2002. To Clinton-haters these successes do not matter because Bill and Hillary Clinton do not merely pursue policies which are wrong-headed. They actually *represent* moral decline. The Clintons are seen by some, in Speaker Newt Gingrich's words, as the 'enemy of normal Americans', bearing the burden of an entire generation which began to subvert the old order in the 1960s, captured the White House in the 1990s, and is responsible for America's anger and anxiety as we approach the year 2000.

The youthful Clintons promised 'hope' and 'change' in 1992. Instead, by 1993 their failures over health care reform, homosexuals in the military and the ineffectual way in which they ran the White House, contributed to the sense that what triumphed was not a New World Order. It was a strange *dis*order which right-wing critics regarded as the coming to power of the valueless and clueless 1960s counter-culture. The generation of Americans which had defeated Hitler, contained Stalin and built the American middle class had lost out to the generation of hippies, rock music and flower power.

In August 1992, the wife of Vice-President Dan Quayle, Marilyn, captured the tone. She addressed the mean-spirited Republican Convention in Houston, picking up Pat Buchanan's declaration of a 'cultural war' by placing the Clintons firmly on the enemy side. 'Not everyone,' Mrs Quayle said, 'demonstrated, dropped out, took drugs, joined in the sexual revolution or dodged the draft.'

These generational fissures and the undercurrent of a cultural war resurfaced in the 1996 presidential campaign. They will dog the Clinton administration until the end. 'It is demeaning to the nation,' Senator Bob Dole told the 1996 Republican Convention in San Diego, 'that within the Clinton administration a corps of the élite who never grew up, never did anything real, never sacrificed, never suffered and never learned, should have the power to fund with your earnings their dubious and self-serving schemes.'

Senator Dole eloquently expressed the anger of a parent telling his teenage child to clean up his bedroom, do his homework and get his hair cut. This had been the yelled conversation in American living rooms throughout the 1960s between the generation which refused to go to war in Vietnam and the generation which tried to send them there. The resentment about Bill Clinton was palpable, because his was a generation whose formative experiences were flower power and flared trousers in Haight Ashbury, not firepower and military uniforms at Anzio or Guadalcanal. How, we must wonder, can Mr Clinton restore trust in the institutions of government, the central task of defusing political anger in the United States, when of all the emotions he inspires, 'trust' is the one in which he appears weakest?

It will not be easy. It may not even be possible. The Clinton presidency has inspired more than harsh words and character assassination. There have been threats of a real assassination and real violence. In the aftermath of the Oklahoma City bombing, Mr Clinton became the first president to close Pennsylvania Avenue to traffic for security reasons. The threat of significant domestic or foreign terrorism is among the worst fears of the Secret Service, who are well aware that an Oklahoma-sized bomb at the north-west gate could flatten much of the key working areas of the White House operation. The Clinton White House has, in fact, been violently attacked several times, once by a man with a Kalashnikov rifle who loosed off a few rounds at someone he thought was Bill Clinton. No one was hurt, though the west wing was peppered with high-velocity bullets.

On the south side of the White House there was a dive-bombing attack by a kamikaze light aircraft in the middle of the night. The plane hit a magnolia tree underneath the president's bedroom window, killing the pilot.

Every president attracts the angry and the deranged seeking to make a political point. Kennedy was assassinated. Reagan was shot. Ford was attacked. Nixon was hated, especially after Watergate. Johnson was the target of the loathing of Vietnam war protesters. Harry Truman suggested that if a man needed a friend in Washington he should 'get a dog'. But Bill Clinton and his wife bring out the worst in a minority of their fellow countrymen in a way which goes beyond the rowdy conduct of public life or the actions of a few crazy people.

It is difficult to think of a president in modern times who inspires quite as much *personal* loathing as Bill Clinton does. In the words of the 1960s feminists, for Bill Clinton's enemies the personal *is* political. He and his wife are symbols of the 'Bad Generation' that lost (or refused to fight) in Vietnam as opposed to the 'Good Generation' that won the Second World War.

In the 1992 election, America was finally changing the guard, losing an older generation, an old order, and older habits of mind. It is hardly surprising many citizens found that a wrenching experience. Gary Aldrich was one of those. Aldrich was an FBI agent employed in the Bush White House and retained for a time by the Clinton administration. He clearly despised the Clintons, their policies, their personalities and their people. Aldrich wrote an unusual book, *Unlimited Access*, grumpily retelling the shortcomings of the newcomers in the White House.

The Clinton people, he recounted, were scruffy, untidy, long haired, undisciplined. Some of the men wore earrings. Some of the women had unsuitably short skirts. He claims one woman wore no underwear. (Though he does not explain whether underwear inspections were an important part of his FBI duties.) The most revealing passage of Gary Aldrich's book comes when he reports that another FBI agent told him he should remember the Clinton people from previous encounters. Aldrich does not understand at first. Then the agent gives him a clue, singing one of the anthems of the Vietnam anti-war movement. 'Kill the pigs. Ho, Ho, Ho Chi Minh, the Viet Cong are gonna win. That's who they are, Gary. *They're the people we used to arrest.*'

No doubt they were. The Clinton White House 'looks like America' as Bill Clinton promised, in the sense that every kind of racial, ethnic or social grouping seems to be represented. But there is one obvious exception. The military veterans, so common in every American administration of the past fifty years of the old order, are conspicuously under-represented. Nevertheless, to supporters the Clintons are the best of 1960s idealism – a sense of liberation, of community activism, civil rights, colour blindness. But to their detractors, including Mr Aldrich and the proponents of the cultural war, the Clinton administration amounts to little more than the triumph of everything they had fought against for thirty or even fifty years of the old order: the enemy within; the counter-culture; the pinkos; the long hairs; the druggies; communes; free love. To them, the Clintons are not the *solution* to the United States of Anger, but its *source*. They are agents, as well as symptoms, of decline.

'What is broken in our society, most Americans recognize,' the political commentator Michael Barone argues, 'is not the economy. It is our *culture*.' (My italics.) And Barone, like most

American conservatives, is in no doubt when the break occurred. The 1960s and 70s: 'The worst of the cultural wreckage was done between 1965 and 1980,' he asserts. 'Over those fifteen years the US crime rate tripled. Drug use exploded . . . Illegitimate births as a percentage of all births increased 139 per cent from 1965 to 1980, and another 60 per cent since . . . The percentage of children on AFDC [welfare] rose from 4 per cent in 1965 to 12 per cent in 1980.'[1]

In Barone's view this cultural decline was not an accident. It was driven by what he calls three really bad ideas. All three were espoused by 1960s liberals in the baby boom generation. All three reached their peak in the 1990s. And all three can be tied to the way in which the angriest conservatives perceive Bill Clinton both as a man and as a president.

First of the three bad ideas is what Barone calls the 'liberation from established norms'. That translates into Sixties-speak as 'do your own thing' – smoke dope, sleep around – precisely the kind of moral turpitude of which Mr Clinton repeatedly stood accused. The rules of American life have not only changed. There are no 'rules'.

Second, Barone targets 'a preference for ambiguity over clarity'. Translation: in different situations there are different versions of what is right or wrong. There are no absolutes. Situational ethics. In Sixties-speak: 'if it feels good, do it'. Bill Clinton's political kleptomania and ideological promiscuity fit in exactly here.

And third is 'a sense of entitlement to desired economic and personal outcomes'. In other words, the selfish 'Me generation' believes it *deserves* to prosper and thrive. Without mentioning the Clintons by name, Barone talks of 'a generation of males who refused to fight for their country as their fathers had, and a cohort of females who refused to raise their children as their mothers had'.

We know exactly whom he has in mind. But there is something rather dim about complaining that the middle-aged Bill and Hillary Clinton of the 1990s are unfit for leadership because as teenagers thirty years or so ago they were part of a rebellious 'Sixties' generation. To judge from Mr Clinton's intellectual engagement with issues, his conservative stance on crime, his support for the death penalty, his fiscal conservatism and his toughness on welfare, his administration does not represent the political triumph of the 1960s counter-culture. Far from it. Instead, at its worst, the Clinton administration does represent the triumph of the culture of victims. It is an administration which was *never* in tune with the wide-eyed idealism of hippies. But it is frequently in tune with the much more cynical values of lawyers, perfectly designed for a United States entering a new millennium with one million attorneys in the population. Michael Barone's three 'bad ideas' — no rules, no absolutes and a selfish sense of entitlement — explain precisely why in America the rule of law has indeed become the rule of lawyers, right up to the White House itself. It is not merely that Mr Clinton has faced legal challenges about the alleged sexual harassment of Arkansas State worker Paula Jones, or over the Whitewater affair.

It is that the Clinton administration constantly postures like a group of lawyers defending a client rather than political leaders promoting a vision of government for the future of the United States. Jonathan Swift allows his hero to define the common traits of lawyers in *Gulliver's Travels* when Gulliver says 'there was a society of men among us bred up from their youth in the art of proving by words multiplied for the purpose that *white* is *black* and *black* is *white*, according as they are paid. To this society all the rest of the people are slaves.'

He could just as easily have been describing the Clinton administration, or indeed much of the legal-political élite which rules Washington. Consider again, in the light of this, the routine abuse levelled at Mr Clinton from the angriest Americans. As Glenn Wilburn from Oklahoma or talk radio host Rush Limbaugh or millions of angry Americans would put it, Mr Clinton is supposedly a 'draft-dodging, pot-smoking, womanizer'. These are the 'hippy' charges. Now consider Mr Clinton's defences to these indictments. He admits he smoked marijuana but 'did not inhale'. He *avoided* the draft, but did not 'dodge' it. He wanted to maintain his 'political viability'. There was trouble in his marriage, but he has never admitted specifically to the word adultery. He denied having an affair with Gennifer Flowers, who publicly accused him of a long-standing relationship. And he did not recall meeting Arkansas State employee Paula Jones who claimed he sexually propositioned her in 1991 in a hotel room in Little Rock.

Bill Clinton is not just Commander-in-Chief. He is also America's Lawyer-in-Chief. Smoking marijuana but not inhaling is an argument which *only* a lawyer could deliver with a straight face. Avoiding the draft without 'dodging' it is classic lawyerese, a distinction without any real difference. And committing adultery in the abstract but not with any named human being is a *Kama Sutra* of the mind, a feat managed only by lawyers and politicians. This slippery quality led to the revival of the adjective most often used by Americans about lawyers but increasingly used about Bill Clinton. He is 'slick', with lawyerly ways which leach into his policies and his presidency, so that without any obvious embarrassment he will argue from time to time that white is black or black is white.

He can plead for political reform while simultaneously accepting hundreds of thousands of dollars from donors to the Democratic party who have been rewarded by receiving White House coffee or a night in the Lincoln bedroom. He can raise taxes while calling for tax cuts. He will reform welfare while arguing that welfare reform goes too far. He will insist that the era of big government is over, then offer small government – but big amounts of it. Other politicians perform the same feats, but none so well as the leader of the society of men bred from his youth in the art of proving by words multiplied for the purpose that black is indeed white, or white is black. To this society, all the rest of the people are slaves.

Even those who admire the Clinton presidency, or at least prefer it to the alternatives, recognize this slippery quality. At best it means that Mr Clinton is engaged in a perpetual plea-bargain with the American people, in which he forever accepts a little responsibility and takes a little blame in return for a light sentence of mild approbation. At worst it means that precisely those qualities which Mr Clinton possesses in abundance – political charisma, vision, eloquence – are lost because he is trusted even less than most politicians in an extremely untrusted profession.

What, then, are the prospects for America in the future under Mr Clinton's leadership or that of his successor? Is this increasingly divided, culturally fragmented country more likely to come together or come apart? The way ahead is best seen by examining two extreme possibilities: the benign and malign scenarios. Both are necessarily speculative and rough, but they suggest the stark nature of the choices facing the United States in the coming decade.

In the benign scenario, the United States will come together by living up to its best traditions. *E Pluribus Unum*. Hard work. Tolerance. Heroism. The American century will push through into the next millennium. President Clinton (or his successors) will preside over a new progressive era, probably across party lines and similar to that of the early years of the twentieth century. Reformers from the Republican and Democratic parties – Senator McCain from Arizona or Senator Kerry from Nebraska, Senator Feinstein from California or Governor George W. Bush from Texas – will help create a new consensus in the sensible middle of American politics.

The 'vital centre' as President Clinton and others have called it, will indeed hold. There will be a New Covenant between the government of the United States and its people. The principal task of this New Covenant will be, in the words of Senator Bob Dole's 1996 election promise, to 're-create the American Dream' for ordinary citizens by ensuring all Americans feel they have the opportunity to prosper. Political reforms, including reforms of the ways in which campaigns are run and money raised, will ensure that the institutions of government may not be loved but they are once again generally respected. In this benign scenario, rose-tinted glasses firmly in place, politicians will bleed money from the system which elects them by choosing any of the half-dozen or so campaign reform initiatives currently before them. Then, emboldened, they will imaginatively leap far further, grappling with the unspeakable dirty secret of American politics, obvious to outsiders but ignored by most Americans. That secret is this: the United States has too many elections. America does not suffer from too little democracy, it suffers from too much of a uniquely unnerving type. As Professor Anthony King demonstrates,[2] unlike British MPs who spend five years in office with strong backing from their political parties, members of the US Congress spend their lives constantly worrying about two interconnected problems: being re-elected every two years and personally raising enough money for their re-election campaigns because their parties mostly cannot help.

These two factors – the dependence on campaign contributors who demand favours of one sort or another, and the constant worry about imminent re-election – mean that members of Congress are typically far from energetic when it comes to *leadership*. They are energetic in *followership*. They bend quickly in the prevailing political winds rather than sailing ahead with unpopular (even if well-conceived) policies. And they are forced to worry about challenges within their own party in primary elections as well as running against the opposing party. The result is that many American politicians choose to chase rather than change public opinion. They excuse this weakness by claiming that they are 'responsive' to the needs of the electorate. In truth they are scared. They are most dynamically responsive only to those who threaten to make trouble or those who offer to give money. This leads to the typical Washington spectacle of flatulent, empty politics.

The populist solution to all this is to pass 'term-limits' to throw out politicians after, say, twelve years in Congress. Professor King's more ingenious solution is to extend the length of congressional terms to four years, giving House members a little time to establish themselves and cutting the number of elections suffered by American voters in half. President Lyndon Johnson suggested precisely this in his 1966 State of the Union address. President Clinton could do the same in the interests of good government in the twenty-first century. Senate terms could be extended from six to eight years, half retiring every four years. Fewer elections would be far less costly but more 'special'. Voters might, conceivably, take an interest, and would still be able to sweep away the deadwood politicians should they choose.

In this benign scenario, sweeping political reforms would revive American democracy, ceding more power back to the states, and from the states to local communities. For American readers who will say such sweeping reforms are impossible, there is one compelling question. The United States frequently instructs other countries on the virtues of democracy. Would you seriously export to a developing country, hungry for democracy, a precise copy of the 1990s American system of government? A system replete with parasitic lobbyists, intolerant pressure groups, apathetic voters and presidential elections which seem to take four years to complete and require hundreds of millions of dollars? Or would you prefer to export the American ideal of democracy which appears to have been buried under the rubble but is still there, somewhere, and still worth fighting for?

Most Americans would, presumably, be more comfortable championing the ideal of American democracy rather than its corrupt reality in the 1990s. In which case, why should they settle for anything less for themselves than real and sweeping reform?

The problem, according to former Republican Senator Warren Rudman, is that one of the least enviable characteristics of Americans is their desire to procrastinate. For the benign scenario to begin to work the American people will have to recognize – as many do – that something is seriously amiss in their political system. Then they will have to come together to put it right.

But – and we are still pursuing the rosiest of possibilities – the richest and most talented citizens may decide they can prosper whatever the failings of their politicians in Washington. In this benign scenario the world's most powerful economy will not merely roar ahead in the twenty-first century, but the rising tide will again raise all boats. According to the Census Bureau figures released in early 1997, the number of Americans living in poverty dropped significantly between 1994 and 1995 from 38.1 million to 36.4 million. 'Only' 41 million Americans lacked health insurance, no change from the previous year. (At least it did not go up.)

Median household annual income, however, was still not as high as in 1989, but there were measures which could result in fewer Americans being left behind by rapid economic changes. President Clinton could, for example, fulfil his promise to ensure every American eight-year-old can read up to standard, every twelve-year-old can operate computers and connect to the Internet and every eighteen-year-old has the opportunity to go on to further education. No one expects the United States to betray its strong traditions and decide to use taxation to redistribute wealth. But in the benign scenario, the White House could try to distribute knowledge more widely by using education funds, scholarship money and tax breaks to help poor Americans learn the skills they need to prosper and change with a changing economy. Above all, in this America, the best American traditions of freedom, opportunity, personal responsibility and community would reassert themselves through the efforts of millions of individuals who want to prosper.

For an idea of how this might look, consider a thriving black church in Texas. Windsor Village United Methodist Church in south-west Houston is an example of the best of America's spirit to succeed. The church's extraordinary preacher, the Reverend Kirbyjon Caldwell, is an impressive figure. He is in his early forties, well over six feet tall, with the athletic build of a basketball player. He built his mega-church of 10,000 members from a tiny congregation of just twenty-five using business methods he learned as an investment banker on Wall Street. He could have made millions, perhaps tens of millions, of dollars as a talented young black man at the heart of American capitalism. Instead, he decided he would not only save souls but also provide economic salvation.

During sermons he asks those parishioners who know of job vacancies and those who need jobs to meet together after church, to try to ensure that all his flock have jobs and a chance of prosperity.

Parishioners are trained in interviewing skills and given help to apply for jobs. Pastor Caldwell has used a bond issue to raise money for a multimillion dollar 'Power Centre' which helps black entrepreneurs obtain investment capital. He offers deferred or low-cost rent to black businesspeople who are struggling to get started, and he has even managed to attract a commercial bank to the Power Centre when, on strict financial criteria, many banks would tend to avoid less prosperous black neighbourhoods as too risky.

In a culture which often stereotypes black children as failures, Pastor Caldwell has helped create a church school which has raised expectations that young African-Americans will succeed. 'Children do *not* fail here,' the uncompromising school motto says, 'because we do not allow it.'

Instead of whining complaints about the iniquities of racism, Pastor Caldwell practises trickle-down salvation, instructing his parishioners that the only way forward is to help themselves and that the best cure for racism is black success. Although, in this case, it involves a black community with a Christian message, the self-help principle extends to those of different faiths and no faith, and to white, Hispanic, Asian or other races. It is, in a sense, the triumph of America in the anecdotal, of ordinary people punching above their weight. This is the key to overcoming the most dismal aspects of the United States of Anger in the 1990s.

'The pre-eminent mission of our new government,' President Clinton said at his Second Inauguration in January 1997, 'is to give all Americans an opportunity – not a guarantee, but a real opportunity – to build better lives ... we need a new sense of responsibility for a new century ... Everyone who can work, *will* work, with today's permanent underclass a part of tomorrow's growing middle class.'

But is any of this benign scenario realistic for America as a whole? How many Americans think that their permanent underclass will indeed become tomorrow's middle class? Is not the real American fear – the malign scenario – precisely the opposite? In the words of one of the Dayton workers, Jeff Woodward, the malign scenario begins with the anxiety that America's middle class has embarked upon a long, slow slide from prosperity. For some, tomorrow could bring membership of a growing underclass.

The malign scenario is, at its worst, very frightening indeed: America will come apart, increasingly divided on class and racial lines, staggering under a top-heavy bureaucracy with an out-of-touch governing élite incapable of reform, buffeted by extremists, religious bigots and unscrupulous populists offering simplistic solutions to a shrinking middle class fearful of change.

Among the most eloquent pessimists, Jonathan Rauch, author of *Demosclerosis*, argues that serious reform is essentially impossible in a 'sclerotic' American political system.[3] President Clinton boasted that the era of big government is over. But the era of small government may also be over. The expansion of government in the past fifty years cannot, in Rauch's view, be reversed. Mr Rauch persuasively insists that the lobby to keep agencies like the Pentagon, the CIA, the Environmental Protection Agency intact, plus entitlement programmes such as Social Security, Medicare and Medicaid, is roughly equal to the lobby against raising taxes. In Newtonian physics, every action has an equal and opposite reaction. In Washington that means political gridlock, behind a show of posturing reforms with no real substance. Or, as Mr Rauch argues, Washington is now what it will be in the future – not a pleasant prospect.

The reason I cite Mr Rauch's characterization of political paralysis at the beginning of an outline of a malign scenario for the United States is that one option for the future has to be ruled out: doing nothing. The trends and fears that make up most of this book will not stand till. Mostly they are changing for the worse. The undercurrents of anger against the political system can only increase unless the federal government overcomes its reputation for incompetence, beginning with balancing the US federal budget. This has become not merely an economic and political matter but almost a moral issue for a society in which tens of millions of citizens are in debt and a record one million filed for bankruptcy in 1996.

The traditional American shame about personal debt has evaporated because it is so commonplace in a credit card culture with a persistently spendthrift government. A popular TV game show called, unbelievably, *Debt*, captures the new tone. Those in financial difficulties appear before a live TV audience, admit how many thousands of dollars they owe, and compete against other debt-ridden contestants with the promise that the producers will pay off the winner's debts at the end of the show. The host, the 'Duke of Debt' Wink Martindale, smiles as he announces: 'The country's in debt. You're probably in debt . . .'

But, sadly, there are no TV producers able to wipe away America's budget deficit or the political posturing behind which it has grown. In the malign scenario, therefore, the various means by which politicians try to balance the budget will fail by early in the 2000s. Voter cynicism will increase again at a time when a definable crunch is coming. As a people, Americans are getting older. The retirement of the baby boom generation will exacerbate every one of the tensions which anger, frighten or unnerve voters most when they consider their future – tensions over the family, morality, the angry society, the anxious economy and the divisions between rich and poor. The Congressional Budget Office estimates that in 1950 the United States had seven working Americans for every one pensioner over sixty-five. By 1990 the ratio had dropped to five to one. By 2030 it will be below three to one. The CBO calculated that the burden, without tax increases or spending cuts, could cause the national debt to *triple* and the budget deficit to explode *sixfold*.[4]

According to a study by Brown University in February 1997,

a solid majority of American workers – 58 per cent – still felt they were not sharing in the prosperity of their companies or their country. Around half believed they had not benefited from a strong economy, and the same numbers believed their retirement will not be as secure as their parents'.[5]

In this malign scenario, the inequality between poor Americans and the rest, which has always been an accepted fact of America's opportunity society, will become far worse. The middle class, those who are not computer literate and do not demonstrate special skills, will compete for lower-paying service jobs and fall further behind.

Political unrest, from those who expected to do better, will fuel the growth of more extreme anti-government militia groups who will continue to have easy access to powerful weapons. The tiny minority of dangerous extremists will find – on the Internet and in the new media – that they can easily link up and use their small numbers to maximum advantage. Extreme Christian and new age groups will be utterly devastated when, after the millennium, the second coming of Christ or the new age does not appear to be at hand. Some will commit suicide, like the thirty-nine Heaven's Gate cult members in Rancho Santa Fe, California, who thought their leader was Jesus and that they were about to rendezvous with an alien spaceship in the wake of the Hale-Bopp comet. Others, like the Branch Davidians in Waco, Texas, will find themselves in angry confrontations with the secular authorities. A tiny minority will decide to give the Lord a helping hand by 'cleansing' America of sinners, bombing abortion clinics, gay bars and the usual targets of the most unreasonable people in an Armageddon of armed domestic terrorism. At worst, rhetoric about a cultural and religious war could become a reality with a repeat of the Oklahoma City bombing.

The rich and well educated will continue to vote and be puzzled that fewer of their fellow citizens choose to do so. The vast majority of Americans will switch off from politics and snuggle up in the tranquillity of a couch in front of the TV or the solitary abuse of hours on the Internet. The angriest will become even more angry. Populist movements led by the successors of Pat Buchanan, Ross Perot and Louis Farrakhan, will seek to bring about the collapse of one or other of the main political parties. Eventually they will succeed. A genuine third force will destroy either the Republicans or the Democrats – though by that point no one will care which party collapses since they will be almost indistinguishable. Class divisions will increase dramatically following the next recession. Current inequalities between workers and their bosses will be made even worse by rising unemployment. Labour disputes will turn violent, harking back to the period from the 1890s to the 1930s.

There will be generational divisions too. Older Americans will demand their entitlements to Social Security and Medicare. Increasingly resentful younger Americans – many of them Hispanic and Asian – will want to escape the tax burden of paying for somebody else's grandfather.

A severe correction to the stock market (43 per cent of Americans now have some investment in equities) will leave millions of middle-income Americans wishing, as in the 1920s, that they had not invested their life savings in a way that can go down just as dramatically as it went up.

The computer-literate workforce, a new techno-élite, will prosper. The richest will move to stockaded communities protected by armed guards and increasingly isolated from a demoralized, low-paid service workforce.

In this malign scenario, while America may not decline as a world power for many years, its share of world GDP will drop, fuelling the scaremongers into demanding solutions along protectionist and isolationist lines. The shock will quickly spill over into foreign policy, with the search for new enemies. The Chinese? The European Union? Mexico? Arabs?

Immigrants will be the most notable scapegoat for 'stealing American jobs'. Anti-immigrant panics will end in race riots in the inner cities. By the year 2050, according to the Census Bureau's report, *The State of the Nation: 1997*, one in four Americans will be of Hispanic origin compared to one in ten in 1997.

Instead of assimilating, in this malign scenario, poor Hispanics will be viciously cut out of the American Dream, regarded as an alien wedge. Relations with Mexico will sour. Violent crime will rise again when the children of the rootless, amoral, predatory criminals of the 1990s become the new predators of 2005, teenagers with guns and ambitions but without hope or a developed sense of right and wrong. And in a flourish of imperial nostalgia the United States will try to hold on to its collapsing prestige by spending ever-increasing proportions of its national wealth on advanced weapons which will never be used.

Which will it be? The benign or the malign? The best that American promises or the worst that it threatens? Coming together or coming apart? That, of course, is a matter for the American people and their leaders, though it is obvious that the rest of the world, especially NATO allies and, most especially, Britain, have interests at stake in the outcome.

The optimists will point out that America has supposedly been in 'decline' for years but has consistently seen off foreign challengers (whatever did happen to Japan?). The United States has remained more or less united despite extraordinary domestic upheavals from the Civil War to civil rights.

The former Governor of New York, Mario Cuomo, probably America's best-known liberal intellectual, in typical style even finds something optimistic to say about the new sense of discontent. 'This is all a pendulum,' Governor Cuomo explained, speaking of the mood swings of the American people and sense of political drift. 'One school of thought persists long enough to be responsible for the status quo. The status quo is *always* unsatisfactory. People ask for change because they want something better than the status quo. There are an awful lot of Americans dissatisfied with this economy. But this economy is infinitely better than the economy was forty years ago. All of America is stronger, richer. Why are people so unhappy? Because as you become accustomed to the status quo, you want something better.'[6]

That is an eloquent summary of American restlessness for perfection, as a cause of anger and discontent. Yet pessimists will counter that America in the 1990s is not so much looking for 'something better' as decadently living off the perfume of a withering flower, a great empire at its peak and beginning an uneasy decline.

Some Americans, contemplating the future, suggest a dislocation for Western society far greater than anything I have addressed in this book. The 'futurist' Alvin Toffler and his wife, Heidi, have formed a friendship with Speaker Newt Gingrich and his wife, agreeing that the next few years for the industrialized world are likely to be as exhilarating and as terrifying as the Renaissance itself. The Tofflers and the Gingriches are an odd pairing. Alvin Toffler admitted that they sometimes engage in 'shouting matches over politics' but were in agreement about the central point: the magnitude of the changes we can expect to sweep the United States and the rest of the world. 'I believe that the changes that the human species will make in the next ten or twenty years are in fact of a *greater* magnitude than those of the Renaissance,' Mr Toffler told me.

He prophesied it would be a painful period in which 'all existing moral and political codes' would be challenged by the proliferation of computers and new technology. By way of an example he produced the front page of that morning's *USA Today*. The lead story was the launch by Microsoft of its new Windows program. 'Did you ever think the launch of a computer program would make front page news in a regular newspaper?' he asked. Or that we would so easily and assuredly take computer technology for granted?

Then he switched to the largest retail organization in the United States, Walmart, which sells everything from TVs and fishing rods to clothes and toys. This size of operation, Mr Toffler believes, was not achievable a generation ago without computer tracking of inventories. 'The average Walmart has 110,000 different items in it. That was not possible before the informationalization of the economy.'

Toffler talks of these technological, social and cultural changes as a 'convergence of crises' hitting the United States and, eventually, the rest of the world.

If you look at the United States now you see crisis in the education system, crisis in the urban systems, crisis in the health system, crisis in the justice system . . . right across the board. And the question we ask ourselves is why? Why now? Why not fifty years ago, or why not fifty years from now? And the answer we think is that most of these systems, whether they are institutional and organizational or whether they are even the value system, were all shaped by the industrial revolution.

In Toffler's view, we have not merely lost the baggage of the fifty years of the cold war, but of 200 years of the industrial age. These two changes, each enormous in itself, are happening together.

There was a time when everybody was supposed to grow up and go into a nuclear family – father goes to work, mama stays home, two kids under the age of eighteen. That was the one-size-fits-all family unit that preceded the last few decades. Gone. In the United States fewer than 5 per cent of Americans live in that kind of family unit. Now we have a diversity. Single parents, childless couples, twice remarried, three times remarried . . . I am not arguing good or bad, but it's a fact of life.

Another fact of life is that computer technology itself changes so fast it appears obsolete the moment it is available on the High Street. Machines re-inventing themselves every couple of years in new and exciting ways points to the inadequacies of mere humans who used to believe they could train once for a career which would last a lifetime. Now we must expect to train and retrain again and again. 'I think that there is an enormous amount of fear,' Toffler went on. 'Fear of dislocation, fear of losing one's job, fear of what's going to happen to the neighbourhood, fear of what's going to happen to the family because we have moved from a period in which permanence . . . characterized human relationships to a period . . . [of] transience and temporariness . . . and in which old smokestack jobs or manual jobs or low-skill jobs, factory labour, is increasingly vulnerable.'

The changes embrace culture, epistemology, religion, values and family structure. The waves of change after the cold war, in this view, are only part of an enormous tidal wave which is about to crash around us, most violently and immediately in the United States but also in Britain, Europe, Japan and around the world.

My own guess — and it can only be a guess since reporters are always poor clairvoyants — is that for the United States in the twenty-first century, elements of what I have caricatured as the benign and malign scenarios will coexist for many years. There will be considerable unrest and alarming violence, and while the peak of American power is passing, it will pass slowly. There is a clear and present danger of racial explosions, involving the black poor but also, increasingly, the Hispanic underclass. The fragile veneer of American urban civilization was rapidly exposed in Los Angeles in 1992. The veneer has been restored, but for the foreseeable future major American cities will perpetually hover one court case, one police beating, one shooting away from a repeat of that catastrophe. Or something worse.

I am also convinced that right-wing violence, militia activity and theatrical attacks or disturbances from millennialist groups will be a feature of American society for the next decade and beyond. There will be blood on the streets from the intolerant worshippers of unreason. At best, like the Heaven's Gate cult, they will confine their violence to themselves. At worst, strange beliefs will slide into violent behaviour. It takes a very few dedicated and yet deranged people to launch a provocative jihad against government workers, racial or minority groups, homosexuals, abortion clinics or the other customary targets.

But amid the gloomiest parts of the malign scenario I am still optimistic that the centre of American society will hold. It did so through the industrial revolution, the Civil War and civil rights, and so why not now? Most Americans want to live in a genuinely tolerant country, and will be prepared to fight the worst elements in their society in order to do so. The America of the nightly news – corrupt politicians, intolerant religions, angry militias – is, thankfully, not the America I recognize from my friends, neighbours, or from most of the Americans I have met when travelling around the country.

I am also optimistic that the American economy will continue to be endlessly inventive, rebounding from the challenges posed by China and the Asian Tigers in the early 2000s as it has rebounded from the Japanese challenge in the 1990s. But I am irredeemably pessimistic about class divisions in American society as the single most potent source of the United States of Anger. I quoted above the Census Bureau report of 1997 pointing to a decline in poverty between 1994 and 1995. This is hardly surprising in the middle of an economic boom with the stock market spiralling upwards. But the same report also revealed that 40 per cent of those living in poverty were children under eighteen. This is where the people and the American Dream come apart. If America has always organized itself around a dream for the future, then the future has always meant children.

America is in very deep trouble because children in the United States are in greater jeopardy than in any other industrialized country in the world. Nearly three-quarters of all the children murdered in the industrialized world are Americans, according to the Centers for Disease Control.[7] In the 1990s a baby is born to an unmarried American mother every twenty-five seconds. Every thirty-two seconds an American baby is born into poverty. Every thirty-four seconds a baby is born to a mother who did not successfully complete high school. Every four minutes an American child is arrested for a violent crime. Every two hours a child is killed by a gun.[8]

There is no prosperous country which even comes close to desperate statistics such as these, yet this is the generation which will inherit either what remains of the American Dream, or the bleaker parts of the United States of Anger — the benign or the malign scenarios.

At an elementary school in Mississippi I talked to teachers about this future generation, about whether President Clinton's plan to ensure every child could read up to standard by the age of eight was realistic, or just another inflated promise. The school, on the outskirts of Vicksburg, was planning how to rewire and cable up to try to take advantage of the Internet, to leap with enthusiasm into the information age. The teachers, typically bright and engaged, welcomed the Clinton literacy project, the computerization of school, the challenges of the future. But then they pointed out the catch. The children they see coming to school at five years old are so diverse in ability, teachers doubted if they could succeed in teaching all of them to read at grade level by the time they are eight. 'Some five-year-olds we see here perform like nine-year-olds,' the head teacher said of the induction class. 'And some perform like two-year-olds.'

She explained that, in the worst cases, five-year-old children arrive at school without ever once having had a parent or guardian read to them. These children may never have seen a book, because there are no books in their homes. They cannot follow the connection between pictures telling a story and have no idea that the black squiggles on a page are words with a meaning and a relation to a narrative. These children, in a nation which has the finest universities in the world and the most Nobel prizewinners, would find it difficult to compete in industrial America. In information age America they are destined to become another lost generation.

A teacher in a school in the mid-West nodded in understanding at such stories. She told me she had been especially concerned by the poor performance of a nine-year-old girl in her class. The girl was being brought up by her mother who had never come to school for any consultations. The teacher thought extra help with reading would benefit the child. She sent a note to the mother suggesting that the woman might help her daughter to read. The mother wrote back: 'When you come and do my work,

I'll do yours.' The teacher was at first appalled, but then concluded that the mother – like tens of millions of other single parents – was probably doing the best she could, working hard, and resentful at being nagged that she was not doing enough for her daughter.

These comments from teachers could, undoubtedly, be heard from some of their British counterparts or teachers in poor areas of Europe. But they go to the heart of what keeps the United States together. It is not the flag, or the Constitution, important though these are as American symbols and as a kind of operating manual for democracy. It is not even the belief in freedom. It is the idea, a constant theme in this book, that children will do better than their parents.

The glue of America has always been this belief, rooted in the most optimistic hope of all, that the past is less important than the future. It does not matter where your parents emigrated from, whether they were aristocrats or beggars, how plummy their accents sounded or whether you were bankrupt last week. What matters is how well you can work today and how strongly you can pursue your hopes tomorrow for your children and their children. My greatest optimism, therefore, comes from spending years with ordinary Americans – mostly open-minded, tolerant, and inventive – who, like the Morins of New Hampshire, still desperately want to keep this dream alive.

My worst pessimism derives from observing the American style of government in Washington – fossilized, inept and corrupt – which often stands in the way. The tussle for America's future will be between the best that its people can offer and the worst that its broken style of government can retain. I hope, naturally, that the people will win. To do so means recognizing that the challenges now are just as important as they were in the past fifty years of the old order. They are not, however, quite so clear-cut. But one piece of wisdom from the start of the cold war still applies to America facing the new millennium. It comes from the diplomat George Kennan in his famous essay published in *Foreign Affairs* in 1947. Kennan's analysis of Soviet doctrine scared the American élite and the American people into action, but his essay concluded on a positive note, quite different from his otherwise grim analysis.

His words about the struggle against Communism could equally apply to the struggle against the most outraged voices in the United States of Anger, the cynics, defeatists, racists, religious bigots and violent extremists: 'The issue,' Kennan wrote, 'is in essence a test of the overall worth of the United States as a nation among nations. To avoid destruction the United States need only measure up to its own best traditions and prove itself worthy of preservation as a great nation.'

'Only measure up' is a fitting motto to end the United States of Anger. American citizens, as well a their politicians, need to measure up to their own best traditions, to come together rather than to come apart, and above all to stop whining that whatever goes wrong in life, the alligator in the pond is someone else's fault.

POSTSCRIPT
AFTER ANGER

In the summer of 1996 Juanita Tanika Maddox was murdered. She was shot to death two months after her fourteenth birthday in a poor neighbourhood of Washington DC. Another fourteen-year-old girl was wounded in the same incident. Such stories are no longer big news in the United States, not on front pages across the country or on the nightly national TV newscasts. Unlike the murder of the rich, white, six-year-old beauty queen Jon-Benet Ramsay which made headlines around the world for months, Juanita's killing was just another local story of an American kid who died before she had lived. She was the fifth teenage girl murder victim in Washington in 1996. Tia Mitchell, aged sixteen, had been shot to death on 4 July while riding her bicycle.

The generation of Juanita Tanika Maddox will soon inherit the United States. There is no shortage of reformers offering versions of the Promised Land in which children like these will thrive in a better America in the new millennium. Ross Perot wants political reform. Louis Farrakhan wants to reform the hearts of young black men. William Bennett and numerous other authors of 'virtue' books want to start a moral revival. The Christian Coalition and evangelical groups want to turn America back to Christ. Bob Dole wants to 'restore the American Dream'. President Clinton wants to be the 'education president'. Alvin and Heidi Toffler foresee an America of millions of computer-literate people no longer having to travel to factories to work, instead going on-line from their computer cottages, working from home.

America's future hovers between the greatest excitement and opportunities for change and the sad reality of the death of Juanita Tanika Maddox or the grim statistics about America's children. This remains, in other words, a continent of almost unlimited possibilities and hope for the future, coupled with levels of despair and wickedness unparalleled in any other industrialized country. The anger Americans feel about the condition of their society is a *good* thing. It is the anger of those involved in a passionate love affair with a country that they wish to rescue.

How the United States channels that anger and simultaneously comes to terms with its profound economic, social and political distress will set the tone for much of the world in the twenty-first century.

This remains a land of paradoxes, not just between the successes of America in the aggregate and the chronic problems of America in the anecdotal. This is the land of Microsoft and snake-handling churches, of easy tolerance and violent bigotry, of generosity and terrifying crime, of information Haves and Have-Nots, of splendidly rich and hopelessly poor. It is a country in which black and white want to get along, and yet frequently are too scared and suspicious of each other to do so. It is the nation of *Dumb and Dumber* and also of the Kennedy Center, the Lincoln Center, the Smithsonian Institution and the world's finest universities. It is the sound of gangsta rap and of Wynton Marsalis accompanying Kathleen Battle. It is the land of rugged individuals and whining complaint.

A friend suggested a guiding thought: 'Everything you can say about America is true, and so is the opposite.'

The United States can surf the waves of economic and technological change. But can it also tackle the sickness of a society in which fourteen-year-old girls being murdered in poor areas no longer constitutes a big news story?

In his 'Poetry of the Negro', Langston Hughes wrote:

> Oh yes
> I say it plain
> America never was America to me.
> And yet I swear this oath –
> America will be.

Notes

CHAPTER 1

1. All the events and conversations in this book, unless otherwise specified, are from my own reporting. The incident in Sanibel took place in May 1994.
2. The conversation with the Annapolis police officer was in October 1996.
3. In *The New York Times* of 28 January 1997, John J. Brennan of Vanguard Group, the second largest mutual fund (unit trust) investment group in the United States described the giddiness of America in the aggregate. Funds were flowing into Wall Street, he said, because 'everybody remembers that the market went up 23 per cent last year and 37 per cent the year before that'.
4. There have been numerous surveys reflecting American anxiety and pessimism concerning the apparent decline of the United States. While it is wise to treat opinion polls with a degree of scepticism, what is alarming is the consistency of their findings, especially concerning the decline in confidence in government over the past forty years. I found *The State of Disunion* survey conducted in 1996 by Gallup for the University of Virginia Post-Modernity Project most useful. Face-to-face interviews were conducted with more than 2,000 American adults for up to three hours at a time. It is one of the most detailed and rich studies of its type conducted during the 1990s.
5. The conversation with Senator George Mitchell was in October 1996, after he had helped Mr Clinton rehearse for the debates.
6. The *Washington Post* series, 'The Economic Perception Gap – A Nation that Poor Mouths its Good Times', began on Sunday 13 October 1996.
7. President Clinton made his extremely perceptive 'off the cuff' remarks on Air Force One in 1995, and then retracted them. Presumably he felt his comments were too close to President Carter's pessimistic diagnosis of America's 'malaise'. Unlike Mr Carter, of course, Mr Clinton was re-elected.

CHAPTER 2

1. Robert J. Shapiro, writing in *Building the Bridge*. The book was produced by the Progressive Policy Institute (a Democratic party think-tank) to coincide with President Clinton's inauguration in January 1997. Will Marshall (ed.) (Lanham, Maryland: Rowman and Littlefield).

2. On wage stagnation and deterioration I found the Economic Policy Institute report, *Profits Up, Wages Down*, published on Labor Day, September 1995 especially helpful. It concluded that after-tax profits in 1994 were the highest for twenty-five years. But 1989–95 hourly wages 'have been stagnant or declining for the vast majority of the workforce'. The hourly wage of the median male worker declined '1 per cent per year over the 1989–94 period, continuing the trend apparent over the prior business cycle from 1979–89'. See also the EPI's *Jump-Starting Wage Growth* of 28 February 1996. This concluded that 'the typical American family has seen either little or negative growth since 1979. Middle-class incomes fell in the 1989–92 period and have not grown since 1992, despite the recovery.' In late 1996 there were moves to recalculate the Consumer Price Index, the CPI, which retrospectively would put a different gloss on these figures. I have taken figures from the original method of calculating the CPI. Even if the new measure were to be used, three key elements do not change: income growth was still far greater in the 1950s and 1960s; incomes in the 1990s did not rise as fast as most Americans had expected; and the wealthy did better than middle-income workers and the poor. Also extremely useful on statistics of economic and class division was *The State of Americans*, a compilation of statistics about the United States from Cornell University.

3. In *The Rise and Fall of the Great Powers*, historian Paul Kennedy writes of the United States' debt (p. 527): 'Historically, the only other example which comes to mind of a Great Power so increasing its indebtedness in peacetime is France in the 1780s where the fiscal crisis contributed to the domestic political crisis.'

4. The excellent Garry Wills article on Ronald Reagan was in *The New York Times Magazine* of 11 August 1996. In the Reagan years increased military spending plus tax cuts resulted in the budget deficit almost tripling while the trade deficit grew fourfold. For most of American history the federal government has run at a surplus during good times and a deficit during bad times. But in the past generation, from the Kennedy administration onwards, with the exception of 1969, Democratic and Republican presidents have run constant budget deficits in

322

bad times *and* good times. In February 1997 the White House released budget figures for fiscal 1998. This put interest on the national debt at 15 per cent of spending. Equally uncuttable for political reasons were defence (15 per cent), Social Security (23 per cent), Medicare (12 per cent), Medicaid (6 per cent) plus other 'entitlements' like veterans' pensions and child nutrition. The remaining 17 per cent of 'cuttable' spending included such things as the FBI, National Parks, roads and infrastructure projects.

5. The statistics on the number of elected officials come from Martin Gross's *The Political Racket.*

6. Jonathan Rauch, *Demosclerosis* (New York: Random House, 1994).

7. *The State of Disunion,* op. cit.

8. I met the Morin family in February 1996 during the New Hampshire primary campaign. Pat Buchanan won the New Hampshire Republican primary, though failed to capture his party's nomination. I first came cross the phrase 'Corporate Killers' in a *Newsweek* cover story early in 1996, though the phrase was often used by ordinary voters to describe the unhappier side of corporate America.

9. *American Enterprise* magazine produced by AEI had numerous useful articles, including March 1995 'Indicators on taxes and suspicion of the government'; September 1995 edition entitled 'Work!' and July 1996 'Economic Anxiety'.

10. *The State of Disunion,* op. cit.

11. The health care problem changed gradually through the 1990s. The Kennedy–Kassebaum bill ensuring 'portability' of health care coverage did not become law until July 1997, more than a year after my visit to the Morins.

12. The *Washington Post* published a survey by the Kaiser Family Foundation on 14 October 1996.

CHAPTER 3

1. In preparing this chapter I am especially indebted to two books by *Newsweek* writers. Robert Samuelson's *The Good Life and its Discontents* lucidly analyses the American paradox, explaining why things are apparently going well and yet Americans still feel bad about them. Michael Elliott's *The Day Before Yesterday* demonstrates not only the triumphs of America in what he calls 'the Golden Age' after the Second World War, it also shows how unusual the trends in this period were.

2. 'Rethinking National Security' by Theodore C. Sorensen, *Foreign Affairs,* Summer 1990, Vol. 69, No. 3.

3. The views of Newt Gingrich come from his 'Citizen's Guide to the Twenty-first Century', the foreword to a book written by the 'futurists' Alvin and Heidi Toffler, *Creating a New Civilization*.

CHAPTER 4

1. Jeff Woodward's story was first published as part of a series of articles by *The New York Times* on economic anxiety early in 1996. I met him in the summer of 1996. The conversation with Senator Mitchell was in October 1996.
2. The American Enterprise Institute publication cited is called the *American Enterprise*. Its cover story of July/August 1996 shows an American worker trying to walk up a staircase. This is a Sisyphean task, since the staircase is never-ending, constructed in such a way that the worker can never really get any higher.
3. I visited the Ford plant in Cleveland in 1995, Dayton and Macomb County at various times during 1996.
4. According to a Brown University poll published in March 1997, 68 per cent of Americans felt companies were less loyal to workers than ten years before and 59 per cent said employee loyalty had also diminished.

CHAPTER 5

1. The phrase 'linguistic Lourdes' comes from Robert Hughes's book, *The Culture of Complaint*, a devastating account of two types of PC behaviour in America: the Politically Correct from the Left, and the equally absurd Patriotically Correct from the Right.
2. Center for National Policy Study, published 18 April 1996: *Diagnosing Voter Discontent – Politics, Identity and the Search for Common Ground*. The study also noted that 'voters tell us that they must work harder today to make ends meet or to achieve the standard of living their parents had when their parents were the same age. Decreased job security is a major concern for many of these voters . . . many already had personal experience of lay-offs . . . most see America as an increasingly violent and dangerous place.' One respondent summed it up this way: 'We are a colder, less caring society, and a colder, less caring people.'
3. The Yankelovich study referred to in the text was published as 'Three Destructive Trends' in the *Kettering Review* of Fall 1995.

CHAPTER 6

1. The advertisement – possibly mythical – was quoted by Walter Olson in *The Litigation Explosion*. His analysis of the over-lawyering of America proved an invaluable aid in writing this chapter.

CHAPTER 7

1. I met Milton and Dr Goetcheus in February 1995.
2. Arthur Fletcher's comments came in a 1995 BBC interview with my colleague Bridget Kendall.
3. I found *Two Nations* by Andrew Hacker an invaluable source. Hacker quoted the FBI crime statistics. According to the Sentencing Project (*Washington Post*, 30 January 1997), the incarceration rate for African-Americans was 7.66 times greater than that of whites. That was up from 6.88 times in 1988. The Sentencing Project estimated that 1.46 million black men out of a total voting population of 10.4 million had lost the right to vote. Laws in thirteen states banned half a million black men from voting as a result of past felony convictions. The remaining 950,000 were ineligible because they were in prison, on parole or on probation.
4. Jerome Miller's prediction was quoted in *The State of Americans*, the Cornell University statistical guide to America in the 1990s, as was the study of the economics of ghetto drug dealing. It was published in 1996.
5. I met Sweet Pea and the inspirational Reverend Hezekiah Stewart on a visit to Arkansas in 1994. At the time President Clinton was proposing a new Crime Bill to put 100,000 extra police on the streets. He was also in favour of a waiting period for handgun purchase (now the Brady Law) and a ban on nineteen different categories of assault weapons. Sweet Pea did not think either law would present much of a problem to his 'organization'.
6. *The State of Americans*, op. cit.

CHAPTER 8

1. Peter D. Salins, author of *Assimilation, American Style* (Basic Books) extract in the *Washington Post*, 9 February 1997.
2. Congressman Lamar Smith was speaking on 25 September 1996. His office produced statistics from the Social Security Administration showing that from 1982 to 1994 'native Americans increased their applications

for Supplemental Security Income (extra aid paid to poorer, older Americans) by 49 per cent. Immigrants increased their applications by 580 per cent. Congressman Smith described this as the 'welfare magnet' effect.

3. Census Bureau Statistics quoted by Carey Goldberg, 'Hispanic Households Struggle as Poorest of the Poor in US', *The New York Times*, January 1997.

4. To put the new immigration wave into perspective, if the 1995 rate of legal immigration had applied to the heyday of Ellis Island there would not have been thirteen million immigrants from 1892 to 1924, there would have been twenty-three million. Illegal immigration, obviously, would increase the figure further, by at least another eight million.

5. George Borjas was quoted in the *Wall Street Journal*, 26 April 1996, in an article entitled 'Painful Figures'.

CHAPTER 9

1. *The State of Disunion*, op. cit.

2. To try to inject some reason into the accepted beliefs propounded by Mr Robertson and promoted by Mr Buchanan and Senator Dole, I asked the Pentagon exactly how many US troops were under UN control. Officially, the US Department of Defense finds such questions embarrassing and refused to talk on the record. Various informed sources helped put together the following picture, current in February 1995 when Mr Buchanan made his statement to New Hampshire voters. Of the 67,000 UN peacekeepers around the world at the time, just 963 were American – a minuscule percentage of the US military which was then 1.6 million strong. Almost all of the tiny American force (846) was stationed in Macedonia. It was under US command, not UN command. The UN patches or berets worn by US soldiers are, occasionally, but a flag of convenience for the United States in pursuit of its own interests. Only in extremely rare circumstances are US troops under UN command. One example, an informed source said, was when two-dozen mine clearing experts, including a couple of Americans, went to assess mine clearing operations in Cambodia. The senior officer in charge was not American.

3. Pat Robertson's remarks were quoted in the Anti Defamation League report, *The Religious Right: The Assault on Tolerance and Pluralism in America*, p. 14.

4. Richard Hofstadter, 'The Paranoid Style', in *American Politics* (New York: Alfred A. Knopf, 1965).

CHAPTER 10

1. Jonathan Alter in *Newsweek* of 7 October 1996 quoted Moynihan and urged a common-sense compromise because 'when politics meets moral conviction, the truth usually gets aborted'. He was unable to find any reliable figures for the number of partial birth abortions.
2. I visited Dr James Kennedy in Florida in 1995. You can hear his arguments with the Clinton administration over 'traditional' morality on his television programmes, radio shows, or in his book *Character and Destiny: A Nation in Search of its Soul.*
3. Newt Gingrich made the 'enemy of normal Americans' comment on the CBS programme *Face the Nation*, 23 October 1994.
4. The quotes from Pat Buchanan come from my own reporting, as does Sarah Brady's speech and the discussions with Dennis Barrie, Congressman Rohrabacher and Congressman Yates. The Minnesota anti-abortion rally is also from my own reporting.
5. T. S. Eliot wrote about the quality of doubt in an essay on Tennyson's poem, *In Memoriam*.

CHAPTER 11

1. *The State of Disunion*, op. cit.

CHAPTER 12

1. Most Republican candidates – including the eventual winner Bob Dole – boycotted Louisiana for reasons of self-interest. Iowa and New Hampshire traditionally kick off presidential election campaigns. These small and unrepresentative states jealously guard their ability to make a lot of money every four years in the middle of winter from politico- and journo-tourism as the candidates arrive with thousands of camp followers in the media. In 1996 the upstart Louisiana decided to go first, but Senator Dole decided not to offend local pride in Iowa and New Hampshire and pretended the Louisiana vote was not happening. Most Louisianans obligingly pretended the same thing.
2. According to *The State of Disunion* survey, 60 per cent of Americans claim that 'people like me' have no say in what the US government does and 81 per cent think politics is often 'like theatre or entertainment'.
3. Martin Gross's book, *The Political Racket*, outlines 'Deceit, Self-Interest and Corruption in American Politics', and is especially good on the

corrupt ways in which campaigns are financed. His *The Government Racket* is also useful on federal government waste.

4. In 1992 President Clinton came second in New Hampshire, but survived the brutal scandals which dogged him there and quickly went on to win his party's nomination. In 1996, Senator Dole also came second in New Hampshire and it was not until the South Carolina primary that his money and superior organization made it clear he would win the nomination. But in elections in the previous forty years the wisdom was that you could not win the presidency (or indeed your party's nomination) without winning New Hampshire. Even if 1992 and 1996 mean Iowa and New Hampshire are less reliable as guides to the final outcome, the general point still stands, that these two states exert an influence utterly disproportionate to their electoral strength while big states like California, Florida, Michigan, Ohio and Pennsylvania only enter the primary process when the race is essentially over.

5. *Diagnosing Voter Discontent*, op. cit.

6. The figures on campaign spending in congressional races in 1996 come from the *Washington Post*, 6 January 1997.

7. *The State of Disunion*, op. cit.

8. Turnout figures come from Curtis Gans of the Committee for the Study of the American Electorate. In 1992, 104.4 million Americans voted, or 55.2 per cent. In 1996 it was 95.8 million or 48.8 per cent. This drop came despite an easing of voter registration rules and five million more registered voters.

CHAPTER 13

1. I visited the Wilburns, Governor Frank Keating and Stephen Jones in April 1996, as Oklahomans prepared for the first anniversary of the bombing.

2. Not true. A member of Congress earns $133,000 a year. But you get the point.

CHAPTER 14

1. The quote from Karl Popper comes from *Conjectures and Refutations* (London: Routledge, 1969, iv, p. 123).

2. Opinion poll figures on government as a conspiracy come from *The State of Disunion* survey, op. cit.

3. George Kennan, 'The Sources of Soviet Conduct' from *Foreign Affairs*, July 1947.

4. The episode of the *X Files* was broadcast in the United States on 1 December 1996.
5. The 1951 quotation from Senator McCarthy was quoted in Kenneth S. Stern's *A Force Upon the Plain*, p. 139.

CHAPTER 15

1. *Time* magazine, 21 October 1996, 'The News Wars'.
2. James Fallows, *Breaking the News: How the Media Undermine American Democracy* (New York: Pantheon, 1996).
3. Or there is 'Who is Deading Whom? KEEPING SCORE.' This fax is dated 30 April 1995. It is divided into two columns. On the left under 'Militias' it counts those deaths caused by anti-government militia activists: 'No reported deaths caused by any militia, anywhere, at any time,' it says. In the right-hand column under the heading of government agents 'BATF, FBI et al', it lists those deaths caused by the US authorities: 'Waco, Texas, 4/19/93, eighty-seven dead including seventeen children. No crimes were committed by victims. Ruby Ridge, Idaho, 8/12/93, two dead. One mother as she held her baby and one fourteen-year-old boy and his dog. No crimes were committed by victims.' It then lists 'thirty bodies more or less' connected to President Clinton – retelling the outrageous allegations of the Clinton *Circle of Power* video or the letter by former Congressman William Dannemeyer.
4. The Kennedy speech was quoted in the ADL report, 'Poisoning the Airwaves', op. cit.

CHAPTER 16

1. *The State of Disunion* survey, op. cit.
2. Senator Dole lost the vote on the constitutional amendment, though it was fated to rise again.
3. The quote from George Stephanopoulos is taken from a Ken Auletta article in the *New Yorker*, 18 November 1996, p. 59.
4. Figures on congressional staff salaries and abuses come from two Martin Gross books, *The Government Racket – Washington Waste from A to Z* and *The Political Racket*, and also from Professor Anthony King's article, 'Running Scared', in the *Atlantic Monthly*, January 1997.

CHAPTER 17

1. Michael Barone, 'High Anxiety' in *American Enterprise* magazine, July 1996.
2. 'Running Scared' by Professor Anthony King, from *The Atlantic Monthly*, January 1997.
3. Jonathan Rauch, *Demosclerosis*, op. cit.
4. The CBO figures on the ageing population are also quoted in Jonathan Rauch, 'Endgame' in *The National Journal*, 7 September 1996.
5. Brown University/*Providence Journal* study published in March 1997. Sixty-eight per cent said companies were not as loyal as ten years ago. Fifty-nine per cent said employee loyalty had also diminished in the same period. Seventy-eight per cent of men surveyed felt 'betrayed' by their companies, pointing, the study said, 'to a breakdown of the social contract. The disparity in workers' experiences has troubling implications for society.'
6. Mario Cuomo's remarks were reported by my colleague, Bridget Kendall, in the summer of 1996.
7. The Centers for Disease Control checked the figures on child murders in the twenty-six richest countries in the world. In the United States, children under fifteen years old also had a suicide record double that of the rest. Many countries told the CDC that they had no homicides involving children under the age of fifteen. The figures were published in February 1997.
8. *The State of America's Children*, Children's Defense Fund Yearbook, 1996.

Select Bibliography

I found the following published sources especially useful:

SURVEYS AND ARTICLES

American Enterprise magazine, especially March 1995 *Indicators on Taxes and Suspicion of the Government*; May 1995 *Crime Solutions*; September 1995 edition entitled *Work!* and the July 1996 edition, *Economic Anxiety?*.

The Atlantic Monthly, October 1995, 'If the economy is up, why is America down?' by Clifford Cobb, et al.

Center for National Policy, April 1996 study, *Diagnosing Voter Discontent*.

Chicago Council on Foreign Relations survey, *American Public Opinion and US foreign policy 1995*.

Citizens and Politics, The Kettering Foundation, 1991.

Congressional Pig Book Summary, 1995, Citizens against Government Waste.

Economic Policy Institute report, *Profits Up, Wages Down*, September 1995. Also, *Jump-starting Wage Growth*, 28 February 1996.

The Final Call, 3 September 1996, 'The CIA Drug Pipeline'.

The Kettering Foundation, *Meaningful Chaos*, a report prepared by the Harwood Group in 1993.

The *Kettering Review* produced by The Kettering Foundation of Dayton, Ohio. Especially Fall 1995.

National Issues Forums. Three reports published in 1996: *Mission Uncertain: America's Global Role*; *The Troubled American Family*; and *Pocketbook Pressures*.

Newsweek, 26 February 1996, 'Corporate Killers'.

The *New Yorker*, 18 November 1996, 'The President and the Press' by Ken Auletta; 4 November, 'The Criminals of Tomorrow' by James Traub.

The New York Times series, 'The Downsizing of America', 3 March 1996 and following.

The New York Times Magazine, 11 August 1996, 'Reagan Country' by Garry Wills.

Poisoning the Airwaves, Anti Defamation League research report, 1995.

The State of America's Children, Children's Defense Fund Yearbook, 1996.

The State of Disunion, 1996 survey of American political culture based on polling conducted by The Gallup Organization, Inc. The University of Virginia, 1996.

Trends in the Well-being of America's Children, 1996, United States Department of Health and Human Services.

University of Michigan survey on 'Trust', quoted in the *Washington Post*, 2 June 1996.

The *Washington Post*, 1 February 1996 feature on Levittown, Pennsylvania, by Paul Taylor.

The *Washington Post*/Kaiser Family Foundation survey, *Why Don't Americans Trust the Government?*, 14 October 1996.

BOOKS

Among the books I found most useful are the following:

Aldrich, Gary, *Unlimited Access* (Washington DC: Regnery, 1996).

Anonymous, *Primary Colors* (New York: Random House, 1996).

Anti Defamation League, *The Religious Right* (New York: A.D.L. Publication, 1994).

Baldacci, David, *Absolute Power* (New York: Warner Books, 1996).

Bronfenbrenner, Urie and Peter McClelland, Elaine Wethington, Phyllis Moen, Stephen J. Ceci, *The State of Americans* (New York: The Free Press, 1996).

Clinton, Bill, *Between Hope and History* (New York: Times Books, 1996).

Coates, James, *Armed and Dangerous* (New York: Hill and Wang, 1995).

Dionne, E. J., *Why Americans Hate Politics* (New York: Simon & Schuster, 1991).

Edmonds, Thomas and Raymond J. Keating, *D.C. by the Numbers* (New York: University Press of America, 1995).

Elliott, Michael, *The Day Before Yesterday* (New York: Simon & Schuster, 1996).

Fallows, James, *Breaking the News* (New York: Pantheon, 1996).

Gingrich, Newt, *Quotations from Speaker Newt* (New York: Workman, 1995).

Gingrich, Newt, *Window of Opportunity* (New York: TOR Books, 1984).

Gottlieb, Alan, *Politically Correct Guns* (Bellevue: Merril Press, 1996).

Gottlieb, Alan, *The Rights of Gun Owners* (Bellevue: Merril Press, 1991).

Gross, Martin, *The Government Racket: Washington Waste from A to Z* (New York: Bantam, 1992).

Gross, Martin, *The Political Racket* (New York: Ballantine, 1996).

Hacker, Andrew, *Two Nations* (New York: Ballantine Books, 1995).

Hughes, Robert, *The Culture of Complaint* (New York: Oxford University Press, 1993).

Jaffe, Harry and Sherwood, Tom, *Dream City* (New York: Simon & Schuster, 1994).

Jamieson, Kathleen Hall, *Dirty Politics* (New York: Oxford University Press, 1992).

Johnson, Haynes, *Divided We Fall* (New York: Norton, 1994).

Kennedy, James, *Character and Destiny: A Nation in Search of its Soul* (Grand Rapids, Michigan: Zondervan Publishing, 1994).

Kennedy, Paul, *The Rise and Fall of the Great Powers* (New York: Vintage Books, 1989).

McCullough, David, *Truman* (New York: Touchstone, 1992).

MacDonald, Andrew, *The Turner Diaries* (Hillsoboro, W. Virginia: National Vanguard Books, 1993).

Maraniss, David, *First in his Class* (New York: Simon & Schuster, 1995).

Marshall, Will and Schram, Martin, *Mandate for Change* (New York: Berkley, 1993).

Mason, Todd, *Perot: an Unauthorized Biography* (Homewood, Ill: Dow Jones, 1992).

Miller, Nathan, *Stealing From America* (New York: Marlowe, 1996).

Moore, Jim Clinton, *Young Man in a Hurry* (Fort Worth, Texas: Summit, 1992).

Noonan, Peggy, *What I Saw at the Revolution* (New York: Random House, 1990).

Olson, Walter, *The Litigation Explosion* (New York: Truman Talley Books, 1991).

Phillips, Kevin, *Arrogant Capital* (New York: Little, Brown, 1994).

Republican National Committee, *Contract with America* (New York: Times Books, 1994).

Robertson, Pat, *The New World Order* (Dallas, Texas: Word Publishing, 1991).

Samuelson, Robert, *The Good Life and its Discontents* (New York: Times Books, 1995).

Stern, Kenneth, *A Force Upon the Plain* (New York: Simon & Schuster, 1996).

Stone, Deborah and Manion, Christopher, *Slick Willie II* (Annapolis: Washington Book Publishers, 1994).

Sykes, Charles, *A Nation of Victims* (New York: St Martin's Press, 1992).

De Tocqueville, Alexis, *Democracy in America* (New York: HarperCollins, 1988).

Toffler, Alvin and Heidi, *Creating a New Civilization* (Atlanta, Georgia: Turner, 1995).

Tolchin, Susan, *The Angry American* (Boulder, Colorado: Westview Press, 1996).

Woodward, Bob, *The Agenda* (New York: Simon & Schuster, 1994).

Woodward, Bob, *The Choice* (New York: Simon & Schuster, 1996).

Zweck, Brad, *The Quotable Clinton Almanac* (Wausau: Politico Press, 1994).

Index